Counselling &
Older People

An introductory guide

Counselling & Older People

An introductory guide

Edited by

Verena Tschudin

BOOKS

Published by Age Concern England
1268 London Road
London SW16 4ER

First published 1999

Editor   Verena Tschudin
Production   Vinnette Marshall
Designed and typeset by GreenGate Publishing Services, Tonbridge, Kent
Printed and bound in Great Britain by Bell & Bain Ltd, Glasgow

A catalogue record for this book is available from the British Library.
ISBN 0-86242-245-0

Bulk orders
Age Concern England is pleased to offer customised editions of all its titles to UK
companies, institutions or other organisations wishing to make a bulk purchase. For
further information, please contact the Publishing Department at the address above.
Tel: 0181-765 7200. Fax: 0181-765 7211. E-mail: addisom@ace.org.uk.

Contents

About the Authors

Richard Adfield is an Anglican priest. After ordination in 1964 he worked in parish ministry in Bedworth, Islington, Notting Hill and Chiswick. In 1992 he did a two-year postgraduate course in counselling at the University of Brighton. Presently he is working as administrator/counsellor for Kensington and Chelsea Cruse – Bereavement Care. He is also part-time chaplain for the Royal Sussex County Hospital, Brighton. Richard is married with two daughters, a son and six grandchildren.

Lilian Bruce was ordained to the ministry of the Church of Scotland in 1971, and has served in parishes in Edinburgh and the south of Scotland, in East Africa, and latterly in the Highlands of Scotland. Pastoral care of older people has been a priority in each of these very different situations.

Tui Grimmer-Fleming was born in New Zealand and came to Europe in the 'swinging 60s'. In mid-life she married a Cockney, Ted, settled in London and studied counselling with distinction at Birkbeck. In her chosen field as a volunteer with Elder Abuse Response she says she is a 'skilled helper'.

Francesca Inskipp first trained as a counsellor at the age of 50, at the University of Keele in 1970. Since then she has worked as a counsellor, trainer, supervisor, writer and broadcaster, promoting counselling and counselling skills as aids for easing suffering and for finding ways to live more joyfully.

Lyn Jennings is a counsellor, educational therapist (with children), supervisor and university lecturer in counselling. She also writes and develops courses in counselling and is an external examiner in counselling for the Associated Examining Board. Lyn is particularly interested in the therapeutic function of poetry. She also runs 'Creativity and Spirituality' workshops.

Dorothy Jerrome is a counsellor at Threshold Women's Counselling in Brighton, and also a Senior Lecturer in Social Gerontology at the

University of Southampton. She has written extensively on intimate relationships in later life and for 20 years has been involved in research and training for work with older adults.

Hugh Mackay undertook full-time counselling training at SCOPE Ministries, Oklahoma, and was accredited by the International Association of Biblical Counsellors in 1988. He was Director of Training for Hope Christian Counselling in Bath until 1991. Since then he has spent five years as Counselling Service Manager for Age Concern Bath and North East Somerset.

Pat Milner is a Fellow of the British Association for Counselling and has been a counsellor, supervisor and trainer for 30 years. She was the founder chairperson of the Association for Student Counselling and has been a tutor to counselling courses in diverse settings, such as the South West London College and the original master's degree in the psychology department at the University of London, Goldsmiths College. She is currently a consultant to the Centre for Stress Management, London and the centre's honorary adviser in counselling in education. She has a long list of publications to her name.

Verena Tshudin trained as a nurse and counsellor and has many years' experience of practice in counselling individuals and teaching nurses. She has written several books on counselling and related subjects, mostly for nurses. She also teaches ethics and edits an international journal on ethics for nurses.

Sandra Williams is Co-ordinator of the Advocacy Project at Age Concern Coventry. The scheme was established in 1996 and is aimed at residents in Coventry aged over 55. Now that the scheme is well-established, it is being expanded to cover advocacy within a care setting.

Sheila Willson's interest in puzzles was sharpened by wartime experience in a government centre for code-breaking. She later spent 20 years as a documentary film editor, and for a rather longer period she has been a Jungian psychotherapist in private practice. She is curious to know what will come next.

Introduction

Dear Reader

Every editor and author has an image of her or his 'reader'. It helps to keep this ideal figure before the mind's eye when writing. To my delight I have usually found that when I met *real* readers, they have been much more human and interested than I imagined, and with a *real* story for why they bought or read the book.

So I imagine you to be an older person in a library or bookshop, by chance or by intention, looking through the choices on offer on counselling. You pick up this book, and you leaf through it, and you find that you recognise certain things which attract you. You might never have thought of yourself as a counsellor, but you notice some things and they ring bells. You give the book a second look and take it home because you have found something which might give you a new vision of possibilities. Should we meet, I am sure that we would both be surprised at who we are and why we have read or edited *this* book.

I also hope that younger people, and students on counselling courses, will read this book and use it. The fact that older people have written for their own peers makes it particularly useful to anyone who works with older people to hear and read what they themselves say about themselves. Too often in helping and social care settings younger people care for older people, each assuming that the other understands what is happening – and then finding it is different. The fact that older people themselves here write for and about themselves makes this book not just valuable, but a fund for insight.

As editor I have had the privilege to work with a group of people who have shown immense courage, enthusiasm and commitment. As we are all older people (over 50) I have found working with this group a particularly good experience. Are older people nicer and better people? This is a biased remark: my experience of working with this group of people and on this book at least has been that they are. I am deeply grateful to them.

In this book you will find a distillation of much experience.

Each chapter is different in style and in approach. Each author conveys not only her or his own unique personality but also a special field of concern. The authors were not only chosen for their experience in their field, but they had to be over 50, and some are many years beyond that. For some it was the first attempt at writing; some are well published authors. These elements give this book an authenticity and slant which is unique.

What all the authors do have in common is that they write as themselves. They give of themselves, they share, and they are generous with their sharing. But more than anything else, it is the sense of individuality and personal uniqueness which came across as I worked with the authors. Each person had a story to tell, and each person tells it in her and his own way, making no excuses, being proud to tell it and sure that it will find an echo. It is as if the fruit of years of life and experience have now really come 'into their own', and they are proud of it. There is no doubt that because all these writers have gone through some form of counselling and awareness training themselves, they are more fundamentally able to listen to themselves and they have grown as persons. They have learnt to see themselves for who and what they are; now they share with others – with you, the reader – what they have acquired, and it is not only fascinating, but often humbling and awe-inspiring what can be achieved.

This is therefore not a textbook in the recognised sense of the word, though some chapters are theoretical in content. But neither is the book simply a good read. All the chapters give examples of human pain and suffering which at times may come very close to your own experience, and bring to mind memories which may be disturbing. But all the authors show and believe that with sensitive listening and accurate empathy they can and do help not only to relieve the suffering, but to use it eventually for good.

All the examples used in the book are from real life, but in every case they have been used with permission and the details have been masked to protect the person's identity.

The book is also unusual in that it has two strands: the chapters, and in between them a series of 'pensées' – thoughts – on memory. As we get older, the memory plays an increasing part in our lives because we have more memories, we rely on them more, and we tend to lose memory. So to weave in some thoughts on this is a way of gently bringing your attention to the importance of memory.

Perhaps the most obvious aspect about the book is its message: dare to be yourself, be different, as this makes you grow even when you are older. You too can be of help in a skilled way with your family, friends and acquaintances. I trust that the book will encourage you to try some of the skills described, because at bottom they are nothing more than effective human interaction. As you read, you may become interested in learning more about counselling and perfecting certain skills which you may recognise. If so, you may consider a course or training. But most of all, as we get older, our teachers are no longer our elders, but our peers, our equals and our friends. As editor it is my hope that you will also find the book itself to be a friend, leading you in a direction which brings further fulfilment and satisfaction.

Verena Tschudin

In Praise of Memory

'What was hard to endure is sweet to recall', says a proverb. People remember the war and what it meant to them.

'The mystic chords of memory, stretching from every battlefield and patriot grave to every living heart and hearthstone all over this broad land, will yet swell the chorus of the Union when again touched, as surely they will be, by the angel of our better nature'. (Abraham Lincoln, *First Inaugural Address*, 4 March 1861).

We remember the sunny days when we were young, when the summer holidays were full of sun and good times.

'Four ducks on a pond

A grass bank beyond,

A blue sky of spring,

White clouds on the wing:

What a little thing

To remember for years –

To remember with tears!' (William Allingham, *A Memory*, 1888).

Memories give us the points of reference in our lives. They help us to make sense – perhaps a long time after the event.

'You will awake, and remember, and understand' (Robert Browning, *Evelyn Hope*, 1855).

Memories are good for us and good to us. Praise memories: appreciate them, enjoy them, treasure them.

(Verena Tschudin)

Personality Styles and Counselling

Pat Milner

Editor's Introduction

Any kind of counselling we do starts with ourselves. Pat Milner has drawn on psychology and sociology in this chapter to describe the differences in personalities and how these can help us to know ourselves and thus help each other.

Our differing personal attributes are too often seen as either 'problems' or 'wrong' and this chapter highlights the differences in order to put them alongside each other and see them as assets. As we get older, our character traits become more distinct and many people find that they are more at ease with themselves. Yet life has also damaged us, and now may be the time when old wounds make themselves felt. Depending on our character, we deal with such memories and experiences differently. Now can be the time to help each other, through counselling and reminiscence, to turn these memories and experiences into assets.

This first chapter outlines some counselling psychology as this, rather than general psychology, informs counselling. Personality differences affect our counselling interactions. Pat writes with her life-long interest in personality theory clearly evident. She is an eclectic teacher and the historical overview she gives is therefore as much for interest as for guidance on the journey of discovery of ourselves and others.

Introduction

'The purpose of psychology is to give us a completely different idea of the things we know best.' Paul Valéry (1871–1945)

Doris and Evelyn are two friends who live in a residential home. They are both in their 70s and widowed and each has a monthly visit from her daughter, who is her only child. For Doris this visit is a highlight which she anticipates joyfully and although she would like to see her daughter more often, she gains strength from the thought that, in the middle of a very busy life, her daughter finds time to make the 80-mile round trip to visit her regularly.

Evelyn's daughter makes a journey of similar length each month, but Evelyn perceives her daughter's visits quite differently. She interprets the monthly timing to mean that her daughter does not love her as much as other daughters love their mothers, and frequently tells her that other daughters visit more often. Because she also believes that the frequency of the visits is a judgement on the quality of the mothering she herself gave, Evelyn becomes quite depressed (adapted from Coleman 1993b).

Although Doris and Evelyn share some similar life circumstances, they are clearly very different in the way they respond to these. In considering their relationships with their respective daughters, we might say that Doris' glass of life is half-full, whilst Evelyn's is half-empty. As potential counsellors, how are we to understand this difference?

This chapter suggests that two things might help our understanding. One is to consider the way in which Doris' personality differs from that of Evelyn, and the second is to take account of the different circumstances and experiences of their individual lives.

Introduction to personality

Any consideration of personality involves a short trip into the realm of psychology, which inhabits an area of study between biology and sociology. This suggests that what is psychologically possible is circumscribed by both our physical bodies and our society. A study of personality styles looks at the many characteristics which can distinguish one individual from another, such as to what extent we are generally cheerful in disposition, like Doris, or more gloomy like Evelyn; whether we are talkative, energetic, quiet or placid.

In describing and drawing attention to the fact that people behave in a variety of different ways, personality theory tries to explain what makes us 'tick'. One of its major concerns is trying to understand and explain why and how some people experience psychological stresses such as becoming very anxious or depressed while other people do not; or why people persistently behave in ways which distress them and make their lives unrewarding; why some of us are more like Doris and some more like Evelyn.

Thus one important personality characteristic may be the extent to which we experience and generate psychological distress itself, which may lead those of us who are troubled by it to seek psychological help in the form of counselling.

Because this is a book by older people for and about ourselves, the examples in this chapter focus particularly on some areas of life change which may lead us to experience distress as we become older.

What makes us 'tick'

Whilst our physical characteristics make us readily recognisable to others, we all carry within ourselves an absolute individuality. No-one else has automatic access to that kaleidoscope of memories and ideas which forms our particular consciousness and includes those thoughts, feelings, habits, hopes and prejudices which are constantly expanding and affecting our lives as we grow older. All this experience is locked away in each of our brains and it is indeed a source of wonder that 'our very personalities and mental processes, our "states of consciousness", derive from a slurry of tissue with the consistency of a soft-boiled egg' (Greenfield 1995: vii). That soft-boiled egg is our very own mind and memory, the foundation of our personal self and our identity.

Our personality may be described as a composite of our physical and biological characteristics (our genetic inheritance of personality) and the creations and products of our complex mind. What is certain is that 'we cannot assume that other people's minds work on the same principles as our own ... others do not reason as we reason, or do not value the things we value, or are not interested in what interests us' (Myers & Myers 1995: 1).

Is it possible to come to the kind of understanding of individual personalities, such as Doris and Evelyn, which may help us to offer support in times of psychological distress?

Different types of people

Throughout history there have been various attempts to create some order out of what has sometimes appeared to be the chaos of human differences.

Physical characteristics

Sheldon *et al* (1940) arrived at their theory of human types by looking at our physical constitution and our personal characteristics. They saw some basically jolly, friendly people, inclined to fatness, and they called them **endomorphic**. Those people who looked strong and athletic and who behaved in a competitive and aggressive way they called **mesomorphic**, whilst sensitive, imaginative, thin people who were not athletic, they termed **ectomorphic**. Although this seems a broadbrush approach which has little to say about the inner dynamics of men and women, in fact, size and shape can have a profound influence on the individual who dwells within the body. Our physical genetic inheritance can lead us to develop habits and behaviour patterns which we may not have chosen, given a different physical constitution, and these patterns may also stress us in later life. Our physical presentation is often our first, non-verbal, communication and can be one of our most powerful. As we grow older, the change in those physical aspects of which we have been most proud, perhaps our beauty or handsomeness or our attractive physique, may affect the foundations of our identity and induce powerful feelings of loss.

Language, thought and emotion

Dollard and Miller's (1950) attempt to reduce the complex phenomena of personality to manageable dimensions led them to look at the way in which our use of language might link with our emotional responses. They reasoned that our emotional reactions frequently resulted from the words we use to describe an experience, not necessarily from the objective characteristics of the experience itself. If I describe a situation as 'dangerous', the upset I experience would probably be a direct response to the label 'dangerous'. To the extent that I had labelled the situation appropriately and was, for example, sitting in a car which had stalled on a level crossing in the path of an approaching train, then the emotion aroused by the label 'dangerous' would be appropriate and might even save my life. However, if I am a person who is anxious and uncomfortable, even among friends, the label 'dangerous' may be describing an inappropriate and unhelpful reaction.

This basic assumption, that our emotions are aroused and lead to 'mal-adaptive' behaviour according to the interpretations that we put on situations, laid the groundwork for the counselling approach of Albert Ellis (1962, 1994). Rational-emotive behaviour therapy proposes an ABC framework in which:

(A) is an activating situation or experience, for example, Fred, an older widower, meets a woman he really likes and wants to know better and thinks 'she may not like me, she may reject me.'

(B) represents Fred's beliefs about (A): 'I must not get rejected, because I will be worthless and a failure; but I can't stand not having a woman in my life.'

(C) looks at the consequences of Fred's beliefs, which are depression, difficulties in sleeping, and avoiding women altogether even though he really likes their company. What a counsellor could help Fred to see is that it is not meeting a woman he likes that is the problem (A), but his irrational beliefs about rejection and failure and their effects on him (B), which result in his depression and avoidance of women (C).

Similarly, many of the other theories concerning the structure of per-sonality have developed around a series of relatively effective therapies, or approaches to counselling, including Freud's psychoanalytic view that our past experiences, particularly in childhood, hold the key to understanding our present predicaments; Jung's psychological types which are discussed later, and Carl Rogers' self-actualising, person-centred therapy with its emphasis on the genuineness, respect and empathy of the counsellor as crucial to effective therapeutic help.

The psychological framework of life

Erik Erikson (1950, 1982, 1986), a psychoanalytic practitioner, developed a theory of personality which has had a major influence on the ways in which growing old is studied. His book *Childhood and Society* (1950, 1965) provides a framework for life which takes the form of a series of psychological tasks to be fulfilled, influenced by and influencing our intellectual, physical and social development.

Briefly, Erikson proposed that in babyhood our first psychological task is to develop a sense of trust, rather than mistrust; in childhood, to develop autonomy, initiative and industry; in adolescence, to grapple with adolescent identity (it was from this struggle that Erikson developed the concept of 'identity crisis', now so often applied to middle age). Early adulthood sees us facing the development of intimacy versus a sense of isolation, whilst in middle age our task is guiding and establishing the next generation, generativity versus stagnation, in which Erikson (1950: 259) suggests that 'individuals often begin to indulge themselves as if they were their own or one another's one and only child.'

The stage which most concerns us here forms the task of old age: to work toward an assured sense of meaning and order both in our lives and in the world, as against stewing in despair and disgust. Erikson calls this 'ego integrity' (Coleman 1993b). How we cope with each life stage has repercussions on our subsequent stages and this cumulative effect makes the issues of old age somewhat different for each one of us, according to our past experience.

However, it is what experiences mean to us personally that counts, not necessarily how they appear to an outsider.

Stability of personality

The most dominant current personality theory, espoused by McCrae and Costa (1995), is known as the 'five factor theory', consisting of the independent aspects of emotional stability, extraversion, culture, agreeableness and conscientiousness. The work of McCrae and Costa (1990) is also relevant to our consideration of personality amongst older people. The authors have followed groups of adults (particularly men) for up to 30 years, using detailed and standardised personality inventories. Their studies indicate that our major personality characteristics are fairly consistent throughout our lives and into old age. However, we are not set in personality plaster because what we can change are our attitudes and perceptions toward ourselves, our habits and our roles. We do develop our personalities as we get older, but in certain basic respects each of us remains recognisably the same person, particularly from about 30 years of age. So who are we broadly?

INTROVERTS AND EXTRAVERTS

The two broadest, generally accepted personality groups are based on the way we experience both our internal reality of thoughts, feelings, images and memory and our external reality of other people in the world around us. Thus we arrive at the two personality distinctions, which sound a little like a '60s pop group, 'the introverts and the extraverts'.

Ninety years ago the philosopher William James proposed two basic types of people, the tender-minded and the tough-minded. He suggested that the types are opposites: the tender-minded characterised by idealism, optimism, dogmatism and rationalism (following principles), whilst the tough-minded are irreligious, pluralistic, sceptical and empirical (following facts). According to James (1906, 1975), the two types think badly of each other; tender minds often find tough minds callous, brutal or unrefined; tough minds think of the tender as soft-headed sentimentalists.

Does any of that sound familiar? Like many opposites these two attract each other and need each other and often marry, but then fight because neither understands that the other is fundamentally different.

Carl Jung, the founder of analytical psychology, was one of the most imaginative and influential writers and therapeutic practitioners who supported the separation of personality into the fundamental groups of introvert and extravert. For Jung (1976) the extravert turns with a ready welcome to the world outside, whilst the introvert prefers the world within the self. He also made further divisions of personality according to four principal ways of dealing with life and its problems: through our senses; through thought; through feeling or through intuition. Whilst we all exercise each of these functions to some degree, Jung (1976) describes our personality according to the one we use predominantly. In part innately and in part influenced by our training and early experience, we tend to rely more on one of these ways of coping with our tasks and problems than we do on the other three. In life, as in bridge, we prefer to play our strong suit.

An insult or differences in kind?

Descriptions of personalities are a potential minefield. They are sometimes taken as 'an insult and a threat to individuality' or as 'profound differences in kind ... which fit people to varying degrees and are intended to help in self understanding, not to be definitive' (Bayne 1995: 12).

What follows is intended to be informative, but not definitive, and written in praise of individuality rather than as a threat to it. We all tend to have both introvert and extravert tendencies and if placed on a line, one end of which represents extreme introversion and the other extreme extraversion, would find ourselves grouped with a majority of other people somewhere in the middle. We each have aspects of sensing, thinking, feeling and intuition. We *prefer* to act in one or another, but no one aspect is better or worse than the others.

A closer look at introverts

If we have an introvert world view, being true to ourselves, to our own ideas and feelings and to our own vision are usually what bring us peace of mind. We tend to preserve our inner integrity at all costs and to be on the defensive against the world outside and somewhat uncom-fortable in it. However, we are not necessarily shy people and if we develop our social skills we can be very personable and enjoy company – in small doses!

It is likely that we will tend to:

- be drained by continuous activity with others and need time apart to restore our energy levels. We prefer a high degree of peace and quiet;
- need time to think before we talk and thus not like being asked to speak on the spur of the moment, though we are fine if we can pre-pare ourselves beforehand;
- seldom disclose what is most precious to us and only share our inner world with people we trust;
- dislike mess or disorder and be fearful of chaos, so make our deci-sions on the basis of organising, clarifying and achieving.

We cultivate a lifestyle characterised by a love of precision, neatness and predictability. To contain our anxiety we prefer things to be done prop-erly and on time. We may not know how to address the needs of extraverts because they seem to be so superficial (Milner & Palmer 1998).

Counselling implications

Clients who prefer introversion tend to feel easy with silence, be less comfortable with action and be less enthusiastic about counselling until trust is established (Bayne 1995: 112).

An introvert counsellor is likely to help a client to explore a few issues in depth, be comfortable using silence and have the ability to reflect on strategies (Bayne 1995: 115).

'Introverts, unless handicapped by a marked lack of self-confidence, have no difficulty in creating order and imposing that order on the chaos around them. To be a successful self they need to learn:

1 The simple social skills that establish and maintain relationships.
2 That everything that exists is in constant change, that all imposed order is temporary and often an illusion and that what they call chaos, is also freedom.' (Rowe 1983: 192)

A closer look at extraverts

If we have an extravert world view, we need to be on good terms with people, things and what happens around us. We can be shy when we think that people will reject us if we attempt something and make a mess of it. For this reason we will sometimes avoid doing things in a group.

It is likely that we will tend to:

- generate the energy to tackle the tasks of life by interacting with others and being active in the world around us. We like lively surroundings and lots going on;
- decide what we think by talking about it and create our own reality and formulate our thoughts and ideas by speaking them aloud;
- prefer the activity and companionship of a life that is directed toward others; it is difficult to develop our inner lives without support;
- savour what is most precious to us by sharing it freely and talking easily about it;
- be fearful of being rejected or abandoned and so make our decisions on the basis of creating and maintaining relationships;
- have a lifestyle characterised by a spontaneous and flexible approach, rather than having timetables and plans. We put off making decisions as long as we can so as to 'go with the flow' and not miss the next bit of information which might make all the difference to our choice! We may find introverts difficult to work with because they seem so impractical. Our characteristics may be overesteemed in an activist society (Milner & Palmer 1998).

Implications for counselling

Clients who prefer extraversion tend to want a more active counsellor, be less comfortable with reflection, be optimistic and energetic (Bayne 1995: 112).

An extravert counsellor is likely to help a client to explore a range of issues, make an easy initial contact and be adept at 'thinking on their feet' – in their chair! (Bayne 1995: 115).

'Extraverts, unless handicapped by a marked lack of self-confidence, have no difficulty in making and maintaining relationships. To be a successful self they need to learn two things:

1 It isn't frightening and forbidden to explore your internal reality, rather it is interesting and very important to do so.
2 If you are completely on your own you don't disappear'. (Rowe 1983: 192)

These thumbnail sketches give an inkling of those aspects of life which may generate difficulties and the ways in which people from the two groups can stress each other in family or work situations, not necessarily from malice, but simply because they are quite unaware of the fundamental differences in these two ways of perceiving the world. In choosing a counsellor you may look for a person who is more likely to respond to your needs as an extravert or an introvert.

Personality and growing older

Although many reviews of the research findings indicate that our personality remains stable as we grow older (Woods & Britton 1985; Stuart-Hamilton 1991), there is a strong suggestion that we do become more pre-occupied with our inner selves, our own thoughts and feelings, and less with the outside world.

Eysenck's (1987) work shows that whilst generally young men are more extravert than young women, this changes with age, so that by their 60s, men are more introverted than women. Gutman (1987) suggests that with age men become less assertive whilst women become more so. Men may therefore fear old age more, whilst women find new strength and courage. This may be unsettling and can be a reason for either looking for counselling help, or indeed for becoming a counsellor.

Another study of personality over more than 50 years indicates changes in personality even from young old age (65–74) to old age (75–84). The older people were rated significantly more open-minded, cheerful and accepting (Field & Millsap 1991). Older people also rated themselves as more accepting of the limitations of old age and seeing their lives as more inevitable, appropriate and meaningful than they remembered them being in the past (Ryff & Heincke 1983; cited in Coleman 1993a: 83).

Reasons for change

There are different possible interpretations for our different behaviour as we become older. If we become less clear thinking than we once were this may be the result of psychological change, the product of biological ageing, or a consequence of living in circumstances which are incapacitating us. If we become less sociable than we once were and have less time for people, this may be the result of a depressive illness, particularly if we are extravert, a deterioration in our hearing, the lack of a stimulating environment, or our 'natural' personality inclination to engage less – part of making our world smaller (Coleman 1993a).

Roles

Our roles in society and in our family often change suddenly in later life and there may be occasions for us to develop different aspects of our personality in consequence. Older men and women who have for many years been productive, achieving and competitive in their work lives may, in retirement, be confronted with a desire for intimacy and a need to nurture which they had not previously developed. A man who was an indifferent father may make a loving and attentive grandfather. Alternatively, women who have worked at home may realise a striving to be assertive and to give time to their own needs which they had previously submerged in order to meet the needs of their family.

Many unhappy and depressed wives and mothers are introvert women who discovered that children and housework do not give them a sense of achievement. For them a lessening of the daily family grind which growing older can offer as children become more independent, may mark the end of their sentence of depression.

If we cannot negotiate the necessary changes in our close relationships or other areas of life, we may become vulnerable to developing emotional problems. It is important to promote a growing awareness of the need for individual or couple counselling and retirement preparation for people in our older age group (Coleman 1993a).

What does growing older mean?

If we are 65 or over, we have a 20 per cent possibility of suffering from pervasive depression (Gurland *et al* 1983) and there are several different ways of trying to account for this possibility. Medical clinicians may point to changes in an ageing brain and prescribe anti-depressants. Psychologists emphasise the changes in older people's self-concepts and offer the support of counselling and therapy which, for some, is a more active and positive resource than taking drugs. Sociologists look at the changes in our social relationships for the causes of our depression and recommend day centres and luncheon clubs or other social activities.

Thus biological, psychological and sociological theories of ageing tend to focus on different aspects of the ageing process without necessarily contradicting each other. They make different assumptions, use concepts in different ways, pose different questions and arrive at different explanations of the ageing process. Their perspectives are not right or wrong, they are different and each has a valid contribution to make to our understanding (Bond *et al* 1993).

Nevertheless, there are fundamental aspects to ageing which are widely accepted (Strehler 1962). Ageing is:

- universal – it occurs in all of us (unlike disease);
- progressive – it is a continuous process;
- intrinsic – it is a fundamental part of our nature;
- degenerative – we deteriorate as we age (cited in Bond *et al* 1993: 21).

Childhood and old age are part of the same story, or as R L Stevenson stoically put it, in his *Virginibus Puerisque* (1881) 'Old and young, we are all on our last cruise'. Consequently, ageing successfully means coming to some fairly satisfactory resolution of the issues we faced earlier in our lives, since the way we handled these can have major repercussions for our later development. It is likely that we all can bring to mind older people we know who, having arrived at the final stage of life and faced with the task of integrating and using their accumulated years of experience and knowledge, sadly die uncommitted and frustrated, feeling that their life is unresolved.

But if we do not know what the task of life is, how can we meet it? If the ultimate journey we make is to die, whether we are introvert or extravert, we fear it for different reasons. If we are introvert we will want a sense of having control over our death and the thought that we will lose control of our lives and lose ourselves in some unknown force is the ultimate dread. If we are extravert it is not so much the loss of control that we fear, but the fact that death is the one journey we each make on our own (Rowe 1995: 72). Counselling is one way through which we can address these issues.

Depression, illness and stress

Throughout life we have various experiences which, for some of us, act to generate stress or depression. Bond, Coleman and Peace (1993) describe many of these in their comprehensive book *Ageing in Society*. A helpful description by Hanley and Baikie (1984) cites the following potential stress factors in growing older:

Loss The removal of people or external circumstances that we have relied on to satisfy and meet our needs, perhaps the bereavement of a partner or a change of home.

Attack An external force which produces discomfort, perhaps our own illness or the hostile reaction of others to us, whether physical or psychological.

Restraint External restriction on activities which have been necessary for the satisfaction of our needs, perhaps enforced retirement, becoming immobile, feeling that we have to stay indoors.

Threat Any event which warns us of a possible future loss, attack or restraint.

Some experiences link all these potential stressors. A heart attack, for example, clearly 'attacks' us, restrains us and may be seen as a forewarning of our loss of life in the future. It is perhaps not surprising that heart conditions are strongly linked to depression (Coleman 1993b: 114).

Personality and illness

In 1997, the Edinburgh Artery Study made links between personality and heart disease which suggest that one feature of personality which seems to protect us against heart attacks (particularly if we are women!) is the trait of low self-confidence and submissiveness. Thus if we are a person who prefers to stay in the background and let others lead and dominate us, we are likely to lack a sense of security, but less likely to have a heart attack (Whiteman *et al* 1997). This parallels the findings of the Western Collaborative Group Study, that submissive men had a lower 22-year mortality rate from all causes than did dominant men (Houston *et al* 1997). Such studies point to the possibility that, taken together with other predictors and lifestyle, personality factors may help doctors to improve their prediction of which of us is at risk of coronary heart disease. An area for collaboration between medical and psychological practitioners perhaps?

However, it is also important to recognise that it is not only major life events such as illness or bereavement which can be related to the development of depression as we grow older. Holahan *et al* (1984) have suggested that there is evidence that psychological distress is more strongly related to daily hassles than to major life events.

Keeping up appearances

Although as we age many of us may appear depressed within ourselves, we can be quite uncomplaining about the things in our environment. We might say that we are 'happy with' our circumstances in life, but do not 'feel happy'. Thus we present an apparent paradox, that as older people we display relatively high rates of depression but express ourselves the most satisfied with the circumstances of our lives. Of course, our reactions to our encounters with stress are part of our 'life-long drama' and those of us who seek to offer counselling need to take account of the commitments, values, fears and hopes shown throughout an older person's life, if we are to understand these reactions (Lazarus & DeLongis 1983).

The value of a confidante

Some researchers have speculated why it is that some of us appear more protected against depression than others. Murphy (1982) and Brown *et al* (1986) demonstrate the importance of having someone in whom we can confide, a person to whom we can speak about our concerns and our problems, who perhaps acts as a buffer in life's difficulties. They call such a person a 'confidante', and perhaps that is a more familiar and acceptable word to some of us who are older than is the word 'counsellor', which may have associations with religion or town hall 'councillors'. The older people studied who were most vulnerable to depression when they suffered poor health and encountered adverse life circumstances were those who reported a lack of confiding relationships (Murphy 1982). However, older people who seek support from a counsellor who is not a person with whom they have a long-standing, reciprocal relationship may experience a loss of self-worth (Brown *et al* 1986). Perhaps this may be seen as an indication of the value of co-counselling (in which two people who feel some compatibility, agree to take it in turns to counsel each other) amongst older people. It certainly suggests a need to be aware of the effects of such a difference in perception of the value of the help that professional counsellors may offer.

It seems important to ask what it is about a confiding relationship that protects some of us against depression. Perhaps the crucial value lies in having someone to whom we can speak out our problems, or perhaps it is the behaviour and attitude of the confidante that matters. The feeling of reciprocal warmth and trust, and most important of all, a sense of being valued and of being understood, are the key to the sense of support that we gain from a confidante (Murphy 1982). This reinforces Rogers' (1961) therapeutic qualities of empathy, respect and genuineness which are at the core of his person-centred approach to counselling.

What is my worth?

How we feel about ourselves has been considered 'the linchpin of the quality of life in old age' (Schwartz 1975). Self-worth is similar to depression in the sense that some of us experience more of it than others. We may be vulnerable in our view of ourselves, perhaps as a result of life's experiences, particularly in childhood, and how we have interpreted them, or as an outcome of our inherited personality. Others of us, again for the same reasons, may have an almost inviolable sense of our own self-worth. If we take responsibility on ourselves for all the negative things that happen in our world and credit others with all the positive things that happen, we are likely to become depressed, even if we have the support of a confidante and do not encounter stressful life experiences. Alternatively, those of us with a strong sense of our own value take responsibility for positive things that happen and are better able to see the responsibility of other people for the negative outcomes (Coleman 1993b). Krause (1987) has suggested that effective social support (which could include counselling) will help to reduce the deleterious effects of stress upon our depression, mainly by boosting our self-esteem or feelings of personal worth.

Our personality influences how we behave in relation to our feelings of self-worth. Introverts who value and accept themselves will be readily able to meet life with the view that although it might take time, they will sort things out. Extraverts who value themselves are more likely to respond with the view that anyone who rejects them is a fool and they are not going to trouble themselves with fools. Neither of these approaches to life is compatible with depression.

Conversely, introverts who feel badly about themselves meet each of life's problems with the devastating thought that they will not be able to cope, whilst extraverts who do not value themselves meet problems with the devastating thought that whatever they do, everyone is going to hate them. 'It is extremely important that you know what is your top priority, having a sense of individual achievement or having a good relationship with other people. Of course we all want both, but life often makes us choose' (Rowe 1995: 59).

In what she terms 'top priority for a satisfactory life', Rowe (1995: 59) suggests that if we are introvert we need to ensure that there is something in our lives which gives us a sense of achievement. If we are extravert, we need to ensure that there is at least one group of people in our lives in which we feel a secure member. As we become older and we make our world smaller, what can we do to ensure that we can meet these top priorities as our room for manoeuvre is diminished? This is surely one of the questions for any counselling which takes account of our differences in personality. Doris, Evelyn and Fred, who we met earlier, are all facing this dilemma.

Perception

The perception of life and other people we each have is influenced by many things, of which our personality is one. We can gain an indication of this influence by asking whether, like Doris, we consider our glass of life to be half-full, or like Evelyn, half-empty. Or perhaps we are like Fred and have beliefs which lead us to fear rejection and thus to impoverish our own lives. Clearly our responses to corresponding life situations and events are affected by the way in which we perceive them.

Mindlessness or mindfulness

As we grow older, our perceptions of the importance of issues such as an expectation of poorer health, or media coverage of rising crime rates and attacks on older people can have an impact on our judgement. If we have an opportunity to discuss things which concern us, which counselling offers, it is less likely that our anxieties will become too intense to manage. We may not feel able to go out because we have exaggerated fears of being mugged or think that because we have arthritis or a heart condition it is dangerous for us to walk about. The opportunity to talk to a counsellor about our anxieties makes it more likely that we can achieve more realistic attitudes to life and develop more sense of control. If we can feel that we have some control of our lives we are less likely to find our morale and eventually our physical health deteriorating.

Langer (1989) draws our attention to the benefits of moving older people from a passive state of 'mindlessness' to an active state of 'mindfulness' (cited in Coleman 1993b: 127).

Some insights into the perceptions of a state of 'mindlessness' which make up a recipe for depression are:

1 Believe that you, your life and the world, are exactly and unchangeably as you see them.
2 Believe that you are, in essence, bad and have to work hard to be good.
3 Believe that you live in a Just World where goodness is rewarded and badness punished.
4 Wait for a disaster to occur to you (Rowe 1995: 81).

As older people we have life experiences which have imbued us with such perceptions and it can be difficult for us to keep up with the pace of present day life and the change in values which accompanies human progress.

Changing values

The changing circumstances of childhood which people have experienced during the twentieth century are well described by Seabrook (1980). Mary could have been a character in that book: now 89, Mary grew up in a world in which she had to be disciplined and stoical, frugal and self-denying. What this taught her, often in bitterness and pain, appears to be of less value to her children, no use to her grandchildren and completely foreign to her great grandchildren, who have all been shaped by dramatically different experiences. In some ways she is like 'a time traveller exiled to a foreign country' (Rabbit 1984: 14). It is not surprising that Mary sometimes feels obliged to condemn modern society, because if she accepts its very different values, this means denying meaning to her own life, as she has lived it. McCulloch (1990) calls this concept 'moral siege' and describes it as the attitudes of people who in comparing the past with the present, emphasise the differences rather than the similarities and give a high moral estimate to older people and a low one to the young. This criticising of young people and present day society is often seen as a fault in older people. 'It would perhaps help if we were more sensitive to the very understandable reasons why they do so criticise' (Coleman 1993b: 109). The attitude of 'moral siege' is a way of coping with social changes which helps us as older people to retain some satisfaction with our own past lives. Counsellors working with people like Mary need the sensitivity and awareness to help her to retain the value of her past whilst choosing her own realistic accommodation with present society.

Another of McCulloch's (1990) concepts is that of 'questioning' which is that state of confusion arising from changes in values and beliefs which leaves us in a wasteland between our own past values and beliefs and those of the modern world. When we can transcend the differences between our past and our present we are able to achieve a sense of continuity or progress with which we can identify. However, it is not easy for anyone to achieve a state of harmony with a rapidly changing world. We are often caught between two sets of values, for example a life training in the importance and dominance of paid work may act against us in retirement, when a lack of occupation feels like sinful idleness, particularly if we are introvert. One of the bonuses of modern society is an increase in new leisure pursuits which, together with creative activities, can become more important in retirement. If we have the resources, we are entitled to take a full part in such a new pattern of life, but it is a particularly cruel deprivation for older people that in recent years the cost has increased and the provision of adult education has been reduced. Young people who cannot find things to do with time which hangs heavily may be led to delinquency or drugs, and counsellors readily recognise this. What is perhaps not so frequently acknowledged is that at the opposite end of life, reduced mobility, a less active but by no means passive mind, and time which passes slowly may also exact a price in human misery.

Mutual caring

The suggestion of this book that as older people we support others by being available to them as confidantes or counsellors can be seen as part of the growing mutual aid movement. Richard Titmuss (1970), in his study of blood donors, used the term 'gift relationship' to describe an altruistic exchange between people characterised by unseeking generosity. Perhaps with age, we come to value such altruistic social exchanges more, and may grow to perceive counselling each other as a 'gift relationship'.

Reminiscence

'When the theatre of the mind becomes the only show in town, archival memories begin to be actively explored for scripts. Remote memories are increasingly rehearsed for recreation and the pattern of memory accessibility across the life cycle is changed' (Rabbit 1988: 503; cited in Coleman 1993a: 81).

As potential counsellors of older people, what can we learn from the existing experience of 'reminiscence therapy' and its value? Coleman (1993b) credits the work of the American psychiatrist Robert Butler (1963), as giving positive encouragement to the view of reminiscence as a normal activity in old age; as a means of reviewing and coming to terms with our lives as we have lived them. So reminiscence as a life review is seen as a way of achieving Erikson's final stage of 'integrity'. In addition to the support of life review theory, the value of reminiscence is promoted by identity maintenance theory which claims that a greater identification with our past life and past achievements is helpful to us, particularly in situations of deprivation and loss. It is particularly at such times that the discrepancy between how we would like to live our life and how we are actually living it can be minimised by stressing the value of the life that we have already lived, thus invoking in us a valuable sense of self-worth (Coleman 1993b).

Whether or not as older people we stand to gain from reminiscence or reviewing our lives in counselling depends as much on our past experiences as it does on our present needs. The problem for an active older counsellor working with a frail, disabled person is that the comfort and appreciation which the one gains from thinking back on memories may be quite incomprehensible to the other. This emphasises the importance of a thoughtful matching of counsellors and clients, just as in the gift relationship of blood donors we need a gift from someone with a compatible blood group.

Conclusion

The story of Doris and Evelyn which introduced this chapter illustrated how apparently similar events can be experienced differently. To comprehend the significance of those differences requires counsellors to understand the experience and perception of Doris and Evelyn and also those of Fred and Mary, who we met later, whilst also acknowledging the influence of their differing personalities. This is because whether we are introvert or extravert, older or younger, we can help each other to work toward our own 'ego integrity'. This is a journey we can choose to make alone, or in the company of another, but we only have that choice if there are others available. Growing older can mean that there are fewer people in our lives, which is one reason for the encouragement of counsellors and counselling amongst older people which this book makes.

'It is by discovering the self-confidence with which we were born and by learning what we need to learn that we are able to achieve our own individual synthesis of being an extravert and an introvert. Of course as a born extravert we keep looking around for some extra stimulation, and as a born introvert we keep organising, but, tolerating our long established idiosyncrasies, we achieve not merely the idealised notion of being both an individual and a close-knit member of a group, but the real lived experience of being one's unique self and an integral part of the continual life of the planet, as much a part of life as a wave is part of the ocean' (Rowe 1988: 280).

References

Bayne R (1995) *The Myers Briggs Type Indicator: A critical review and practical guide*. London: Chapman and Hall.

Bond J, Coleman P, Peace S (eds) (1993) *Ageing in Society*. London: Sage.

Brown G W, Andrews B, Harris T, Adler Z, Bridge L (1986) 'Social support, self-esteem and depression'. *Psychological Medicine* 16: 813–831.

Butler R (1963) 'The Life Review: An interpretation of reminiscence in the aged'. *Psychiatry* 26: 65–76.

Coleman P G (1993a) 'Psychological Ageing'. In: Bond J, Coleman P, Peace S (eds). *Ageing in Society*. London: Sage, 68–96.

Coleman P G (1993b) 'Adjustment in Later Life'. In: Bond J, Coleman P, Peace S (eds). *Ageing in Society*. London: Sage, 97–132.

Coleman P G, McCulloch A W (1990) 'Societal change, values and social support: exploratory studies into adjustment in late life'. *Journal of Ageing Studies* 4: 321–332.

Coleman P G, Bond J, Peace S (1993) 'Ageing in the Twentieth Century'. In: Bond J, Coleman P, Peace S (eds). *Ageing in Society*. London: Sage, 1–18.

Dollard J, Miller N E (1950) *Personality and Psychotherapy: An analysis in terms of learning, thinking and culture*. New York: McGraw Hill.

Ellis A (1962) *Reason and Emotion in Psychotherapy*. Secaucus, NJ: Citadel.

Ellis A (1994) *Reason and Emotion in Psychotherapy* (revised and updated). New York: Carol Publishing.

Erikson E H (1950) *Childhood and Society*. New York: Norton.

Erikson E H (1965) *Childhood and Society*. Harmondsworth: Penguin.

Erikson E H (1982) *The Life Cycle Completed: A review*. New York: Norton.

Erikson E H, Erikson J M, Kivnick H Q (1986) *Vital Involvement in Old Age: The experience of old age in our time*. New York: Norton.

Eysenck H J (1987) 'Personality and ageing: an exploratory analysis'. *Journal of Social Behaviour and Personality* 3: 11–21.

Field D, Millsap R E (1991) 'Personality in advanced old age: continuity and change'. *Journal of Gerontology* 46: 299–308.

Greenfield S (1995) *Journey to the Centres of the Mind*. New York: W H Freeman & Co.

Gurland B J, Copeland J, Xuriansky J, *et al* (1983) *The Mind and Mood of Ageing: Mental health problems of the community elderly in New York and London*. London: Croom Helm.

Gutman D L (1987) *Reclaimed Powers: Toward a new psychology of men and women in later life*. New York: Basic Books.

Hanley I, Baikie E (1984) 'Understanding and treating depression in the elderly'. In: Hanley I, Hodge J (eds). *Psychological Approaches to the Care of the Elderly*. London: Croom Helm, 213–236.

Holahan C K, Holahan C J, Belk S (1984) 'Adjustment in aging: the roles of life stress, hassles and self-efficacy'. *Health Psychology* 3: 315–328.

Houston B K, Babyak M A, Chesney M A, Black G, Ragland D R (1997) 'Social dominance and 22-year all-cause mortality in men'. *Psychosomatic Medicine* 59: 5–12.

James W (1975 [1906]) *Pragmatism and the Meaning of Truth*. Cambridge, MA: Harvard University Press.

Jung C J (1976) 'Psychological Types'. In: *Collected Works of C J Jung* (Volume 6). London: Routledge and Kegan Paul.

Krause N (1987) 'Life stress, social support and self-esteem in an elderly population'. *Psychology and Ageing* 2: 349–356.

Langer E J (1989) 'Minding matters: the consequences of mindlessness-mindfulness'. *Advances in Experimental Social Psychology* 22: 137–175.

Lazarus R S, DeLongis A (1983) 'Psychological stress and coping in aging'. *American Psychologist* 38: 245–254.

McCrae R R, Costa P T (1990) *Personality in Adulthood*. New York: Guilford Press.

McCrae R R, Costa P T (1995) 'Toward a new generation of personality theories: theoretical aspects for the five factor model'. In: Wiggins J (ed). *The Five Factor Model of Personality: Theoretical perspectives*. New York: Plenum.

McCulloch *see* Coleman and McCulloch

Milner P, Palmer S (1998) *Integrative Stress Counselling*. London: Cassell.

Murphy E (1982) 'Social origins of depression in old age'. *British Journal of Psychiatry* 141: 135–142.

Myers I B, Myers P (1995) *Gifts Differing: Understanding personality type*. Paolo Alto: Davies Black.

Rabbit P M A (1984) Investigating the grey areas. *Times Higher Educational Supplement* 1 June: 14.

Rabbit P M A (1988) 'Social psychology, neuroscience and cognitive psychology need each other (and gerontology needs all three of them)'. *The Psychologist. Bulletin of the British Psychological Society* 12: 500–506.

Rogers C R (1961) *On Becoming a Person*. Boston: Houghton Mifflin.

Rowe D (1983) *Depression: The way out of your prison*. London: Routledge.

Rowe D (1988) *The Successful Self*. London: Harper Collins.

Rowe D (1995) *Guide to Life*. London: Harper Collins.

Ryff C D, Heincke S G (1983) 'Subjective organisation of personality in adulthood and aging'. *Journal of Personality and Social Psychology* 44: 807–816.

Schwartz A N (1975) 'An observation on self-esteem as the linchpin of quality of life for the aged'. *The Gerontologist* 15: 470–472.

Seabrook J (1980) *The Way We Are*. London: Age Concern.

Sheldon W H, Stevens S S, Tucker W B (1940) *The Varieties of Human Physique*. London: Harper Row.

Strehler B L (1962) *Time, Cells and Ageing*. New York: Academic Press.

Stuart-Hamilton I (1991) *The Psychology of Ageing: An introduction*. London: Jessica Kingsley.

Titmuss R M (1970) *The Gift Relationship: From human blood to social policy*. London: Allen & Unwin.

Whiteman M C, Deary I J, Lee A J, Foulkes F G R (1997) 'Submissiveness and protection from coronary heart disease in the general population: Edinburgh Artery Study'. *The Lancet* 350: 9077; 541–545.

Woods R T, Britton P G (1985) *Clinical Psychology with the Elderly*. London: Croom Helm.

In Praise of Memory

'Remorse begets reform' has apparently been said by William Cowper (1731–1800). Pain enables change; repentance leads to conversion.

Memory is necessary for any change, any moment forward of mind and body. We remember to get up in the morning, and we remember who we are. We remember our potential.

'Psychotherapists are very familiar with the process of quantum memory, though most might be surprised upon first being told that! The physics by which the wave functions of our various past sub-selves can overlap with, and hence get taken up into, our present self is the physics by which psychotherapists get their patients to relive past experiences in the "now", thus robbing them of their isolation and their sting and wedding them to the present. This moment of psychoanalytic "insight", during which the past is now and both past and present are transformed, is quite different from the simple, intellectual remembering of past events.

'Put in quantum terms, the wave function of a relived past moment overlaps with the wave function of now, and the two unite to form a new way forward. The person gains perspective and becomes more coherent'. (Danah Zohar, *The Quantum Self*, 1991, Flamingo, p 105)

The move forward is only possible because of the move backward.

We remember an emotion, a feeling, a sensation:

'By the waters of Babylon we sat down and wept, when we remembered thee, O Sion.' (Psalm 137, 1)

Not all memories make us change and move on. We can be trapped by memories. Can memories then still be praised?

(Verena Tschudin)

2

Working with Older Women

Dorothy Jerrome

Editor's Introduction

Many more women than men either use counselling services or are counsellors themselves. In this chapter, Dorothy Jerrome considers the gender issues which relate to counselling and counsellors.

The age-old chestnut of nature and nurture turns up again and again in our lives. But analysing which has influenced most does not normally help us to solve a problem. Taking stock of where we are, how we can use what we have, what has been given to us, and what we can make of opportunities is sensitively addressed in this chapter. Dorothy helps us, by the use of examples, to see what motivates women and how counselling can be used to gain new orientations and fulfilment.

Introduction

In the course of this chapter, I shall ask why more women than men seek counselling, and what distinguishes work with women in the second half of life. The invisibility of older people in counselling services and of older women in specialist agencies for women, is striking. I ask why older women are unlikely to seek counselling, finding answers in both professional attitudes and in older women's own reluctance to seek help.

There is a reluctance to acknowledge the need for help and to ask for it directly. This is related to a central theme in women's lives: dependence, independence and interdependence. Dilemmas over dependence and independence reflect the central importance of these states in our culture, where the concept of maturity lays emphasis on autonomy, self-reliance and self-control. Emotional distance from others is rewarded, particularly as a feature of manhood. But women too learn at an early age to be emotionally self-sufficient while providing emotional support to the people around them. People who deny their own dependency needs, or fail to have them recognised by others, achieve a state of unsatisfied independence. A state of imbalance is problematic in different ways. Loneliness is a price paid for independence, and similarly dependence and frustration or anger are two sides of the same coin.

In the course of the chapter I shall show how the dependence-independence dynamic works for some women. Ambivalence towards these states emerges as a life-long issue which creates problems for women and which enters the counselling room in various guises. The therapeutic goal is then to find a way of accepting help without guilt, perhaps for the first time in a woman's life. To illustrate the point I shall use case material from my own work with older women.

Women and men as clients

A striking imbalance exists between men and women as clients, at all ages. In later life, the reasons are partly demographic: there simply are more women. The life expectancy of women still exceeds men, despite improvements in child health and the environment which have allowed baby boys and girls alike to grow up and grow old, and improvements in adult health provision such as the introduction of antibiotics and health and safety measures in the work place, which have improved adult men's chances of survival. So both men and women have more or less equal chances of entering old age. But once in retirement, the equality ends. Women, although suffering from higher rates of chronic illness, outlive men for reasons which are not clear. One possibility is that they are better able to withstand the vicissitudes of age. It is significant, for instance, that older men cope less well with bereavement. It is, for them, a minority experience; while most women can expect to be widowed, most men can expect to be married until they die. The higher life expectancy of women and the tendency for men to have wives younger than themselves, accounts for this pattern. However, those men who do experience widowhood are more likely to die within a short time of their partners than widowed women are.

A clue lies in the different meanings of marriage for men and women. For men, the wife is likely to be a major confidant and the sole source of emotional intimacy. Women are more likely to number women friends and female relatives in their list of confidants. Women have a greater capacity for intimate same-sex friendships, which stands them in good stead in the context of bereavement. It seems that older women have emotional resources possibly lacking in men, such as the capacity to reach out and share in times of emotional distress.

A difference in emotional make-up, which is seen in the way women relate to people from their earliest years, is another possible reason for their greater numbers in counselling. The fact that women are the majority of both clients and counsellors is striking. Perhaps the counselling process, involving self-disclosure, a focus on need and vulnerability, and an emphasis on feelings, is more congenial to women. Research on intimate relationships tells us that men experience discomfort in the use of certain emotion words and express their intimacy needs differently. The language of intimacy is more familiar to women. Counselling is an intimate relationship, and communication about feelings is often easier in same-sex pairs.

A third reason why older women appear more frequently as clients than older men might reflect women's particular life experiences. Pre-occupations in the second half of a woman's life are similar to those of earlier adulthood: roles and relationships, health and illness, sexuality and body image, power and autonomy in relation to other people and the social environment, income, housing and physical security. But ageing brings additional problems and changes the character of existing ones. Mother-daughter relationships change as the two women move along different pathways. The environment over which the older woman seeks control comes to include the activities of caregivers. Physical ageing reduces power and independence. There are fewer opportunities for sexual expression. There are strong cultural pressures towards independence and a coping stance, which are not necessarily appropriate at this stage. Ageism combined with sexism limits activity in the public sphere. The loss of paid employment on retirement from the workforce reduces income and limits choice. The loss of paid work means the end of a particular kind of social involvement. It might also expose long-term difficulties which had been kept under control. The loss of an occupation, whether paid or not, has many emotional reper-cussions.

Lastly, the loss of intimate relationships through death is a more fre-quent occurrence in later life. The bereavement process might be problematic, especially following the kinds of conventional marriage common to those who are currently in their 70s and older. Impending death brings the need for closure and an acceptance of life as it has been lived.

Issues in counselling

The problems which older women present are varied. In terms of fam-ily relationships, there are problems associated with motherhood: difficulties in relating to children and grandchildren, and in achieving a balance between distance and over-involvement, the long-term effects of having given up children for adoption, separation and estrangement from older children, a sense of abandonment. As daughters, older women are still troubled by difficulties experienced for decades, such as separation, responsibility and caring, guilt and resentment. As sisters, long-term sibling rivalry shapes current relationships. There are issues concerning partners, such as a sense of exploitation, unsatisfying patterns of loving and caring, boundary issues, dependence and survival in the absence of the partner, and unresolved grief. Another set of issues concerns the home, possessions, housing and physical space as sources of self-expression and symbols of independence in old age. There are issues of retirement such as the loss of social contact, a sense of achievement and a source of self-esteem. Isolation and loneliness, experienced both as an absence of intimacy and an existential sense of being alone in the world, are serious problems for some older women. Ill-health produces many problems, including unsatisfactory or distressing treatment by health professionals. There are issues of death and dying and frustration and disappointment with life as it has been lived. There is intense regret over childlessness, a failure to take advantage of educational opportunities and to experience the full range of sexual potential. Such experiences make death an object of dread.

To the various life crises and events which assail most of us, we must add the unique individual response which allows one woman to cope unaided and another to require help. Advanced age heightens the possibility of early difficulties being overlaid by others. There has also been more time to develop unhelpful coping strategies which are harder to unravel since they have served for longer as a means of psychological survival. Women may reach old age suffering unaccountably from depression or anxiety which assails them apparently 'out of the blue'. They have coped for most of their adult lives with conditions which most of us would find acutely stressful. They might bring with them painful memories of past trauma, barely kept in check. A relatively stable lifestyle and coping strategy are rocked by an episode of ill health or a profound loss or other acute difficulty. At this point, psychological characteristics such as passivity and low self-esteem, which have been successfully masked earlier in life, prevent the woman from moving on.

Provision for older women

What role does counselling play in meeting such needs? To answer this question we need to look first at mental health provision in general, then see how counselling, as a particular kind of service, fits in. On the one hand there appears to be a shortage of suitable provision for older women. On the other hand, existing services are under-used. Mental health professionals have failed to recognise older women's needs and offer appropriate treatment. But older women themselves do not actively seek professional help for their emotional problems.

Professional help with personal problems has traditionally come through two channels: social services and medicine. Social work provision for older adults has come increasingly to focus on their practical needs. Current legislation requires the assessment of need. But although assessors are often concerned about the emotional and psychological difficulties of elderly people, an increase in referrals and in paperwork since the introduction of the new community care arrangements have left them with little time to address these issues. Social workers recognise the need for skilled listening and for checking that painful issues have been addressed. But they report having no time for interventions in the area of emotional need. An emphasis on practical tasks, time constraints and the problems of purchasing services that once they provided themselves, has led to social work's neglect of older people's emotional needs. Faced with marital problems in relationships that have lasted more than half a century, with intractable disability, with the looming presence of death and with few resources to draw on, assessors have no incentive to identify needs they can do little about. Depression, for example, a common problem among older people faced with traumatic life events and with the painful reality of declining health, is assessed as a medical problem requiring in-patient treatment with medication. For people who are lonely and depressed in the community, a day centre referral is seen as the solution. Individual counselling is no longer an option.

The health service response to emotional difficulties is equally limited, despite official statements of good intent. The mental health needs of older women are recognised in official policy statements such as *The*

Health of the Nation (Department of Health 1992a). Mental illness is recognised as a leading cause of physical illness and disability, and older people (of whom the majority are women) are seen as a vulnerable group. Severe mental illness is as prevalent in older people as in younger. Depression, the most common mental illness, is more common in older adults than any other group. A significant percentage of older people consult their GPs for anxiety states and other nervous disorders, the percentage rising with age (Department of Health 1992b). Depression accounts for roughly a quarter of first admissions to psychiatric hospitals among 60–75-year-old women. The government white paper expressed concern over continuing treatment by drugs, notably benzodiazepines, and noted that behavioural, cognitive and psychotherapeutic treatments might be more effective.

Professional attitudes

Despite this positive approach at the level of national health policy, older women's mental health needs have received little attention. Professional attitudes have inhibited service development, being somewhat ageist. There is a widespread view of old age as a static and unresponsive stage which, in a climate of diminishing resources, encourages practitioners to channel psychological services in the direction of younger patients and clients who are thought likely to benefit more. Personal attitudes to age and ageing interfere with the perception of older people's problems. In some professional workers, hatred and fear of frailty and death, difficult family relationships of their own, guilt and resentment of parents, all make a sensitive response hard to achieve. Ambivalence towards old age and older people interferes with existing practice with older clients, but it puts the majority of practitioners off work with older people altogether.

Although anxiety and depression are relatively widespread in older people, they are unlikely to be recognised, and if diagnosed are not likely to be treated as such. There is a lack of both detection and treatment of depression and anxiety, even if presented to doctors as such. Medical help with mental health problems takes a particular form in old age. Emotional problems causing anxiety and depression tend to be treated with drugs and ECT (electro-convulsive therapy) rather than psychological therapies. While neither of these treatments is intrinsically harmful, they must be viewed with caution. The side-effects of ECT, such as memory loss, are hard to measure with this population. Older people are more susceptible biologically and so respond relatively well to antidepressant drugs, but while drugs and ECT provide the preconditions for psychological interventions, they are not sufficient in themselves. Both work best in conjunction with other therapies which can uncover underlying causes of distress.

But older people are generally not offered counselling. In terms of the age take-up of GP services, relatively few older patients are referred for counselling, even when there is a counsellor based in the practice. Similarly, relatively few older patients are referred to clinical psychology services and hospital-based psychotherapy, even in the psychogeriatric service.

Other obstacles to getting help

A reason for the failure of GPs to detect mood disorders or to treat them as such, in patients of all ages, is that they are rarely obvious. Currently, about 15 per cent of all visits to GP surgeries are for 'hidden' psychiatric problems, such as depression (Mental Health Foundation 1997). In these cases, patients report physical problems for which there is no apparent physical cause. Hard-pressed GPs may find it difficult to make a correct diagnosis and patients can end up receiving expensive specialist treatment – and remaining distressed – while the real nature of their problem goes undetected. GPs are generally untrained in focussing on psychological as opposed to physical issues, and the patient similarly finds it easier to present with, say, physical pain than to talk about heartache or despair.

So women's restricted access to psychological services such as counselling is not just a result of professional limitations. There are difficulties on the potential clients' side too. A critical issue is the way in which emotional problems are presented. There are generational differences in attitudes to mental health and to seeking help with personal difficulties. Older people are more likely to perceive mental illness as stigmatising, and seeking help as complaining. Physical symptoms, on the other hand, are socially more acceptable, and generally easier to diagnose and treat. Older women are more likely to present their emotional distress in physical terms, if they seek professional help at all. It is significant that psychosomatic illnesses occur disproportionately among ethnic minority people, the poor, older adults and women. It would seem that people whose emotional difficulties take on a physical form are typically those who do not expect to be heard if they voice their distress directly.

There is, in any case, a strong relationship between physical illness and depression. Stress undermines the immune system and in the form of depression has an impact on the cardio-vascular system. The reality of their physical symptoms helps to account for the unlikelihood of older women being referred for counselling.

Even more important, though, are the cultural factors, such as the reserve of this generation when it comes to seeking help, the reluctance to construe emotional problems as needing professional intervention and the tendency to see depression and anxiety as moral issues demanding a stoical response. If they unburden themselves at all it is to sympathetic neighbours, adult daughters, work mates, friends, home care workers, or residential care staff. They view 'counselling' with suspicion or incomprehension.

Added to the psychological inhibitions mentioned above are physical disincentives to seeking help. They include practical problems of access to facilities that are on the whole designed for a young and able-bodied population. Housebound women are unable to travel for counselling. Confusion and hearing loss create problems with recall and reflection. Privacy and confidentiality are hard to sustain with raised voices. Another practical obstacle is cost: private services are rarely free, and potential older clients might expect counselling to be well beyond their means.

Older women as clients: issues of dependency

It would seem that older women will come for counselling only if they are directed to do so by their GPs, and not always then. Their ambivalence towards counselling makes it hard to take the step of actively seeking help, especially when this means completing an application form. Typically, older women who are referred for counselling by GPs, community psychiatric nurses, clinical psychologists and other health professionals, are already part of the mental health system. They are long-term users of mental health services and have been passed around from professional to professional. By the time such a woman comes for counselling she is likely to have had many negative and reinforcing experiences. We might be viewed as a last resort. Her prior experiences of health care have possibly made her resistant to counselling, which she perceives as yet more unhelpful intervention.

A smaller number of women have been referred for this kind of help for the first time, in response to life events which have undermined their life-long coping skills. Such women are easier to work with, though the problems they bring may seem quite intractable. Finally there are those – a minority – who come on their own initiative, because they have heard or read about the benefits of counselling, because family or friends have recommended it, and because they are desperate.

Existing in a culture where independence is highly valued, and dependence acceptable only in childhood, women grow up accustomed to being strong for other people. For the majority of women who come for counselling, even childhood has been a time of enforced emotional independence. Women find it easier to care for others than to receive care and attention. Having been encouraged to deny their emotional needs, they find the expression of need, even in counselling, a struggle. Unaccustomed to having their needs acknowledged, they find it difficult to concentrate on themselves. Invited to talk about themselves, they respond by talking about the people they care for – children and grandchildren, husband or elderly parent. The counselling process here mirrors women's habit of turning everything they are given into giving to others. The process can be observed in daily life in, for instance, the

acknowledge a compliment by turning it back to the giver,
feel guilty about solitary pleasures. This kind of client asks how
you are even as she mounts the stairs to the counselling room, is anxious not to distress you with her sadness, apologises for taking up your time, and imagines there are far more deserving cases than she.

The stigma of dependency in our culture means that the client has mixed feelings about showing the full extent of her need for support. She has a powerful longing to be able to depend on the counsellor but also a powerful belief that she should not. There is a fear of dependency, a sense that she should not be needy and that her needs represent a shameful, self-indulgent side of her which should remain hidden.

In the rest of this chapter, the themes of dependence and coping are illustrated in relation to two women, Elaine and Mavis. Their different needs give some idea of the range of issues and challenges brought by work with older women.

Take two women ...

Elaine, a woman in her mid-60s, came to counselling on the recommendation of one of her daughters who herself had benefitted from therapy. She was feeling desperate and confused about a choice she had made to leave her husband of nearly 50 years to live by herself. She continued to love her home and mentally ill husband, returning at weekends to shop and look after him. A major issue was her relationships with her three adult daughters and her grandchildren: was she responsible for their happiness? Did she need their permission to go back home? Other issues included the significance of her family roles for her sense of self, and the loss of a dream of a happy retirement shared with her husband. In terms of ageing, the focus of our work together was on coming to terms with disappointment and exploring the possibilities for change and choice in late middle age. Elaine had coped with her arduous family responsibilities over the years by managing her husband and children, and not thinking much about herself.

In the counselling relationship she was able to explore these issues, to identify the pattern of investments she had made and value them as a positive choice, despite being castigated by her daughters as weak for her continuing loyalty to her husband, and giving herself a hard time for having put up with his behaviour for so long. A major focus of the work was loss and endings.

In the counselling relationship, Elaine experienced sharing with someone who did not judge her as her daughters did, and was not both demanding and unsympathetic as her own mother had been. She explored her difficulty in making her own needs felt, afraid that she might overwhelm me as her youngest daughter overwhelmed her. In the course of the ten weeks we worked together, Elaine had been able to explore three themes in her life: responsibility, burden and space. By the end it seemed that she knew what she wanted for the forseeable future: space for herself, more independence from her daughters, and a workable contract with her husband so that they could live together again in the future. Elaine had begun to express some feelings which normally did not get an airing – sadness and irritation. Stronger feelings were kept in check, though their presence was revealed through her body language. I respected her need for control as the way she had coped so far in her life. We concluded that Elaine's family were still central in her life, and possibly always would be.

Mavis, 85, wanted my help in dealing with unpredictable and inexplicable depressions which assailed her with increasing frequency. This was her first experience of counselling and a friend associated with the counselling agency had recommended it. She described herself as a loner, who had had two brief partnerships many decades earlier, had moved to the town on retirement 25 years ago and was unused to sharing her feelings even with old friends.

During the counselling several issues came to light. Feelings of inadequacy had dogged Mavis all her life, and there was evidence of an emotionally disturbed childhood with an alcoholic mother. It was possible that her depression in late life might be a product of low self-esteem in childhood. Mavis described her success in coping through her early and middle adulthood but found the feelings of inadequacy emerging with full force in her advanced old age. She found that it helped to see how her current feelings might be linked to childhood difficulties and began to dream in a comfortable way about people from her past.

In counselling she learnt that her earlier strategy for coping with low self-esteem and depression – hard work – was no longer helping her. She needed to retire from her voluntary work as she was too tired to carry on. But the prospect of giving up was terrifying. She had always valued herself in terms of what she did, and to retire and do nothing useful would be a living death. We explored the implications of Mavis retiring, as she felt she was bound to do. The difficulty of simply being, as opposed to doing, was immense. Mavis did not want to contemplate it. She was ready to die and did not particularly want to go on living.

Over the ten weeks of our work together, Mavis identified feelings of profound loneliness, a lack of intimacy and fear of emotional dependency. She had a dream about a vulnerable child being rescued by a woman who seemed to be the mother. The appearance of this woman relieved Mavis herself of the need to intervene on the child's behalf. As we discussed the dream, Mavis identified herself as the vulnerable creature and I became the woman who acknowledged her dependency and need for support. The dream session was very moving, though Mavis did not express her feelings directly. We talked instead about the power of great music to move her. I myself experienced feelings of intense sadness as she spoke, and Mavis responded by talking about her own sadness, the sadness of losing everyone, and of not being understood.

By the following week, the dream had been 'forgotten'. Mavis was now concerned to bring the counselling to a close, lest she become dependent on me. She was sure there were other women with a greater entitlement to my time. We talked about her life-long emotional self-sufficiency and choice to continue in that mode. Since starting counselling she had had no more depressions, apart from an episode on holiday recently, brought on by fatigue and a sense of being unable to keep up with her hostess. Mavis was ready to stop seeing me, on the understanding that if she needed to she could come back for the occasional visit.

Conclusion

The themes in these stories are the expression of need, the denial of need, and the displacement of feelings in various ways. All of these themes emerge in work with older women. Counselling provides a unique opportunity for nurturing, though for women who have always done the giving it is initially hard to accept without guilt. Sometimes, the counselling can only be justified in terms of its benefits for the rest of the family. Older women clients (and younger ones too) characteristically discount their own needs in favour of the more deserving. But in counselling they experience a level of sharing never known before. Their needs are, perhaps for the first time, recognised and acknowledged. So Mavis, for instance, felt that she could now leave the counselling relationship and perhaps bid farewell to life. Elaine felt strong enough to defend her right to life on her own terms.

These two women were able to seek help, unlike many who suffer in silence, their emotional distress unrecognised or dismissed as unworthy of attention. I have tried to explain the surprisingly low rates of older women in counselling in terms of both professionals' and older women's reluctance to accept the need for it. I have identified self-denial on the older woman's part and a tendency in providers of services to minimise the mental health needs of this group, or treat them inappropriately. With women's increasing awareness and with the growth of professional interest in the needs of older adults (of which this book is an example), the future looks more promising.

References

Department of Health (1992a) *Health of the Nation*. London: Stationery Office.

Department of Health (1992b) *The Health of Elderly People: An epidemiological overview*. London: Stationery Office.

Mental Health Foundation (1997) 'Lifting the curtain on "hidden" psychiatric problems in GP surgeries'. In: *Talk Back*, Mental Health Foundation Newsletter: May 1997.

In Praise of Memory

'A memory is what is left when something happens and does not completely unhappen' (Edward de Bono, *The Mechanism of Mind*, 1969, Penguin).

The Memory is something to be cultivated and respected; the fact that the nine Muses are the daughters of Zeus and Mnemosyne ('Memory') makes this connection hard to miss.

'I sit beside my lonely fire,
And pray for wisdom yet –
For calmness to remember
Or courage to forget'. (Charles Hamilton, 1830–1904, *Aïdé*).

'I shall remember while the light lives yet
And in the night time I shall not forget' (Algernon Charles Swinburne, *Erotion*, 1866)

'Memory fades, must the remembered
Perishing be?' (Walter de la Mare, 1873–1956).

'A very fair scholar I was too; no thought but a great memory' (Samuel Beckett, 1906–1989, quoted in *The Times Educational Supplement*, 2 June 1978)

'But the Iniquity of oblivion blindly scattereth her poppy, and deals with the memory of men without distinction of merit to posterity' (Sir Thomas Browne, 1605–1682, *Burial Urn*).

'He who is not very strong in memory should not meddle in lying' (Montaigne, 1533–1592).

'You can close your eyes to reality but not to memories' (Stanislav Lec, 1909–1966).

(Verena Tschudin)

3

On Being a Witness

Lyn C Jennings

Editor's Introduction

Lyn Jennings describes a very distinct form of listening: that of being a silent – or almost silent – witness. 'Witnessing' is something which we normally associate with seeing or speaking more than with listening. The essence of this witnessing is *being there*. In such presence there is communication which can be powerful, restorative and empowering.

When we have the opportunity to tell our story we 'see' ourselves in a fresh light. There is a sense in which we become human through talking; we certainly remain human by telling each other our stories. For stories to be made valid, they have to be heard, and telling our stories to a wall is never enough. Counselling is about talking and responding: as each person speaks the other responds, thus making the conversation therapeutic. But as Lyn shows, sometimes the responses have to be minimal because telling the story itself is so important. Because few words are spoken by the counsellor, the listening and the hearing – and the sharing – become that much more important.

Introduction

This chapter explores the concept of the counsellor as 'witness' to the disturbing and distressing experiences that clients may never have previously disclosed to anyone. By telling the (suitably disguised) narratives of some of the people with whom I have worked, I have attempted to show different aspects of the function of 'witness'. In my work of counselling, counselling supervision and the training of counsellors, learning never stops. I feel that it is my professional duty to try to keep abreast of ideas and thinking about counselling and therapy, consequently I attend seminars and read as much as I can, but it is often from my students, supervisees and clients that I learn much that is relevant to the process of my work. Henry was one such client and it is for this reason that I have chosen to tell part of his story here. He was approaching middle-age when he was referred to me.

Henry's story – but what does he want from me?

The person in the chair before me sat with his long gangling legs constantly changing their position, first one way then the other. I tried not to be distracted, needing to concentrate on the great river of words he was pouring forth, but there was a sense that his restless legs were also trying to convey something of how difficult it had been to walk the strange rocky path that had suddenly been set out before them.

This was Henry and it was he who helped me understand, in an unexpected way, what it is that people sometimes want from counsellors. It was Henry who firmly put me into the role of 'witness', a role that has become increasingly meaningful in my work with older clients.

Henry was in his mid-forties when he came to work with me. To his very great surprise, he had suffered what he described as 'a complete nervous breakdown'. He worked in a very well-paid and highly responsible job. He was very good at his job, he told me. 'In fact, I'm a bit of a perfectionist' he said somewhat sadly, as if that role would never be an easy one to occupy again. Henry had been trying to do the work of three people, because of cutbacks, and had been taking work home regularly, as well as staying late at the office. Then Henry found he was unable to sleep and when he did sleep he had such vivid and disturbing dreams that it was a relief to wake up. He began to dread going to work. He found himself feeling irrationally tearful. He began to make mistakes and forget things. He became irritable with his wife. He started feeling nauseous and dizzy, and in the end felt so bad that he went to see the company nurse who recognised what was happening and sent him to the doctor.

Finally Henry 'broke down'. He was off work for four months and in that time, in spite of (or perhaps because of) his medication he experienced terrifying feelings of 'existential dread' that were totally foreign to him. He began to question the 'meaning of life'. He began to say things like: 'And is this all?' He wept for the state of the world. He feared for the safety of his wife when she was out. He felt sure that he was going to die in the midst of a panic attack when he could not breathe. All of these things he steadfastly maintained were not things he had ever worried about before. 'I'm a pretty shallow kind of bloke' he said. 'I just stick to the job in hand, enjoy life with my wife, enjoy a drink with my friends, never read a book, like to play sport and watch the box, if its not complete trash, but (and here Henry put his head in his hands as if to hide his embarrassment) last Friday I was out for a walk because of the restlessness and I heard a bird sing, I heard a bird sing and it was so b....y beautiful I cried – me – I cried at the beauty of birdsong, I've never even noticed birds singing before. (And here he looked up at me, searching my face) Something has happened to me and I'm not sure if it was all bad.'

I was deeply moved by what he said and I was also wondering why I had not been able to interrupt his flow of words with some sort of reflection (for example, 'So you feel that it is very difficult for you to accept what was happening to you?') to enable him to have some sense of my empathic understanding. I recalled saying to my Counselling Diploma students 'Its OK to interrupt a person in full flow if you need to check something, just put up your hand if you feel they are not letting you in at all and say "Could I just stop you there a moment?"' I had tried everything, but Henry had not let me in, I had said almost nothing throughout the session. Even when I tried simply to reflect back what he had said, he brushed my words aside like an annoying fly that had buzzed against his hand.

I took the sessions with Henry to Supervision. (The British Association for Counselling requires all of its practising members to have regular supervision from either a more experienced counsellor or a qualified supervisor. It is essential that, in a rather isolated profession like counselling, one is able to discuss one's work with someone who can be trusted. Respect for client confidentiality is maintained at all times; BAC 1996.) I can remember saying to my supervisor, 'I feel so de-skilled by Henry, what is it he wants from me? He certainly doesn't seem to want any clever interpretations. He doesn't want me to make any comments about what he is telling me. He won't accept a reflection of his own words, often saying "No", even when all I've done is to paraphrase what he has just said. What is it he wants from me?' My supervisor is one of these patient people who will wait for me to reach my own conclusions rather than impose his opinions upon me – he did just that at this point. Suddenly it came to me 'I know!' I said, 'Henry needs a "witness", someone to "see" and understand what it is he's been through. All I have to be is a "faithful witness" to Henry's pain, terror and confusion, something he's not prepared even to allow his wife to be'.

Next time we met, Henry was a little calmer, and I felt that I could be, what Carl Rogers termed, 'congruent' (meaning genuine) in sharing my understanding of what I felt was happening between us. 'Yes', he said without hesitation, 'it has all been so frightening that I was scared I might die without anyone ever having really understood what it was I went through. You were my last hope of really being heard and I couldn't bear you to say anything in case I forgot something vital. I just didn't want to be alone with all this any more'.

Henry only came six times. I felt that we could have done some more worthwhile work, but for Henry it was enough that I had been a 'witness' to a happening that had changed his entire life. It was enough that I could bear simply to be there alongside him whilst he sought to find meaning in his desperation and fear.

What it means to be a witness

I am certain that the idea of the counsellor as 'witness' is neither new nor original, but it was new to me and has become a useful concept in all areas of my involvement with counselling issues. It was with some interest that around this time I read an article in the *Observer Life* magazine (5 January 1997) about the treatment of older people suffering from schizophrenia at the Maudsley Hospital. Regarding the work that is carried out there, the Chief Nurse, Christine Bleathman, was quoted as saying, that:

> '... much of her team's work is that of being *witnesses*, listening to memories of these long lives that would otherwise go unheard. They make the patients feel that their recollections – their lives – are important.'

How much more important it might be if the memories are painful and have never been divulged before.

How can one be a 'witness' to events one has not seen? The definition of the word 'witness' in the *Concise Oxford Dictionary* (1990) reads thus:

> 'witness: a person present at some event and able to give information about it ... testimony, evidence or an indication of ... bear witness to: attest the truth of, state one's belief in ... confirmation.'

How can I, or any other counsellor, call ourselves 'witnesses' to events in our clients' lives if we were not present when these events occurred? This is where it becomes difficult to give words to the 'essence' of the therapeutic relationship. Carl Rogers came closest to clarifying what it is that happens in the counselling situation, when he used the term 'empathy'. These days it has almost lost its true meaning by becoming over-used and often inappropriately used. Carl Rogers' rather more extended definition of empathy runs like this:

> 'To sense the client's private world as if it were your own but without ever losing the 'as if' quality – this is empathy ... To sense the client's anger, fear or confusion as if it were your own, yet without your own anger, fear or confusion getting bound up in it, is the condition we are

endeavouring to describe. When the client's world is this clear to the therapist, and he moves about in it freely, then he can both communicate his understanding of what is clearly known to the client and can also voice meanings in the client's experience of which the client is scarcely aware.' (Kirschenbaum & Henderson 1996: 226)

It is this ability to move about freely within the client's world that enables the counsellor to 'feel' as if she/he has actually been a witness. If there is desire and ability to empathise with the client then the counsellor begins to 'see' from the inside.

David Howe, in his fascinating book that looks at the experience of counselling and therapy from the client's viewpoint, makes an interesting comment on what he terms the 'narrative' or client's story and the telling of it. He says:

'The narrative is recognised as a particularly effective way in which we organise experience ... It is within such structures and sequences that the actions of ourselves and others are *recognised* and understood.' (Howe 1993: 152)

and

'People rework their past experiences as they tell their tale. In this model, the individual *reconstructs* her past rather than *recovers* it ... In bringing the past into the present, experiences are *reconstructed* to make sense in the individual's *current* framework of understanding ... We continually reconstruct the way we understand ourselves. This is what clients seek to do in therapy, hence the need to talk and tell one's story.' (Howe 1993: 155, emphasis added)

It seems that what Howe is saying is that when people come into therapy or counselling they appear to need to 'reconstruct' their experiences in a narrative or story form in order to give meaning to the happenings that life has thrown at them. It is during the reconstruction process that the therapist becomes a 'witness'. Howe calls it being 'recognised'. He states that:

'There is no fixed truth to be found when a counsellor hears a client describe her experience. Whatever meanings emerge are a product of the encounter between the client and the counsellor.' (Howe 1993: 162)

It seems that the counsellor, because she/he is drawn willingly into becoming a witness, is also able to 'confirm' with the client the 'truth' of what is being reconstructed. What is important also about the function of a witness is that she can often 'see' things that the client is unable to see because he is completely involved. (Like the witness to an accident who is able to say which car was in the wrong because he had a good view of both vehicles.) A counsellor-witness, in the reconstruction, enables the client to 'see' things from another viewpoint, thereby broadening his/her vision, and perhaps adding meaning and possibly influencing the way the client is able to deal with future events.

Marcia's story adds another dimension

The way in which some clients relate stories that have never been told before is both vibrant, vivid and graphic; they make me see and feel what happened.

Marcia was in her late 50s when she was referred to me. She was described as being very depressed and suffering from psychosomatic symptoms which often took the form of acute abdominal pain. One of the first things Marcia told me about was the death of her cat, a deeply loved tabby that had certainly led a good life and had recently died from a heart attack due to old age. Marcia's eyes filled with tears which soon overspilled. She apologised, saying that I probably thought her stupid to grieve like that over an animal. (She was unaware that there were two much loved 'moggies' lying on my bed upstairs!) But, of course, she was not only grieving the death of an animal, it later turned out that she was also grieving the death of both her parents. I worked with Marcia for some time and gradually she began to piece her appalling story together. She had lived with a violent husband for almost 35 years. They had had three children, two girls and a boy, and Marcia had spent a great deal of her energy making sure that it was she who received the beatings and blows and not the children. With some spirit she described how the three of them would dance around the house whenever her husband went away. As I listened week by week it soon became clear that Marcia had never told her parents about her awful life, she had always pretended that everything in the garden was rosy, she didn't want to worry them. No-one knew of the horrendous happenings in their house, there were no women's refuges when she was a young wife, and the maxim was 'You've made your bed, now you must lie on it'.

Marcia cried bitterly one day for her dead mother and, through her tears, said: 'She never knew what a b.....d he was to us all, she never knew how he beat me and hurt me and threatened to kill the kids if they ever told anyone. She's dead and I wish, I wish that I had been able to go to my mum who loved me and tell her what was happening. My dad would have killed him!'

For Marcia there had been no-one to witness the horror of her secret life, she bore the pain for all of them alone and now, older and unable to take any more, she was experiencing in her body the unspeakable pain that she had taken care to hide throughout her married life. I had become for Marcia the witness that she had never been able to find. Through the way I received her story she knew that I was indeed feeling her pain as if it were my own. One day she even brought a drawing she had made of the way she visualised the awful pain. It looked like a large round mouth and just inside the mouth were huge shark-like teeth; there was also a large eye at the topmost rim. 'Its always watching me' she said, 'and it constantly tears into my side with its huge sharp teeth. Sometimes it feels like its going to tear me to pieces!' With this powerful image, Marcia had added another dimension to my 'witnessing' as if she really wanted me to see, hear and feel her anguish.

It seems that not only do we have 'witnesses' who were not really there, but we also have unspoken cries that are 'heard'. (Again, an indication of how difficult it is to describe accurately what it is that occurs within the therapeutic relationship.) Communication by impact and the capacity to witness from the inside had the effect on this occasion of enabling me to use a form of blank verse to express my understanding of some of Marcia's feelings. (I was also able to use the poem in my supervision session.) I called it 'Marcia's Song' and I wrote it in response to a session in which I had a real sense that I was witnessing a longing in her to have some space or place of her own in which to recover a sense of herself as a person in her own right and not as an appendage to anyone else. In the poem I, the counsellor, am making full use of the 'as if' quality in my work. I spontaneously began to write 'as if' I were Marcia. It is rather like becoming a type of internal witness to her feelings.

Marcia's Song

Am I there?
Do I exist?
Is there enough space
in the world for me?

Who am I?
Don't call me 'mother' just now.
Don't call me 'wife',
Or 'aunt' or 'gran'.

Call me Marcia,
Call me by my name.
I want to be me,
If you get in the way
I'll never know who I am ...

Give me room to breathe.
Don't choke me to death.
Let me try these
small crumpled wings
I've never had a chance to use ...

Don't look at me.
Don't watch
while I re-discover
this poor body of mine.

Don't look at me
while I feed
this hungry 'child' inside me
and hold her to my breast ...

Don't listen
while I sing to her

and rock her
    and cry for her.

Leave me alone
    to find the space
    in which to move and grow
      and try to love
        the woman I'm becoming.

(L C J, unpublished anthology, 1997)

To 'witness' and to look away

It is noticeable that the language used in this 'song' is very much related to seeing and not seeing. Through the client's mouth I seem to be pleading with myself as counsellor that, having been a 'witness' to Marcia's unspeakable anguish, now is the time to allow her the dignity of privacy, something that she never seems to have had. Now I am, in a sense, telling myself and unconsciously everyone else, to give her some space while she begins to learn the immensely difficult task of allowing her body and spirit to heal.

I often tell over-eager counselling students whom I have observed almost staring unblinkingly at their 'practice' clients, who may (in role) be relating a horrendous story, that sometimes it is kinder to just look briefly away when a client's story is deeply humiliating, to give a sense that we are not sensation seekers who are just plain nosey about the lives of others, revelling in the 'gory bits', but that we are people who have deep respect for the pain and anguish in the lives of those who come to find, at last, somebody to be a 'witness'. There are times when a witness can make a decision **not** to rob a person of his/her dignity by looking at things that are best unseen. The empathic counsellor/witness knows when to 'see' and when to look away.

Becoming a 'here and now' witness

I worked for two years with Edith. I was, at first, reluctant to take her on, believing her to be beyond the scope of my training, but my supervisor felt that even if I provided a 'holding' function for her, it would be useful. Edith, in her late 60s, had both paranoid and obsessive tendencies. She badly wanted me to 'see' the distortions in her world that were immensely real to her. She so wanted a believing witness. Whilst seeking to stay with her in her world, it felt important to keep hold of a sense of reality for us both. But how could I maintain the witness function with Edith? Of all the clients with whom I have worked, Edith is perhaps the one who most visibly carried her story in her body. She was painfully thin and dreadfully pale, she wore nondescript clothes with almost no colour, she carried herself as if she was ashamed of having to take up space in the world. Her every look and movement was apologetic. After Edith had been coming to counselling for about three months, I noticed that she was beginning to sit a little further back in the armchair. (When she first came, she had sat rigidly on the very edge.) I was able tentatively to remark on the slight changes that I was witnessing. It felt important to give this poor downtrodden woman some sort of sense that she did have a place in the world; that she had a right to take up some space. In this case the witness function was very clearly divided into two parts. I did strive to be a faithful witness to the painful and confusing event that had so marked her life, even whilst holding onto the fact that I was only hearing Edith's perceptions of what had happened. I had to enter into her truth no matter how difficult. But I also became a recording witness to the present changes that I saw in her for she was too unwell ever to have noted them for herself. There is not a miraculously happy ending to this story, but before Edith left she had managed to get a little part-time job which had greatly improved her quality of life.

The strange desire for a 'false' witness

There is another function of a witness that, as an ageing person myself, I am beginning to understand more fully. Behind it lurks the desire for a 'false witness', and this is in connection with the ageing process itself. Undoubtedly we have all heard old friends greet each other, after not having met for about 20 years with 'You haven't changed a bit!' And oh, we so want to believe that! Ann Orbach, in her book about psychotherapy and ageing, speaks of the dualism that seems to exist between the inner and outer 'I'. She compares the infant looking in a mirror and loving the image she sees as an ideal, with an older person looking in the mirror who is shocked at the obvious signs of ageing. I can remember sitting on a tube train not many years ago and catching sight of a reflection in the window opposite. I thought to myself 'There's a woman who looks just like my mother.' I turned round to look at her, only to realise that it was my own reflection that I was seeing. I could hardly bear to look again, although I had always thought my mother was a good-looking woman, I did not want to look so much like her just yet. Orbach (1996: 21) says:

> 'The new image is far from ideal, and the old person's narcissism, which still persists, is now internal and in contradiction with the outer "me". We become alienated from our bodies, strangers to ourselves.'

Sometimes the dualism becomes more of a 'split' in the concept of the self. Often as one ages, maturity is sometimes 'pricked' by an unexpected feeling of vulnerability. I have noticed this particularly with people who have had successful careers and have often been perceived as 'powerful' by those who knew them. They begin to have a sense of their power diminishing, and are taken by surprise by these vulnerable feelings. They often do their best to hide them. They experience a not uncommon split between feeling like a child but being perceived as a mature person. A client in therapy who found it helped to express herself in blank verse reveals this 'split' quite clearly. In the poem, she is wondering why she finds it so difficult to read some words she had written to the therapist, then at last realisation dawns, and she writes:

For this is about 'nakedness' you see.
   Not the nakedness of young
      smooth, supple flesh
         that invites the eye and touch.
This is about the nakedness of age,
   of greyish skin instead of gold,
      of bluish veins that sketch
         their history just beneath the skin,

of folds of sagging flesh,
  of slack and untoned muscle,
   of breasts, no longer heavy with life-giving juice,
but heavy with the weight of 'let go' age.

And, still struggling, she continues:

And still I have not written here,
  on this page, the simple word-picture.
My mind keeps pushing it away.

Then, at last she was able to get it out:

So now...
  The layers
  peel away,
  the years
  slip off me
  like the
  sloughed skin
  of an adder,
    and here
    I am
    crouched
    foetal-like
    exposed
    an old grey
    woman's body
    curled round
    the raw sharp edges
    of the feelings
    of a frightened child ...

(used with permission)

Not appealing imagery, but in the writing of the words, in the creating of a graphic word-picture, the client is unconsciously asking the therapist to stay with her as she looks into the external mirror, and also, to be there as she faces the childlike feelings. It feels like a pleading with the therapist not to be 'disgusted' by what she is being asked to witness, but to stay alongside and respect and understand, to become a 'present' witness. Anne Orbach again gives an added clarity to the concept of the 'present' witness when speaking about the loss of self that can be felt in both the very young and the old:

> 'If this nameless fear of loss (annihilation of self) preoccupies the child, I would suggest that it is never totally resolved and will be felt again in old age when a person's hold on life is weakened. Perhaps, even at this late stage, a 'facilitating environment' – someone in the room who is awake and alive (like a counsellor or therapist – my addition) – can mitigate the fear by restoring a sense of life's continuity through the realisation that others will go on living, remembering and being enriched by the life that has to be given up.' (Orbach 1996: 38)

As counsellor, I am awake and alive for my client in order to perform the function of a witness by the way in which I choose to reflect both feelings and underlying meanings. I am also helping the client to hear any discrepancies or notice any gaps. My 'witness' function perhaps 'lays the ghosts' of personal history, thus enabling the person to move on.

Perhaps I, as a counsellor, am only able to enter into the fears and dreads of others and become their witness if I am able to acknowledge my own fears.

Robert Hobson, in his insightful book about the 'heart of psychotherapy', writes compellingly of this usually unspoken fear of what he calls 'no-being':

> 'In striving to express what I mean by no-being, I am attempting the impossible. It is indescribable. Perhaps a calm acceptance of silence is the ideal. But in our isolation, most of us can only fall into either despair, madness or suicide; or else, in halting sentences, we can attempt to move from crude metaphor to the curious clarity of poetry in the hope that we will evoke a glimmer of comprehension in another, and be rewarded by the gift of a sad smile of friendship.' (Hobson 1985: 272)

It seems that what Hobson terms 'a glimmer of comprehension in another' is very close to what I am describing as being a witness. It is that sudden insight into the despair of another which lets me feel it and lets me 'see' in some sense what may have contributed to its cause. How often throughout our lives do we confidently expect to have those close to us act as witnesses to our significant life events: weddings, graduations, naming ceremonies for children and countless other occasions? As children we often beg our parents to 'come and see' the play we're in or to 'see us' running on sports day. We must have someone there to be a witness to our success or failure. We need the affirmation and the recognition in order to have a sense of the developing self. As we get older, having outgrown the urgent need for a witness and becoming used to solitude, there still are times, particularly during illness or bereavements, when the 'existential dread' overwhelms us and we are thrown back into remembrances of unutterably painful events and suddenly there arises a need to tell someone, to feel that all the awfulness and sadness need not go unrecognised.

Conclusion

I have tried to show, by using clients' stories, how a counsellor can find him/herself in the role of 'witness'. I have pointed out aspects of 'witnessing', but in the end perhaps the concept of the counsellor as witness can be summed up in these words from client to therapist:

> I know you cannot change my life
>   or hold back the weight of these advancing years.
>   You can't be there,
>   when in the impenetrable darkness of the night
> I lie awake and sweating in the midst of existential fears.
>   Your training denies even the comfort of a touch,
>   a hand to hold when loneliness engulfs.
> But lonely I was pushed into the world
>   and lonely will depart.
>   All that I ask is that you're there
>   when I relive my pain,
>   to give me recognition when I speak,
>   let me see myself reflected in your eyes,
> let me know my 'being' is affirmed.

Hear with your 'inner ear' the unspoken words
 that fearfully I'm holding back.
See with the eyes of understanding who it is
 I am, and where it is I've been,
  and for pity's sake let me not
 feel rejection in your look.
I'm only brave enough to look into the past
 if you stay by my side.
  I only have the courage to look into the mirror
 if you look with me and are not repulsed.
More than death itself,
 I am afraid to die unwept,
  unrecognised, unheard,
   my desolation – unwitnessed.

(L C J, unpublished anthology, 1997)

References

British Association for Counselling (1996) *Code of Ethics and Practice for Counsellors*. Rugby: BAC.

Concise Oxford Dictionary (1990). 8th Edition. Oxford: Oxford University Press.

Hobson R F (1985) *Forms of Feeling: The heart of psychotherapy*. London: Tavistock.

Howe D (1993) *On Being a Client*. London: Sage.

Kirschenbaum H, Henderson V L (eds) (1996) *The Carl Rogers Reader*. London: Constable.

Observer Life. 5 January 1997, 1147.

Orbach A (1996) *Not Too Late: Psychotherapy and Ageing*. London: Jessica Kingsley.

In Praise of Memory

Macbeth   How does your patient, doctor?

Doctor   Not so sick, my lord,
As she is troubled with thick-coming fancies;
That keep her from her rest.

Macbeth   Cure her of that:
Canst thou not minister to a mind diseas'd;
Pluck from the memory a rooted sorrow;
Raze out the written troubles of the brain;
And with some sweet oblivious antidote
Cleanse the stuff'd bosom of that perilous stuff
Which weighs upon the heart?

Doctor   Therein the patient
Must minister to himself.

(William Shakespeare, *Macbeth*, Act 5, Scene 3)

4

Losses in Later Life

Richard Adfield

Editor's Introduction

When we are young, we can easily think that older people only talk about who has died and whose funerals they have attended. This was Richard Adfield's experience as a boy, and he is not alone in this.

Older age is easily compared with the evening of life, when the world gets darker and one becomes sleepy; or with the autumn of life, when the leaves fall off the trees and the world looks greyer and bleaker, implying that colour, vigour and interest have all been lost. But we forget that sunsets can be spectacularly beautiful, and bare trees show their full might. Yes, in later life we have many losses, but they do not necessarily mean that we therefore become diminished. On the contrary, people's character is formed more clearly and strength is often gained from loss.

Many such losses are addressed in this chapter with great sensitivity. All of us will have experienced some of them, and more. When we can see them not simply as losses, but also as gains – including our own death – then we will be leading fulfilled and meaningful lives.

Introduction

Jack is sitting with his dog in the waiting room of the veterinary surgeon. Patch is 16 years old and has developed an inoperable cancer. Jack is waiting to have him put to sleep. This is very hard for Jack.

Now in his 79th year, it was only six months ago that he buried his life-long partner, Ruby. They had celebrated their 50th wedding anniversary one year, and she had died, quite suddenly, the next.

Five years previously they had sold their large house and moved into a retirement flat, complete with warden. That had been a wrench for both of them. They had lived in the same house for over 40 years and seen their three children grow up there, so it was rich with memories.

The two daughters and the son, all married now, live miles away: one daughter in Yorkshire, the other in Wales and the son has emigrated to Australia.

Jack himself has not been feeling well. Each winter he suffers with bronchitis which usually leads to a short stay in the local hospital. All the staff know him there, it is almost like a second home. But now the local hospital is to close and will be incorporated into the large acute hospital. Even when he is well, Jack's breathing difficulties mean that he cannot walk too far.

So in a relatively short space of time, Jack has lost his wife, home, health, mobility, and now his dog.

It is not surprising then that he is feeling depressed: 'What's the point of going on?'; anxious: 'Who's going to be around for me?'; angry: 'No one seems to bother about old people these days'; guilty: 'Perhaps there was more I could have done for my Ruby. She waited on me hand and foot'.

In this chapter, I shall be looking at what it is to grow old and some of the inevitable losses that we experience. So it may help you to know that I am 66 years of age. I am an Anglican priest and I have worked for 28 years in parish ministry. At present, I am working as a hospital chaplain for three days a week, and running a bereavement counselling service for the other two days.

I shall start by telling you about a couple and how they experienced their losses and how counselling helped them. After that, I shall describe in more detail the various aspects of loss in relation to old age.

Jenny and **George** retired 15 years ago. Last year they celebrated their 50th wedding anniversary. George is now 80 years of age, and Jenny is 71. Before retirement, George had a fulfiling job in a caring profession. They moved from London to live on the south coast when George came to the end of his working life. His job had given him a clearly identifiable role in his community. When they arrived in their new home, he had for the first few years been able to continue similar work in a voluntary capacity. But a change of management had brought this to an abrupt end. The failure of the new manager to enlist his help had made him feel inferior and in-valid. Added to this, George's health had been deteriorating.

Five years ago he had a prostate gland operation which had not been successful and was still causing problems. Two years ago he had a hip replacement, and recently he has had a slight stroke and a heart attack.

The car has had to be sold, because for health reasons George can no longer drive it.

He has now lost his confidence and has become housebound. Even the thought of arranging a taxi to take him and Jenny to the sea front for a walk fills him with great anxiety.

In the past two years Jenny has lost her sight, due to a late diagnosis of diabetes. Although she is in good health generally, the loss of sight has restricted her ability to move about independently.

I met Jenny and George and offered to see them six times, initially, for an hour each time. This seemed about right to them. When I met them for the first time I invited them to talk about their losses and how they felt about them.

The loss of attractive appearance, black hair turning to grey, smooth skin becoming wrinkled, was uppermost in their mind. They both mentioned diminished interest in sexual activity.

George thought they were much worse off financially, but Jenny thought differently. In their case, this may have highlighted the fact that the male partner, who has been the wage-earner, may feel the loss of earned income more keenly that the non-earning partner.

Jenny's loss of sight has made her very dependent on others in order to leave the house. She was learning to go for walks locally, but was longing to be able to go to the nearest large town on her own. She often feels angry about the loss of her sight. This was sometimes directed towards George, although she realises that this is unfair.

Sometimes she will weep, especially when she realises that she will never be able to see her grandchildren again and see the changes in their appearance as they grow up.

Both said they feel 'rotten' about the losses they have had to face, and a feeling of depression was common to both of them.

Fear was also very real: fear of the future, fear of wondering whether they will be able to cope. George referred to his loss of confidence and anxiety. This inability of his to get on with life was affecting Jenny and this made him feel guilty.

At the end of the session I asked them what they found was helping them. In different ways, they both said that one-to-one contact with sensitive, caring people was a tremendous support. For George it had been a former boss who had made contact with him by phone. The man knew him and had always valued his professional abilities. Jenny was receiving support from friends and was herself now giving emotional help to another woman in need.

Jenny and George are both, naturally, anxious and fearful about how they will cope in the future. Jenny's partial sight makes her feel vulnerable and dependent. For someone who has always been so active, and to whom others have turned for help, this is a major adjustment. She has experienced a great loss, and often she feels sad and depressed. George has been withdrawing from normal activity. He has lost the confidence to go out and to make even the most minor decisions. They are both grieving.

As their story unfolded, I noticed the various elements of loss and at the end of this first session, I told them in my own words what I had heard them recount: they experienced loss of a job, health, confidence, attractiveness and being in charge of their lives. They wrestled with fear, guilt and anxiety. They thought that this more or less summarised their situation. We agreed to meet again.

In order to do the same here on paper, a closer look at what this entails for older people is called for.

Counselling the older person

For many people the word 'counselling' is unhelpful. They may feel it is associated with the severely mentally ill. For the older person it can sound as though they are expected to wash their dirty linen in the presence of a stranger. This sounds disloyal and inappropriate. We need to assure those who need help that a counsellor is simply a trained listener.

Jenny and George felt they needed one-to-one support. The first thing we need to remember is that those who are seeking help will need our commitment. They need to know that we will be there for them, hopefully, for as long as it takes. If possible, an informal agreement should be discussed. We should offer to see them once a week, or fortnight, say, for six sessions. This can always be extended if necessary. But clients also need to realise that we cannot offer a lifelong friendship. Our relationship with them is for a limited period only.

It is vital that they can trust us. People who have suffered loss will need to be completely honest. This may mean them expressing anger towards individuals. They will be reluctant to do this if they fear their private matters will become public knowledge. So we must assure them that whatever they say will be treated as strictly confidential.

Carl Rogers (1980) says that there are three things which are vital in a counselling relationship: empathy, unconditional positive regard and congruence (see also Chapter 9).

Empathy

Empathy is not sympathy. When we sympathise we say, 'there, there'. If we are being empathic, we try to see the whole situation through the other person's eyes.

Tschudin (1997: 92) says:

> 'Sometimes empathy is described as "walking in the other's shoes", but this is a wrong image. It is not walking in the other's shoes which is called for – that would mean pushing the other out of his or her own shoes – but trying to imagine and understand what it is like for the other to walk in his or her kind of shoes: "entering the private perceptual world of the other and becoming thoroughly at home in it". This world may be full of anger, resentment, confusion, grief, fear and lostness. Trying to become at home in it does mean accepting and acknowledging that the other person is feeling these things and that they are real. But "becoming at home" in them does not mean that we as helpers make these feelings our own. We do not identify with the client to the extent of becoming "involved with" him or her. We go alongside that person, hear what he or she has to say, give that person the security of acceptance, from which changes can be made. We cannot make the changes; we can help to provide the climate from within which changes can be made.'

When we can acknowledge the other person's losses and get this across to them in a way which is meaningful to them, then we are empathic.

When an older person loses a pet, perhaps because they are entering residential care and animals are not allowed, they can feel devastated. If the counsellor is not an animal lover, this may appear to them to be over-reacting. Empathy will enable us to see that this person's life may have been centred on that pet, especially if, as in the case of Jack, they have recently suffered the loss of a life-long partner.

Perhaps more difficult is to be with older people who tell stories of many losses and some of them are very similar to our own. We are then perhaps tempted to compare and advise, but this is not helpful. Being empathic means staying with the other person's feelings and story, entering into their world and being with them, but not being overwhelmed by this and not being clinical either.

In the case of Jenny and George, each aspect of their losses is high-lighted and therefore made important. When we give due weight to something, they can take it further or let it drop, as is most suitable to them; what matters is that it was acknowledged.

Unconditional positive regard

This concerns the attitude that we have towards those we are seeking to help. Carl Rogers (1980) talked about the need for us to 'prize' our clients; to affirm them; to make them feel totally accepted by us no matter how they look or what they reveal.

Mearns and Thorne (1988: 59) put it thus:

> 'Unconditional positive regard is the label given to the fundamental attitude of the person-centred counsellor towards his or her client. The counsellor who holds this attitude deeply values the humanity of her client and is not deflected in that valuing by any particular client behaviour. The attitude manifests itself in the counsellor's consistent acceptance of and enduring warmth towards her client.'

A young man came to see me 18 months after the death of his mother. At the time of her death he had been pursing a successful career; at the age of 27 everything seemed to be going well for him. But following her death he became very depressed and he had not held down a regular job since then.

After the first two sessions, he began to arrive late for his appointments and then began to cancel at the last minute. After a period of not seeing him for four weeks because of cancellations, we explored the reasons for his difficulty in maintaining the counselling relationship. He explained that he could not face seeing me because he had always failed to make any progress in the intervening week.

He was projecting onto me the image of the 'disapproving parent'. My empathy for him, and unconditional positive regard, made it possible for me to assure him that I realised that his depression had been so severe that he had been in a state of withdrawal for 18 months; that it would take time for him to feel strong enough to take up his career again, and that I was there not to judge him, but to support him during that process.

As he left, he thanked me and said, 'I'll try to be here on time next week'. The following week he was five minutes early!

Congruence

Congruence has been described as being 'transparent' with the client.

Tschudin (1997: 81) writes for nurses, but it is not too difficult to see that her example is also valid in other situations. She says:

'Being congruent can mean something like the following. A nurse is with a patient who is trying to become stablised on insulin. The patient gets frustrated and does not want to hear any more what the nurse is saying. The nurse realises that this may be due to a sense of grieving going on for the patient, in which she adjusts to the diabetes and the new status of a chronically sick person. The nurse says that he understands and that they can go over the procedure again. This nurse has made allowances for the patient's feelings, but not for his own. He may feel just as frustrated as the patient: at her for not wanting to learn, and at himself for not getting through to her.

'… the nurse would be congruent if he told the patient something like: "I can see that you are getting frustrated, and I can well understand you. I am also getting frustrated because I am not helping you well enough. In this way we are disabling each other. Let's take a moment to see what we could do to help each other."'

When my young client kept arriving late, and then did not turn up for sessions, it made me feel frustrated and resentful. So it was not sufficient just to show him unconditional positive regard. I also had to be transparent with him and share with him that we had a problem which we needed to explore together. We had made a contract that he would attend and by him not coming I could not keep my part of the contract.

If I visit a client in their home, and the television is on, I need to be congruent about the difficulty of counselling in such a situation. So I would probably say something like: 'I cannot give you my full attention with the television on, would you mind switching it off, please?'

Professor Fred Zimring in his foreword to Eleanor O'Leary's (1995) book, says that *she* is urging counsellors to accept the empowerment of the older person as an important goal:

'This goal stands in contrast to the more usual one of trying to solve the older person's problems. That is, in seeing the older person as a full person, rather than as someone in a declining pathological state, she shifts the emphasis from fixing problems to facilitating the client's effort to live a fuller, more satisfying life.'

Let us now look at some of these aspects of loss and (see also Chapter 1). I will point out under each heading how these ways of counselling can be applied.

Old age

What does it mean to grow old? Does it have to be all gloom and doom?

In the hospital where I work, a 93-year-old woman was recently given a hip replacement. Earlier, a man I knew in his 90s was fitted with a heart pace-maker.

We are constantly being told that life expectation has moved on from the Biblical 'three score years and ten'. If someone dies at 70, we now regard that as relatively young.

Society may refer to anyone over the age of 60 as geriatric, but those who live to be 90 and over will have had over 30 years as an older person. In an attempt to differentiate such a large group, the 65 to 74 years age group are sometimes referred to as 'young old', and anyone who is 75 or over, as 'old old'.

O'Leary (1995) says that Western society assumes that there is a general deteriorating in all adults once the demarcation age of 65 has been reached. Therefore we confuse chronological ageing and biological ageing. This leads to an undue importance placed on age which may not exist. So, for instance, why is it generally assumed that people should cease to work at the age of 65? Nonetheless, we do change throughout our lifetime. Some of these changes are now detailed.

Biological changes

The ageing process shows itself in the human body by increasing signs of wear and tear. Skin becomes paler and wrinkled and blotches can appear. As we grow older, the colour of our hair changes, turning eventually to grey or white. Most people experience hair loss; the vast majority of men become bald. Our eyesight tends to worsen; for many this means having to wear glasses. Hearing can gradually become less acute; it is estimated that one-third of older adults have inadequate hearing. Mobility is affected. Joints begin to stiffen and/or become tender, which affects movement and strength.

We have to come to terms with changes in our body over which we have little or no control. This can cause us to fear the future. Or, in the loss of physical attractiveness, we might feel that we will be rejected. We need to be able to share these feelings with another person. Counselling can enable us to put these fears into perspective and to see that some of them may be fantasies.

Sexuality

There is a stereotype image of the older person becoming 'sexless' and sexually inactive. A daughter was shocked when a neighbour (a woman in her late 60s) told her that she would love to 'put her slippers under the bed' of her 63-year-old father. The daughter, like many younger people, had never thought that older people thought about, let alone continued to engage in, sex. The capacity to make love continues for the majority until extreme old age, and for some right into their 90s. In spite of this, there are changes in most older people's sex lives. Intercourse takes place less frequently, and some people experience problems.

A great friend of mine developed cancer of the testicle at the age of 72. He refused surgery, and opted for hormonal injections, even though he knew it was unlikely that he would have a sexual relationship in the remaining years of his life. His sexuality was vitally important to his sense of wellbeing and also his bodily image. Counselling enabled him to talk through his anxieties and make the informed decision not to have surgery.

Mental capacity

Memory loss and confusion are often associated with old age. Although some slowing of thought and memory process does take place, 75 per cent of the population can expect to retain sharp mental functioning if they live into great old age. Only a small percentage will be victims of dementia. O'Leary (1995: 12) puts it into perspective when she says that: 'old adults for the most part retain their intellectual ability as measured by intelligence tests throughout life. Poor health is the most likely contributory factor to deterioration.'

All the same, most people will experience some slowing down of their mental capacities. Some get very frustrated by being more forgetful than they used to be, and this gives them a sense of being unreliable and therefore sidelined: 'I won't ask her, she forgot last time'. When a person brings this to a counsellor, we can help them by exploring what it is that is so painful about being forgetful. The usual response is too easily some platitude that we are all forgetful. Taking it seriously and discussing what is important about it can help the person to see that she or he is still valued.

Social changes

As we grow older, our roles begin to change. I remember a well-known preacher, let's call him John Brown, once saying that for years his son was referred to as 'Mr John Brown's son'. Now, in later life, he is known as 'Mr Jeremy Brown's father'. In other words, his son is now in the spotlight, and he is not.

In mid-life we experience our grown up children marrying and leaving home. The relationship between parents and sibling goes through a radical change. In future they will turn to their partner for help and support, not their parents. Many sons and daughters move miles away from their parents' home, some to the other side of the world.

Many people experience the changes in their roles as significant losses. As children move away, the role the parents have filled for 15–20 years suddenly comes to an end and they have to readjust. The pain which many people experience can be acute. Sometimes when people are helped to see that this and many other losses in life are similar to bereavement, they can understand better what is happening to their feelings and emotions.

When children move out there is a gap, but for many people this is being filled again when grandchildren come along. While this may be a joy for many people, others can experience it as one more sign of older age advancing, which can evoke crises and periods of uncertainty and depression. When such people are able to talk through their feelings and experiences, they may be helped to turn a time of turmoil into one of new insight, awareness and understanding.

Loss of social standing

O'Leary says that:

> 'Americans believe that age brings an inevitable decline in health, intelligence and sexuality; that people become dependent on others; that they become locked in their opinions, that they suffer from depression and the fear of death; and that they become grouchy, passive and childish. But younger folk did perceive them as wise, experienced and kind.' (O'Leary 1995: 35)

My son recently celebrated his 30th birthday. Amongst his many humorous cards was one which read: '30 – You've reached your peak'. And inside the words read: 'From now on it's all down hill'. Perhaps, like me, you stand in shops browsing through the birthday cards. So many of them make detrimental remarks about old age. There is always an inference that growing old is something to be dreaded, as it cannot be avoided.

> 'Ageism is distinct from all other forms of discrimination because it cuts across all of society's traditional classifications: gender, race, religion and national origin. If old people show the same desires, the same feelings and the same requirements as the young, the world looks upon them with disgust, in them love and jealousy seem revolting or absurd, sexuality repulsive and violence ludicrous.' (O'Leary 1995: 36)

For some time I was the facilitator of a group for the over-60s dealing with loss. They met regularly in one particular building of the mental health unit of a hospital. Suddenly the hospital management decided that this accommodation would in future only be available for those under 65. The group was therefore rendered 'homeless'. Alternative accommodation was eventually found but the feeling of rejection and anger felt by the members of the group was intense. They had experienced ageism in a world where they thought they would receive care and support. And their constant cry was, 'No one wants you when you are old'.

A woman went to see her doctor with a particular pain, and his response was: 'You're over 70; what do you expect at your age? You must learn to live with it.' Fortunately, she was able to assert herself and request that he take her ailment seriously and prescribe some pain relief, if it could not be cured. Although she had been able to get help on this occasion, eventually she felt that as a 70-year-old she could no longer expect any serious medical assistance from her doctor. This caused her to feel depressed. However, counselling enabled her to get in touch with her anger: both with the doctor and with the negative aspects of growing old. She was also enabled to explore existing, and possible new, opportunities for a fulfiling life.

Retirement

The greatest change that many people in their 60s have to face is the loss of full-time employment. Initially, retirement may be a welcome change from the old routine: a 'honeymoon' period. But for many, the novelty of not having to go to work changes into boredom and loss of purpose. Many retired people say that they wake up each morning not knowing how to fill the coming hours.

Retirement can also put new pressures on a marriage. The wife has to adjust to the husband being in the house, all day, every day. And if the man is finding retirement difficult, he may well be 'under her feet' which she finds frustrating and irritating. One friend told me that her husband had decided to re-organise her kitchen. He felt sure there was room for improvement! There probably was, but he had not asked her what improvement was important to her.

Retirement also brings the loss of a regular income. The last weekly pay packet, or monthly cheque, is daunting if the retired person does not have an adequate pension to supplement the State one.

Most people develop friendships with their work colleagues, and the loss of daily contact with them can leave a big gap. Work itself is mostly fulfiling and gives one a sense of being useful and needed.

When we meet friends and acquaintances who seem troubled about these issues, we can help them with some of the ideas and skills mentioned in this book. Most of all, we can listen to their stories and indeed encourage them to tell their stories.

Our empathy means that we take people seriously and listen to them. We let them know that we have understood them. We accept them as they are: we do not try to change them into copies of ourselves. We acknowledge that what they say is what they mean to say and we do not interpret their meaning or finish their sentences. When we do this, we may well share experiences with them, but only in order to give them other points of view which they may use to shape their own thoughts further. Perhaps just by listening to them we may help them come to realise that their problems are more imagined than real – but this is not an assumption that we as helpers can make.

Residential care

Those who decide that they can no longer cope living on their own may move into residential care. This is a big decision to make and brings with it tremendous change. Moving into residential care brings with it the realisation that we have reached the stage in life where we can no longer live as independent people. It may make us wonder if this will be the last home we shall live in before we face our own death. It can be very helpful to share such thoughts with others, especially someone who is not going to question the pain of it, but acknowledge it as real. We need to take such feelings and experiences at face value before any change to them can be made.

Spirituality

Old age can bring new possibilities for spiritual growth. Our lives have a significance that transcends death. Our values are not limited to our achievements.

Many religions and faiths pay great respect to older members. In this country we know that in many churches the majority of members are over 60 years of age. But as people become much older, many become housebound. This means that regular churchgoers are prevented from attending their place of worship. If the local congregation is not a caring one, this can lead to isolation and loneliness.

Many people feel that not being able to attend church or religious services is just the last straw in a whole litany of losses. Some people can feel intensely guilty when they are no longer able to fulfil their religious obligations.

Not all people, counsellors included, are at ease in talking about religious and spiritual issues with others (see Chapter 6). But what we can all do is listen as people tell us about about what matters to them, their deepest feelings and what life means to them. Perhaps we can help people to see that faith and spirituality are not necessarily tied to rituals – although these are immensely important – but that, particularly in this area, we do continue to grow and develop, and that faith can move mountains if we can allow it to happen.

Local religious communities rely heavily on their older members. Most of the cleaning, catering and visiting of the sick is done by the over-60s. This not only provides for a wonderful opportunity for continuing usefulness, but draws people of similar age groups together for a common purpose. New friendships are formed which spark off new social opportunities. Sharing spiritual pains and joys can also form new friendships and new forms of worship and faith.

Multiple losses

I remember, as a boy, making the obligatory visit to elderly aunts with my grandmother. It always seemed as though they spent most of the time telling each other who had died and which funeral they had attended.

But in old age we have to face the loss of friends and relatives. And sometimes there can be a number of deaths within a short space of time. This not only brings sadness and a sense of loneliness, but may raise fears about our own death.

We often feel that 'bad luck' comes in multiples, and as we get older we are much more likely to hear not just of one death, but of several. This increases the sense of 'I am the only one left', or 'I will be the next one to go'.

But it is not just death which makes us aware of our frailty. Like Jenny and George, it is one thing after another which we have to give up or let go. The accumulation of people and things lost can feel overwhelming. Often the death of a close person reminds us of another death and brings back unresolved memories. Or losing yet another friend reminds us of past wrongs or brings certain guilt feelings to the surface. This is quite normal and should not be seen as 'bad' or 'wrong'. When we meet with people who have lost others, we can often help them simply by saying that we are aware of the fact that a bereavement often calls to mind an earlier one and brings back memories which may be painful. This can sometimes be an opening for two people to share with each other and to help each other.

Our own death

A few years ago, a woman stood up at the Annual General Meeting of a branch of Cruse and stunned those present by saying: 'I have a pathological fear of dying, and no one will let me talk about it. All the obvious helpers and organisations just don't want to know. But surely there must be hundreds of old people who are afraid to die'. This cry from the heart led to advertisements appearing in the newsletters of local organisations for older people. The advertisement invited those who were fearful of their own death to join a self-help group. We were encouraged when five people responded.

One person realised that this was not what she was looking for. But the remainder came on a weekly basis for six weeks. It became clear that specific issues were the basis of their fear of death.

One person was having a very painful and distressing relationship with her son. She could not bear the thought of dying without being fully reconciled with him. Yet this seemed almost impossible to achieve.

A woman who had remained single felt that not having been married or having had children meant that her life was unfulfilled. She felt as though her life had been pointless and that she had not achieved anything.

Another dreaded the thought of dying alone in her flat and no one discovering her body for days.

The group met for eight sessions and the members found that by sharing their fears with each other they were able to focus on the issues that were underlying their great fear of death.

Conclusion

All the changes I have mentioned create a sense of loss.

A short while ago, my wife and I went to visit a friend in a hospice. We were asked to wait in the lobby. Eventually we were ushered into the room. Our friend said, 'Oh, it's you. I wondered who it was. The nurse just said, "There's an elderly couple here to see you."' Shock, horror: my wife and I are now seen as an 'elderly couple'.

This made me realise that I had lost forever the physical attractions of youth and middle-age.

A very bright 93-year-old said to me: 'When I reached the age of 80 I decided it was time I prepared for old age'. When I enquired what the 'preparation' involved, she replied, 'I moved my bed downstairs so that I could live on the ground floor'.

This is an example of someone with a pragmatic approach to life, and it is encouraging to hear of such people. But not everyone is like this and other people will not be so easily adaptable.

The last loss we have to come to terms with is our own life. For many people this is the greatest fear and the biggest loss. Yet many people also adjust to this and are able to face this loss with equanimity. Those of us who have been able to help someone to face death know what a privilege it can be to accompany such a person on this journey. When a dying person can share with another what is happening, then this can be transforming for both. We cannot make it happen, but when it does happen, we can be willing to be there. And perhaps 'being there' is the best we can ever offer anyone at any time and in any situation.

References

Mearns D, Thorne B (1988) *Person-centred Counselling in Action*. London: Sage Publications.

O'Leary E (1995) *Counselling Older Adults*. London: Chapman & Hall.

Rogers C R (1980) *A Way of Being*. Boston: Houghton Mifflin Company.

Tschudin V (1997) *Counselling for Loss and Bereavement*. London: Baillière Tindall.

In Praise of Memory

Memories are the basic stuff of counselling, as they are of biography, of art, of friendships and feuds, of most conversations and of all enduring relationships. Vagueness, clarity, confusion, enlightenment, humour and pain are all part of the contradictory environment created by memory, which often seems to follow its own inclination, tossing us fragments of story that catch the light like broken glass, beckoning us towards the past, beguiling, tricking, threatening and delighting us in turn.

We generally take the faculty of memory for granted – unless and until it misbehaves, snatching away the name that is on the tip of our tongue, or plaguing us with an unwanted visitation in the form of a disturbing episode from the past. To our chagrin, we can neither coax back the one nor banish the other. What, then, are we to make of this wayward servant, whose absence can be so infuriating, whose presence so distressing, yet who at other times commands our gratitude by giving us access to a treasured hoard of moments, magically preserved with all their original sparkle and vitality? And if memory can be a blessing, so too can forgetfulness, when it marks the end of a healing process: an injury has been forgiven, and a particular memory need never again return to haunt us.

What should we do with our memories? And, even more importantly, what do they ask of us?

(Sheila Willson)

5

Bereavement

Richard Adfield

Editor's Introduction

Sooner or later each person will experience a bereavement. These days, many people are well into their adulthood until a death may come close to them or before they even see a dead body. However much we may be prepared when a loved person dies, the pain of loss is unique to each one of us.

In this chapter Richard Adfield tells the stories of two people's experiences of bereavement and then puts the elements of grief into a theoretical framework. To have such a tool can be of enormous help to counsellors and any who accompany bereaved people in their time of grief. Being able to indicate signs of change and movement can be very helpful. But as helpers in whatever capacity, we must never forget that what may happen theoretically, happens to the person 'in the flesh', and it is often that pain which is paralysing, but also necessary; it is devastating, but also a sign of love and growth.

We have only recently come to see many more aspects of loss as very similar to bereavement, therefore this chapter is of great importance in the whole field of counselling older people in a holistic way.

Introduction

The death of someone we love has been described as one of the most devastating things that we have to experience. When a young or middle-aged person dies, the death seems untimely and cruel. But what about the death of a life-long partner or friend, when we are in the last years of our life? Does that make it any easier to bear?

I remember sitting by the bedside of a woman in her 80s who was dying. Her 78-year-old husband sat opposite. I was shocked when he told me that they had both witnessed the death of their two sons. One had died 15 years ago, and the other the previous year. He said rather pathetically, 'Soon I shall be the only one left. What's the point of going on?'

I am a trained counsellor and have been working for Cruse for the last 16 years. Most of our clients are self-referred; in other words they make contact with us themselves. They may do this because they have been advised by their doctor, nurse, social worker, relative or friend to seek bereavement care. I am therefore drawing on my experience in this chapter, as we look together at the natural responses we make when a loved one dies and how we can support older people through their pain of bereavement.

It will probably help us to think about real-life situations. So I have asked two people to share with us their own experience of bereavement. In bereavement training, we often find that the trainees are surprised to find that the whole subject of loss stirs up old memories of loss and pain for them. You, too, may find that many aspects of their stories 'ring bells' with you, either from your own experience or that of people close to you. You might like to be aware that this is happening, and what you feel as it happens.

Netty's story

Netty was 67 years of age when her husband, Ian, began to show alarming symptoms. When Ian went to see his own GP, he told the doctor that he already knew what was wrong: he had cancer of the lung.

Tests eventually proved Ian to be correct, but he was assured that the treatment would give him another year to 18 months of life. But after hearing the diagnosis, he went straight to the local undertaker to make arrangements for his funeral. He was convinced he would die within three months: he lived for only two.

Ian made it clear that he wanted no funeral service whatsoever. So the body was cremated without any member of the family being present and his ashes were taken to Wales, his birth place, for scattering. Netty did this with her close family. But she felt as though she was leaving Ian miles away from the home they had shared together and where she continued to live.

In the relatively few weeks that Netty had between the diagnosis and Ian's death, she often cried, albeit in secret. After his death she felt intense anger. She felt abandoned. She would often cry out to her late husband, 'Why have you just gone and left me?' Although she has three devoted sons, their response to her sadness was, 'Would you really want dad back, sitting in that chair, with all the suffering he was going through?'

Friends were helpful, but she felt that when she began to talk about her feelings of loss, they were thinking, 'Here she goes again'. That made her feel that her need to talk was making her a nuisance to her friends.

A neighbour was different: she was a great help. When the neighbour discovered that Netty was neglecting to buy and prepare food for herself, she would make sure that she went to the shops and cooked meals. 'You cook that and I'll be in to check that you have'.

When her GP discovered that she was feeling depressed, he prescribed antidepressants, which made her feel worse. When the doctor heard this, he recommended that she should see a bereavement counsellor. Netty agreed with some reluctance and apprehension. She had never experienced counselling before and didn't know what to expect.

However, two months after the death, Netty called the local Cruse office. The counsellor allocated to her was John, and he explained from the outset what he was offering: he would visit her in her home and the visit would last one hour, during which time she would be able to share with him how she was feeling about Ian's death.

When the counselling began she felt intense relief: 'Thank goodness I've got someone to help', she said to John.

At the beginning, the counsellor saw Netty twice a week. It was then reduced to a weekly session.

Several months later she went on a trip to Australia to stay with her son. She was still feeling very distressed that she had been unable to say goodbye to Ian at a funeral service. When her son heard this he mentioned this to his pastor who made arrangements for a Memorial Service in which she was able to say her farewell to her husband.

Before she left for Australia, John had said that he would continue to see her on her return. Netty made contact with him immediately she returned home and the counselling resumed.

The sessions continued for over a year. Then John was offered a different job and had to move on. He therefore referred Netty to a support group. This was a group for the over-60s who had experienced major loss. There were about eight people in the group and they all met together, with two facilitators, every week. Netty found it helpful to be able to share her own experiences with people who had similar stories to tell.

At the beginning she was a silent member. But eventually she was able to share her feelings with the others. The group finally ended when most members felt they had reached the stage where they had new activities and new interests.

Five years after Ian died, Netty now attends two clubs a week, one is a social club which arranges a variety of events each month; the other is a luncheon club which is held three days a week. She has made several new friends whom she sees regularly, and together they go on their own outings and shopping expeditions or just meet for coffee together.

She feels she has only recently accepted the fact that Ian is not coming back. Occasionally she can still hear his key in the front door or thinks she can see him standing in the doorway. 'I still miss the hugs and cuddles. And when I'm feeling low, I feel what's the point of going on.' The summer months are much better than the short, dark winter days. And when she is not well, the anxiety and sadness return and she tells

Ian off for having left her. This is a common experience of the bereaved. Although they enjoy life again, illness or an anniversary can make them feel as though they are going back. But such times and occasions tend to pass more quickly and less painfully with time.

Netty's experience gives us several reminders about the process of grieving.

Normal grief

What we need to remember first of all is that grieving is natural. If the person we have loved for years dies, of course we shall feel as though our world has been turned up-side down, and it will take time.

> Time is too slow for those who wait
> Too swift for those who fear
> Too long for those who grieve …

Netty says she is only just beginning to feel as though she can cope with life again. And it's five years since her husband died. Many a newly bereaved person will ask: 'How long? How long is it going to take to get over this?' The answer of course is that we don't know. We all deal with our grief differently, and the time it takes will vary.

Abnormal grief

I prefer to use the term, 'complicated grief'. If we find that we are experiencing one of the four types of complicated grief, the last thing we need to hear is that it, or we, are 'abnormal'!

There are four types of complicated grief:

- Chronic reaction
- Delayed grief
- Exaggerated grief
- Masked grief

Chronic reaction is when the grief is excessive in duration and never comes to a satisfactory conclusion. In chronic or prolonged grief the counsellor and client assess which of the tasks of mourning is not being resolved and why.

Delayed grief may mean that the person did not respond emotionally at the time of the death. At a future date they may experience the symptoms of grief over some subsequent loss. The classic example is when a person appears to be unaffected by the death of a partner, and when a year later the canary dies they have a severe emotional crisis.

Exaggerated grief is when the person is conscious that the reaction is excessive and disabling and seeks help. The anxiety can develop into a phobia, often centred around death.

Masked grief is when people experience symptoms and behaviour which cause them difficulty but they do not see or recognise that these are related to loss. It can turn up as a physical symptom, perhaps even displaying the same symptoms of the illness from which the deceased suffered.

Rites of passage

The other point we need to take note of is the importance of rites of passage.

The funeral service is an opportunity, with our relatives and friends, to say goodbye to the person who has died. The actual moment when the coffin disappears in the crematorium, or when it is lowered into the ground at a burial, can be immensely painful. Often mourners cry out, 'Don't leave me'.

If we try to avoid the reality of death by not attending a funeral service, we may merely postpone the feeling of grief and this can lead to complicated grief.

Ian's intentions by deciding not to have a family funeral service may have been to spare his loved ones pain. But it may have complicated Netty's grieving. It was not until she went to Australia and attended a memorial service that she was able to move on.

The natural process of grieving can be complicated if a person dies abroad and is buried without the family being present. When there is no body, there can be no grave, and therefore no place to visit in the months and years after the funeral. Many people derive great comfort from visiting the cemetery, or crematorium, following the funeral. To begin with this can be as often as once a week; although this may become less frequent a few years after the death.

Netty's family were giving her practical support, but found it difficult to understand her emotional needs. She, naturally, talked about her longing to have her husband back. But her sons made her feel guilty by inferring that to want him back with the pain of his illness was selfish and cruel. Members of a family are bound to grieve in different ways. This is natural. Often they are reluctant to share their feelings with others in the family in case it upsets them.

Jean's story

Jean was 59 years of age when her husband died. She tells her own story:

> 'I was married for 32 years and when my husband died, nothing in my past experience of deaths prepared me for the pain and devastation that I felt. I had lived with him much longer than I had lived with my parents.

> 'When I hear of parents whose children have died, I feel a little guilty at the depth of my grief for a man who lived a long, full and happy life working at a job which gave him great pleasure and satisfaction.

> 'It is always painful when someone we love dies. The death of a long-term partner has added dimensions of pain. On top of everything, the entire routine of daily life is shattered. It seems to me if two human beings live together happily for so many years, each has had to make concessions and both personalities are honed and carved and entwined till they fit effortlessly together. Their minds are in tune, they complete each other's sentences, they find the same jokes hilarious. And then like a plant that a gardener tears in half and divides, the remaining half is replanted and left to face the wind and the rain alone and it feels a different plant because the other half has gone.

> 'Each night he would put his arm round me (he had a rule that all rows and tiffs were settled before nightfall) and suddenly the door has

slammed shut; no more kisses, no more hugs. A great deprivation. No more talking, arguing, gossiping about friends and family; my best friend was gone.

'When they told me he was dead, I felt like a rag doll that has been thrown against a brick wall, winded, numbed and then the start of that nagging pain. That pain lasted all day, all night, month in, month out. After five months, I was forced to admit it would never go. Weird things happened. I developed his medical symptoms. I asked the doctor to examine me but she gently refused and told me this was common in bereavement.

'I believed I saw him standing to the left of the altar at his own memorial service and thought: "Why is he wearing his old gardening coat when we are all dressed up?" But of course his son, our son, was reading the lesson and he was wearing his father's best overcoat.'

The yearning we feel after the death of a loved one can show itself in our constant searching for the person. A similar-looking person can make us feel that it is the deceased. And then we realise, when they get closer, that it is not. In Jean's case, the sight of her son, wearing her husband's overcoat, triggered off this feeling.

'One morning, a few weeks after the funeral, I was having a bath alone in an empty house when I began to feel seriously ill: tight chest, palpitations, cold sweat, it was difficult to breathe. Did I have a stroke? A heart attack? Whatever it was, I was dying. I was so very sorry that my children would have to face my death on top of their father's. I was even too ill to pray. Just to breathe was an effort. Then a voice said, "Get up. You are not dying. You are not ill". And I got up and functioned for the rest of the day.'

It is common for the bereaved to feel physical symptoms in the early stages of grief. It has been said that a large percentage of bereaved people will go to their GP within the first six months of bereavement with physical symptoms, sometimes the exact symptoms which the deceased experienced.

'After six months a neighbour said I needed a holiday. I sat at the table and wept. I realised then that holidays had no meaning without him.

My neighbour introduced me to a friend of his, Mary, who was a Cruse bereavement counsellor.'

The thought of the first holiday without her husband brought home to Jean the reality of her husband's absence. It is difficult for bereaved people to face certain events for the first time. The first Christmas, or New Year; the first anniversary, birthday or wedding; going back to the supermarket where they always shopped together. The second and third times may be less painful.

'I was to visit Mary eight or ten times, but the very first visit marked the turning of the tide for me. The effect was magical: the practical help she gave me reduced the physical pain; the sympathetic under-standing and listening was of a high order and enabled me to express my true feelings with no fear of hurting or distressing anyone. Many people find raw grief scary.

'Now after five years, when I look back, it has been a very painful experience but also a strangely interesting one.

'At the end of my first session with the counsellor, I was decidedly bet-ter and the pain in my stomach had gone. Mary had introduced herself to me and said that the first session would be exploratory. If at the end I felt it would help for me to have counselling on a regular basis, then she would see me on a weekly basis.

'After she had also explained that everything I said to her would be treated confidentially, she invited me to tell my story. So I just shared with her all the details of my husband's illness and death. It felt such a relief to be able to talk to someone else.

'Occasionally I slipped into a day of desolation but these periods grew less frequent as time went on. One day, three and a half years after he had died, I woke one morning and knew that I had left the tunnel for good and was in the light. I could live alone. I could be truly happy again. I could look back without pain and be grateful for the fun and the happiness we had. Of course I miss him, particularly to discuss the news, and progress of our children. Although time is a great healer, I am convinced that the help I received from the bereavement counsellor has enabled me to regain the happiness I once had, albeit in a different way.

'Since then I have taken two courses in bereavement counselling myself and now work for Cruse. My husband will be pleased that I'm trying to use the experience I have so painfully gained. I know he will have approved of that.'

Emotional response to loss

We have already seen some of these in the experiences of Netty and Jean. But there are others.

Denial

One person, with a medical background, struggled for months with this feeling. A part of him knew that his wife had died of cancer; but the other half, deep down, truly believed that she would eventually return. So he would talk about keeping the house just the way she would have wanted. 'I must do that,' he said, 'because I've got this feeling that she is going to return and when she does she'll be furious if things are not in order'.

After several months I began to feel concerned that he was stuck in this particular phase. We talked about this in a session and he agreed, but felt unable to do anything about it. He just could not lose this feeling that she had not actually died. Soon after that, he went on holiday to his wife's home in Scotland. They had been there for family holidays for years. But when he went there for the first time after her death, and she wasn't there, the reality of the death dawned on him and he no longer had to keep the house ready for her.

Anger

Anger, too, was the common experience of both Jean and Netty. Netty was able to cry out to her husband for leaving her. Jean's anger was directed at the well-meaning friends who made thoughtless remarks. One of her friends said, 'He was older than you, you must have always known he would die first.'

Some bereaved people fear that anger is overwhelming. They can direct the anger at all sorts of people: the hospital; the doctor; God. And sometimes in counselling they are helped to realise that they are feeling a great deal of anger towards the deceased as well. A young woman whose husband died, leaving her with three young children and many financial problems, was furious that he had left her to cope with such problems. Counselling gave her 'permission' to get in touch with these natural feelings.

Fear

Another natural response to the death of a loved one is fear. I remember when the police arrived at our home to tell us that my father had died in hospital, my mother's first words were: 'Who is going to do my odd jobs in future?' It struck me at the time as being incredibly callous and selfish. But I now realise that my mother was fearful of the future. How was she going to cope without my father who had always done all the practical jobs around the house?

Guilt

Guilt of course, is common. Sometimes it is justified because we could have done more for the dead person. We could have shown more care and affection. Perhaps there are things we said which we now regret.

A young man returned from his honeymoon, and waiting to meet him at the airport was his brother. His brother was there to tell him that their father had died suddenly of a heart attack two days earlier. He was shattered. When he came to see me he could not stop shaking. As he told me his story it became clear that he was overwhelmed with a sense of guilt. His father had not wanted him to get married. He implored him to wait until after he had completed his time at university. But the young man had gone ahead. So he and his father had not been on good terms.

At the wedding reception they did not speak to each other and he left for his honeymoon without saying goodbye to his father. He had to live with the fact that he would never be able to say 'sorry' to his father.

I didn't have the opportunity of offering counselling to this young man. If I had, over a number of weeks I would have worked towards the time when he may have been able to say 'sorry' to his father. This could have be done by writing a letter to his father. Or, perhaps, by placing an empty chair beside him and suggesting that his father is sitting there. He could then 'talk' to his father and tell him just how he was feeling and that he wanted to put things right between them. Not all clients would feel comfortable in doing this, but it can be of immense help to some.

Guilt is often irrational. For example, the person who sits by the bedside for hours and hours, and when they leave the ward for 10 minutes, that is when the patient dies. The feeling of guilt for not being there at the time of death is overwhelming for many people. In counselling they can be told that this happens frequently. When the patient is on their own, they then feel 'free' and not constrained by visitors who 'hold them back'. This determination on behalf of the patient can be seen by the bereaved relatives as something positive and inevitable, and can possibly help them to feel less guilty.

There are two other things we need to remember when offering counselling support to the older person. One is that the manner in which the person died may affect the grieving process.

In Netty's case her husband's death was relatively quick. Two months after the diagnosis he was dead. This could almost be called 'sudden death'. There was certainly little time for Netty to prepare, although her husband appears to have known intuitively that there was little time left. The other is the type of relationship which the bereaved had with the deceased.

Attachment theory

One person, talking about her grief, said, 'It feels as though I have lost half of myself. I am no longer a whole person.' In some relationships, a great degree of dependency develops. The two people have literally done everything together. Some have few, if any, friends. When one of them dies, they feel devastated because they have never had a life apart from the one they enjoyed with their partner.

A woman of 62 whose husband had died came into counselling. She was feeling utterly depressed and fearful of the future. Her son lived miles away. Although she had good friends she could see sometimes during the week, the evenings and weekends were particularly hard. Going back to the empty house after a day's work was almost unbearable. On Saturdays and Sundays her friends were tied up with their families. They were not free to spend time with her, making her weekend a misery and something to dread.

During the counselling sessions, it became clear that she and her husband were completely devoted to each other to the exclusion of everyone else. Five minutes after she got to work he would be on the phone to make sure she had arrived alright. He would ring after lunch, and then later to make sure that she was leaving on time.

She received six sessions of counselling with me. During that time she unloaded a great deal of her pain and grief. But she was longing to meet other people who were having a similar experience. So at the end of the sixth session, it was arranged that she would join a bereavement support group. This provided her with the extra help she was seeking. The group agreed to meet together over eight weeks, and at the end of that time she had begun to find things to do over the weekends. One of them was joining a group who went for walks around different parts of London on a Sunday.

The older client

How do we counsel the much older person who may be mourning the loss of a person with whom they have had a relationship over many, many years? I believe it is important to remember that these clients may need a different type of counselling than the younger client.

A woman was sharing with me the help she received when her husband died. Two different people had called to help. One was a trained bereavement counsellor from a local counselling agency; the other was a volunteer from the churches' bereavement service.

'I didn't want the bereavement counsellor. There was nothing wrong with me. But the churches' volunteer was wonderful. She came every Wednesday morning and took me by car to a local restaurant for coffee. It was lovely to get out.'

When I asked her what they talked about, she replied that they spent the time over coffee talking about her dead husband.

This shows how important it is to discover what the client is needing. Some bereaved people are looking for new social contacts. They are lonely and wanting to make new friends and do new things. That is why many branches of Cruse provide a social activity group where the bereaved can meet every fortnight, or every month, for a varied programme of activities.

When this woman said she did not need counselling as there was nothing wrong with her, she was voicing the concerns of many older clients. The British Association for Counselling lays down strict codes of practice and ethics which means that counsellors must work within clear boundaries. The time spent with the client must be limited to 50 or 60 minutes. There must be no social contact with the client, and offers of tea, coffee or something stronger should be declined.

So it may mean that in order to help some older clients, we will need to sit with them over a cup of coffee. And they may need our support on practical issues as well as sharing with us the pain of their loss. The point being made here is the distinction between 'counselling' and 'using counselling skills' (see Chapter 9).

It is essential that we are aware of our own boundaries. From the beginning of our relationship we should make it clear what it is that we are offering, and that this is not unlimited and that there will be an end. It may be wise to offer to visit the person on a weekly basis in the first instance for perhaps three months. When the agreed time is drawing near to an end, we can then discuss with the client whether or not there needs to be an extension.

Counsellors are under pressure to keep to strict time boundaries. The 50-minute or one-hour session should be kept to at all costs. And although with the older client perhaps a more flexible approach can be used, it is still important that the counsellors do not give the impression that they are available at any time and for any length of time.

The tasks of bereavement

Worden (1983) suggests that there are four tasks which the bereaved have to do:

1 To accept the reality of the loss.
2 To experience the pain and grief.
3 To adjust to life where the deceased is missing.
4 To withdraw emotional energy and re-invest in other interests.

To accept the reality of the loss

We can help the bereaved by encouraging them to talk about the dead person and to share with us the details of the illness, death, and the funeral. The family photograph album can be a great help. The telling of the grieving person's story increases the reality of the loss and helps them realise the permanence and finality of death.

A woman received a call from the police to tell her that her son had been killed in a car accident. He was living 400 miles away from home in Cumbria. She and her husband went immediately to the hospital. But when they arrived they were advised by the police not to view the body as it was so mutilated. It took them a long time to come to terms with the fact that their son had died. They had only seen him occasionally since he moved to the North. But as the mother, in counselling, kept repeating the story of the telephone call from the police and the funeral, she finally accepted his death.

To experience the pain and grief

We need to help the bereaved to identify and express feelings of anger, guilt, sadness, anxiety, helplessness and panic. It may be that we are the only people who are still willing to hear how the client is feeling about the loss.

Older clients find that members of the family sometimes discourage their parents from talking about the deceased, but they do need to do this. A person telephoned me to say she was concerned about her father. Her mother had died nine months before. She and her family were now living a long way away from the parental home. She was worried about the emotional state of the father: 'We told him at the funeral he must be brave and not cry for mother. And whenever he starts to talk about her and get distressed, we have to be quite firm with him. "Now come on, dad," we say, "mother's been dead for nine months. It's time to forget about it. Do get on with things. What about all those jobs around the house that need your attention?"'

Families that live miles away from the parental home are naturally anxious about the surviving parent. Their concern is sometimes based on their desire to relinquish any feeling of responsibility for their mother or father. But if the older person is denied the opportunity of sharing feelings of loss with other people, it can not only retard the grieving process, but can make for more isolation and more grief. Helping this daughter to understand this was not only helping her, but indirectly helping her father also.

To adjust to life where the deceased is missing

The client may need to overcome various difficulties in taking on new roles, skills, or in making decisions independently. This is a slow and worrying business for many, and there is a need here for praise and reassurance to boost a lack of self-confidence.

Some women clients may never have changed a light bulb or changed a fuse. It is not unusual to discover that the client does not know how to write a cheque. Many men do not even know how to boil an egg, have never used a washing machine, or done any ironing.

I remember one friend whose wife died suddenly just before they were due to retire. For a week or two he was in such a state of shock that he did not feel safe to go out alone. He realised that his wife had always done all the cooking. A part of his coming to terms with his new situation was that he signed up for an evening class to learn how to cook.

Another man who was in a similar position is now a superb cook. Before his wife's death, it was the family joke that he had never used a drying-up cloth.

To withdraw emotional energy and re-invest in other interests

The client may need assurance that it is all right to change. Although his or her loved one will always remain in their heart, it is not disloyal to take on new interests and friendships. The time to stop grieving has to come. And with it has come a time to say 'goodbye'.

This last task may be more difficult for the 'older old' than the 'younger old'. Clients in their 80s or 90s may feel that there is no time left to seek new directions.

I remember seeing a television documentary about bereavement. In it, an old man was interviewed whose wife had died after a marriage which had lasted nearly 60 years. At the time of the filming, the man was depressed and negativistic, refusing offers of help and without hope for the future. When the presenter asked him what one thing he would find helpful, apart from having his wife back, he replied, 'Death. I'd like to die. I can see no purpose in living any longer'. Some time later he was seen again. But this time he was suntanned and smiling, slightly plumper, and engaging in a wide range of hobbies and other activities. Eight years had passed and he estimated that it had taken him five to get back on course. When he was asked what he thought now about his wish for euthanasia, he replied, 'It would have been such a waste'.

One older man, after his wife's death, devoted himself to writing a history of a certain aeroplane. Another 70-year-old took up painting. And eventually she had an exhibition of her work at the local luncheon club.

Conclusion

Counselling older persons in their grief can be a fulfilling experience. Some words from Margery Allingham's (1984: 123) 'The Tiger in the Smoke' are included in the anthology *All in the End is Harvest*. May hers be the last words in this chapter:

> Mourning is not forgetting … it is an undoing.
> Every minute tie has to be untied and something

permanent and valuable recovered
and assimilated from the knot.
    The end is gain, of course.
Blessed are they that mourn, for they
  shall be made strong.
But the process is like all human births,
  painful and long and dangerous.

References

Allingham M (1984) 'The Tiger in the Smoke'. In: Whitaker A (1984) *All in the End is Harvest: An anthology for those who grieve*. London: Darton, Longman & Todd Ltd.

Worden J W (1983) *Grief Counselling and Grief Therapy*. London: Tavistock Publications Ltd.

Further Reading

Mearns D, Thorne B (1988) *Person-centred Counselling in Action*. London: Sage Publications.

O'Leary E (1995) *Counselling Older Adults*. London: Chapman & Hall.

Sanders P (1994) *First Steps in Counselling*. Manchester: PCCS Books.

Terry P (1997) *Counselling the Elderly and their Carers*. Basingstoke: Macmillan Press Ltd.

In Praise of Memory

Think of tiny pieces of coloured earthenware, waiting to find their place as part of a mosaic design; or of a jigsaw puzzle, scattered on the nursery floor; or again, of scraps of fabric, not yet stitched together to form a patchwork quilt. I'm suggesting that to share one's memories in the context of a secure relationship is one way of taking them seriously and of showing respect for them, for when appreciated and re-evaluated they become what they are: each one an essential component of a unique identity. Sharing of this kind is the legitimate business of counselling. And surely, this is what our memories want from us – the chance to rediscover themselves as part of an individual story, just as the jigsaw puzzle, the mosaic picture and the patchwork quilt have waited to disclose their hidden form to the one who is patient enough to look for the unity within their fragmentation.

(Sheila Willson)

6

Religious and Spiritual Issues

Lilian M Bruce

Editor's Introduction

For many people, talking about religious and spiritual things is not easy. This is not the case for Lilian Bruce. She has a gift for relating to people at the level where it matters. In this chapter she is sharing her insights and her practice with us, the readers.

In an age when religions are in decline, the language with which we express ourselves can be alienating. But we find it hard to bypass spiritual issues in our lives. Everything matters, and sometimes the longing to share with others what matters most – however small it is – can be of immense comfort. As counsellors we need to listen more than talk at such moments, but above all we need to be sensitive enough to hear that there is something which needs to be said. Lilian shows us how it can be done, so encouraging us to do likewise.

Introduction

When I was less than 30 years old, and just beginning in my life-work as a parish minister, I remember thinking that it was quite acceptable to describe anyone over the age of 60 as 'elderly'. Now, when the years are rapidly bringing me towards that same age, I am not so sure! At the age of 60, one may have another 30 years to be lived, bringing different experiences in different situations to very many different people.

I also used to think that older people had so much to teach the young about the religious and spiritual dimensions of life. Now that I have spent many years becoming closer to older people, I recognise that there is a certain timelessness and agelessness, a glimpse of eternity, in religion and spirituality, and chronological age no longer seems such a reliable measure of such things as I once thought it to be.

Perhaps when we are younger, we expect those who are older to reveal to us some greater insight into things eternal, as for them the ending of this life naturally draws ever nearer. But why expect from those who are older something that may, or may not, be part of their own personal experience of life?

Those who work with older people will be quick to recognise that there is no such thing as a typical older person, not any more than there is such a thing as a typical teenager. In any sheltered housing complex, or in any residential home, we will find those who will welcome us with a blasphemy, and those who will send us on our way with a blessing. We find those for whom prayer is a real part of their lives, who will be praying for us and who will be deeply happy at the thought that we are praying for them, and we will find those for whom the very suggestion of prayer will stir deep antagonisms, variously expressed.

And so, the questions need to be raised – Are older people spiritually different from any other age group? Why would we expect them to be different? And if one dares to ask about the religious and spiritual experience of the older people for whom we seek to care, it would surely not be unreasonable to ask in a similar way about our own peer group. It is more than likely that we will identify a great diversity of spiritual experience, or lack of it, among our own peer group, and among our families and friends, whatever age they be.

It takes more than the coming of age, the passing of time and the accumulation of life experiences, to create the spirit or to nurture the soul. Like the body and like the mind, the soul or the spirit is given as a gift at the time of our creation. In many of the world's major religions the soul is seen as more important than the body or the mind, because it lasts longer: it is eternal. Other words or phrases may be used besides 'soul' or 'spirit', for example 'the real you'; and 'the real you' is more than your mind and more than your body – which is quite a thought when we think of what may happen to both mind and body as the years go on!

In the care of older people, we know that it takes time and skill and patience to work out the appropriate physical care for any one individual. And it takes different but complementary gifts to identify what is needed for the appropriate stimulation of the mind. I would like to suggest that the same is true of the spiritual care of the individual and likewise it will take the development of the carer's gifts to help to identify and to begin to meet the spiritual needs of the individuals for whom we care.

Who are they? And how well do we know them? Who are they, the older people whom we will meet as we go about our task of caring? Who are they, as they enjoy a fit and active 'old age', or as they begin to suffer the limitations of mind or body? To what extent do the different limitations alter and change their perception of themselves, and to what extent do they alter and change our perception of them? They are not as once they were, but the 'as once they were' is almost always the clue to who they are now – physically, mentally, emotionally, and spiritually.

In this chapter, the focus is on the spiritual dimension of caring for older people. I am writing as a parish minister who has met older folk in a variety of different situations, in very different places: different people, with different needs ... and I would like to introduce you now to three very different people.

Let me introduce you to a midwife. She is now 84 years of age, living in the same community where she was district nurse, still surrounded by the same families. One of the babies she delivered is now her home-help, she knows the woman's parents, she remembers her grandparents, she was there to lay them out when their time came, and she is known and remembered in that community as the nurse who never left a birth or a deathbed without saying a prayer. Like her own mother and grand-mother before her, Mary has the gift of faith, and everyone she meets gets to know of it, usually sooner rather than later. She is 'up front' with her faith, her religion, her spirituality – no one she meets is ever left in any doubt about her relationship with her Lord, and those who dare to listen may learn much.

Now I will introduce you to someone else of the same age. His father did not return from the First World War, two of his brothers and many of his schoolfriends did not return from the Second World War. He does not speak of them, not ever. Their names are there on the village war memorial – they are read out loud, every year, at the service on Remembrance Sunday, and he chooses not to be there, on parade, with the medals and the memories of 'those who grow old'. Instead, on each 11th of November, his choice is to be alone, and to drink himself into oblivion. He swears like a trooper, he avoids any contact with 'church', and in the night his neighbours often hear his nightmare screams fol-lowed by deep sobbing in his sleep. His name is David.

And let me introduce you to someone else who was born in 1914. Helen was fostered out to distant relatives after her mother died in childbirth and her father re-married. The only real home she knew was the one she made for herself and her husband, and the three sons who were born to them. A devout Roman Catholic, she became a reluctant Protestant, to fit in with her husband's family. One son was killed in a farm accident at the age of five. Her favourite, the eldest, died in his 40s. The remain-ing son had a major heart attack at the age of 50, and now suffers serious depression. She is a strong, silent woman, her face serene. If you met her tomorrow, you would not guess her story, and she would not share it. Perhaps you would find one or two clues in photographs, in pictures, in framed texts, in bedside reading. Her privacy is very precious to her.

The same age, the same generation, but three very different people – how would you begin to identify their religious and spiritual needs?

Perhaps these three people, as I have introduced them to you, remind you of people you know, or of people you have known. Or perhaps their stories will begin to stir other memories which may help you to explore this question.

Identifying the religious and spiritual needs of the older people we care for

Perhaps this is an area which you personally would rather not be asked to explore. There are many carers and helpers who would want to back off from religious and spiritual issues, for many different reasons, both recognised and unrecognised. However, that does not mean that the religious and spiritual issues will just disappear from the lives of those for whom we care. And even if it is the case that you find this topic to some degree uncomfortable, you may still discover yourself to be in a situation where you are the person who could make sure that another carer, or group of carers, is introduced into the scenario where their gift or skill is required in order to address the spiritual needs of the person you are caring for in other ways.

As you know, caring for another person means getting to know them, and building up a relationship with them. Think of a person with whom you have a relationship – it could be a member of your family or a neighbour, or someone at work, or someone you meet in some leisure activity.

Perhaps you would consider yourself to be close to that other person – close enough to identify their needs, near enough to meet their needs, and honest enough to recognise that, as in any relationship with any person, different needs will be met by different people at different times in life, and in different areas of life.

How much do you expect of yourself as a carer? Sometimes our own expectations of ourselves as carers are quite unreasonable. Sometimes we may become the victims of other people's expectations of us. Sometimes it may help to separate out the significant areas of the life of the person for whom we care, and to recognise to what extent we may be able to relate to them.

Look at the following list of significant areas of life experience, the examples given, and the questions raised.

The family context

Two sisters who are so close again in their 70s, now that they are both widowed, but may not have seen much of each other during 30 or 40 years of marriage when the one couldn't see any good in the other's husband. How do their families relate to this new situation? And how do carers relate to changing family circumstances?

Family events from the past

Sometimes the most significant family events are those which are never spoken about. What, or who, is missing from the family photographs on display?

The places that have been most important to them throughout their lives

Often getting to know older people is like going on a guided tour through this country, or even across the world. Are the places so familiar to them known or unknown to the carer? Is there someone else around who is able to share the memories of past places and past experiences?

The shape and form of their work

How closely is the person's identity connected with what he or she did when working? Was their work significant to them, or was it more of a meaningless drudge? Would they be happy to have contact with someone who has similar work experience?

Leisure and hobby pursuits

It is not always easy to recognise the rugby cap, or the junior prize boxer, or even the middle-aged cup-winning golfer in the shuffling old man whom we got to know only recently. And how does the almost-blind old lady look back upon the years when her very fine needlework took the trophies at the regional shows? And what about the man whose hobby was to raise pedigree budgies, until he celebrated his retirement by opening all the cages and letting them all fly free?

The religious setting and spiritual experience

Likewise, this area of life may see many changes with the passing of the years. We may meet the sadness of a man who had lived all his life at the centre of the church community saying quite plainly that 'he doesn't believe any of it any more'. Or we may puzzle at an apparently gentle older lady who has a remarkable vocabulary of swear words and blasphemy, yet who will join in faultlessly with the old prayers from the prayer book, and the familiar Bible texts – perhaps none more apt than 'Lord, You have searched me and known me'.

There may be a tendency to think that none of these questions need arise when the caring is being done within a close family circle, where everyone knows everything about everyone else. And when we realise that what does go on within family circles is the stuff that 'soaps' are made of – the question often arises, how well do family members really know each other?

Even in the most close-knit of families it is often helpful to recognise that there are needs which may be met more creatively by someone else, and that caring does not need to be limited to the family circle.

What about the 70-year-old woman, living in sheltered housing, who deliberately came out of her shell to tell the other residents that the 12th of August would be her golden wedding day? When the warden phoned the daughter to find out what was being done, or should be done, to mark the anniversary, the perplexed daughter had to tell the warden that her parents had never stayed together long enough to celebrate any of their wedding anniversaries, and her father had been dead for nearly 20 years. The warden then had an idea. She made sure that she had time to spend with the woman on the 12th of August, and took her some golden roses from a bush in the garden. During the visit, she asked if she could see the wedding photographs. The photographs that were produced turned out to be from the previous generation; they were handled with care, they were spoken about, and the warden was asked if she could get the big one framed. You may imagine the surprise of the daughter, on her next visit, when she discovered, in a prominent place on the wall, the wedding photograph of her grandmother, to her first husband ... her mother had been the second daughter of the second marriage. And where were the photographs of her mother's wedding? There was much still to be unpacked. But would there ever be anyone to do it? Also, how helpful would it be to do it, and for whom?

Perhaps you remember the story of the family who discovered after their father's death that their parents had never been married, and that he still had a wife and son living on the other side of London ... It seems that family situations may often be far more interesting, or complicated, than we assume them to be, or than they are when first presented to us. In some cases, one may discover a certain measure of fantasy at play, but why be surprised when those of us who are younger may often want our own lives to be a little different?

The more that we explore what is meant by the 'religious' or 'spiritual' dimension of life, the more we discover that it is not separate from the rest of life, but is closely interwoven in and through the fabric of our lives.

The word 'spirituality' is much in use at this time, but what does it mean? There are many possible definitions. However, a definition which I find helpful is this, in three parts.

Our spirituality is how we relate to God:

- in and through the created world – earth, sky, sea, trees, flowers, and all other created things;
- in and through other people – awareness of the love of God through the receiving and giving of love and care, in many different ways and in many different relationships;
- in and through our inner selves – the deep places of the soul.

This definition of spirituality seems to have the advantage of being able to be applied to different religions, and to different ways of thinking in the same religion. It should come as no surprise to discover that not all Christians think alike, or that there are many different varieties of Islam. And some people who would resist being attached to any religious label may well turn out to be deeply spiritual people.

So how do we begin to recognise, and to provide for, the religious and spiritual needs of those for whom we care?

Even with close family members we may be surprised. For instance, what may lie behind it when someone unexpectedly begins to speak of 'arrangements', and strongly insists that she is not to be cremated, as her husband was? Or what is going on, deep inside, when an old man starts ripping out pages, one a day, from the Bible that he has treasured for years? Or what does it mean when an old lady, who has loved flowers, begins to pull off the petals, very gently, and to peer at what she may see inside?

The question frequently arises: how well do we know other people, even those in our family circle?

Let me share with you another story about a middle-aged couple, both of them on the staff of a local hospital. They had met and married many years before while she was doing volunteer work in East Africa, and her Asian husband had come to this country with her, and had apparently 'adapted well' to her family's culture. The husband's elderly mother was over here on holiday when the wife was killed in a road accident. Her own parents immediately made themselves available to look after the teenagers, to run the home, and to arrange the funeral, understandably making themselves as busy as possible, which many people do in such circumstances, not only to be 'helpful' but often – subconsciously – to avoid having to come to terms with their own tragic loss.

Unfortunately, and without thinking, they arranged the funeral according to their own custom, which meant buying a plot in their village graveyard. The man who had lost his wife was in a state of shock, and seemed scarcely able to attend the funeral. His mother was distraught, and would not leave her bedroom. The teenagers were unusually silent.

There was still no change in their emotional condition when a friend from work called two days after the funeral. Two weeks later, the husband was still emotionally extremely upset, and unable to contemplate returning to work. He reluctantly agreed to see a counsellor, and it was in the second counselling session that there emerged a previously unrecognised contributory cause to his anxiety and stress. It came out that the husband and his mother belonged to a Hindu family, and that the husband had long since discarded any open practice of his faith. Out of deference to his wife's parents, he had felt quite unable to suggest that cremation would certainly be his preferred option. Neither he nor his mother had been consulted, nor had their deepened distress been noticed. If only a listening ear and a little time had been offered in the midst of their grief.

All of us will have our own lists of 'if only' situations, but I wonder how many of them involve the dangerous assumption that there is nothing that older people are able to tell us or teach us?

Those we seek to care for may be family, or close neighbours, or good friends, or they may be people who are strangers to us, and we are getting to know them as they are, simply because they need our care and attention. Some carers may be volunteers, others may be in employment as carers – either in the community, or in residential homes.

Most carers, either voluntary or in employment, will have received some training in how to be aware of the physical and social needs of older people. However, unless the carer belongs to a church community, or other religious group, it is unlikely that training will have been given to enable the carer to be aware of the spiritual needs of the one who is being cared for.

In whatever setting, be it 'care in the community' or in a residential home, the following checklist may be helpful in order to provide a spiritual or religious profile of the older person we are seeking to care for.

1 Does the older person belong to any particular church? An answer such as 'C of E' could be followed up by a kindly asking of 'whereabouts?' This would ascertain whether it is a 'live' connection, or one which has been lying dormant for a period of time.
2 If there is no answer to 1, is there another religious connection? A simple way of approaching this could be to ask where they, or their family, go to worship.
3 A more personal approach could come by noticing any particular clues, for example a church in a photograph, or a memento from the Holy Land or other religious site, or the obvious presence of a Bible or prayer book, or the wearing of a cross, or a star of David, or other religious symbol.

4 Has the older person been having regular visits from someone from a church, or from any other religious group? Would they like to have such a contact continued?

5 Would the older person like to be able to participate in a service of worship? Are there reasons why this has not been possible? Are they able to be overcome?

6 Does the older person require a large-print Bible or hymn book, or other religious books in large print? Does he or she use audio-tapes?

7 Would it be a good idea to have a visitor who would read to and/or pray with the older person?

8 Does he or she enjoy watching 'Songs of Praise', or any other religious programme? Does he or she listen to the religious programmes on the radio, for example 'The Daily Service'? Someone with limited vision may appreciate some help to discover what is on offer through a radio or television guide.

The responses to explorations such as these will begin to build up a religious and spiritual profile of the older person in your care.

However, it should be noted that this process may well take a considerable period of time, and with many older people it may take a lot of patience on the part of the carer before there is built up the trust that is required to share a very personal part of one's life.

At the same time, the carer may be encouraged to build up a better picture of the resources which are available, or may become available, to meet the religious and spiritual needs of their older neighbours in the community.

Available resources

It is often helpful to expand one's local knowledge by way of a visit to the local public library, who would probably be able to provide an up-to-date list of nearby churches and other religious groups, perhaps with contact telephone numbers. Current information about Sunday services and weekday meetings may also be advertised in the local press.

Facilities on offer

Many churches or places of worship have some or all of the following facilities available:

- A transport scheme for those who need a lift to Sunday service.
- Disabled access.
- A sound loop system.
- A lunch club.
- A mid-week fellowship or service.
- Volunteers who visit the housebound and, if requested, will pray with them or read the Bible.

Discovering the resources, and then linking up an older person with the means of meeting the needs that they have expressed can be a rewarding experience. However, most people who have cared for an older person for some time will have their own stories to tell about caring and careful preparation that can go wrong.

One scenario that happens frequently is that the older person has been prescribed 'water pills' (diuretics), but she doesn't want people to know. Being ready when her lift would arrive on Sunday morning would involve having to rise very early. She tells herself she can do it, but then has to tell the driver that she 'isn't too well today'. After two or three times of this happening in the space of five or six weeks, the driver feels that it is kinder not to come.

Another scenario that I would like to share with you is one which I have met fairly often, but may be more difficult to deal with. All the arrangements have been carefully made, and Maimie greets the driver with a big smile – 'I'm not coming, just come in'. She wanted the company, but she didn't want to go to the service, or to the mid-week church meeting. One day Maimie said, 'You see, there is nothing I can do there any more, and I used to do so much'.

She used to sing in the choir in her local church, she was always baking for parish teas, she was always sewing for parish fairs. Those times are no more, and she felt now 'there was nothing she could do'. However, it was discovered that there was something she could do. When I went to visit, I used to chat to Maimie with different bits of news. One day I was telling her about a young neighbour whose new baby had died. Maimie reached out to touch my arm. 'I lost a baby once', she said, 'tell the mum that I am praying for her'.

Here was something that people like Maimie, and perhaps many others, can do. When carers are able to share in such a way with older people, the older folk themselves often 'open up' and prayer is able to add a new dimension to shared concerns. Only be sure that grace rather then gossip is the order of the day! You may be interested to know that Maimie had already been diagnosed as suffering from dementia. The dementia has, of course, become more of a problem with the passing of the years, but Maimie continues to ask for the young mother, who now has two other children, and she never fails to ask after my own mother with the words, 'Tell her that I am praying for her'.

One begins to appreciate how prayer is so much more an activity of the spirit than it is an activity of the mind. I have found that praying with the very old may be so like praying with the very young, in such a way that the sharing of the silences is so much more significant than the understanding of the words.

'Becoming like a little child' is seen by Jesus to be very important in our relationship with God. In my work with young children, when introducing them to the stories of the Bible, it is true of every new group of children, that they love to hear the words 'Fear not'; God's special message to Mary, and to them, and to so many other people too. Who is there who has never wanted to hear the loving words 'Fear not'? And much has been written about the 'terrors of the night' suffered by many older people who are afflicted by dementia. They too need to hear the words 'Fear not', and to know the security of the love of the Lord for them.

Those who have the care of the very young at heart welcome them into the world and introduce them to life in the world conscious of their need of protection from all that could harm them. The same is true of frail older people. They need to be protected from anything that would seek to harm them or to destroy their peace.

Sometimes it is assumed that a person who is suffering from dementia will not be aware of what is happening around them, and that therefore it does not matter whether carers are using offensive language or carrying on rough and ragged conversations between themselves while seeing to the needs of the older person.

Let me share another of my own learning experiences with you. When I went to my first parish, I was told that there was a very old lady, the widow of a previous schoolmaster in the village, who was in the cottage hospital in the nearest town. 'You don't need to visit her', I was told, 'she doesn't know anybody any more'. For more than two years, I visited her once a month, having a quiet few minutes with her, holding her hand, saying a prayer, and never knowing whether or not there was any real communication between us. Then, one wintry Thursday afternoon, I sat down beside her bed. Her head stirred, her eyes opened, and she spoke to me for the first time. The words were quite clear and matter of fact, 'You're the minister, aren't you? We'll say a prayer.' At seven o'clock in the evening, I answered the phone at home. The sister on the ward told me that they had sent for the old lady's daughter soon after I had left, and she had remained conscious long enough to be able to tell her daughter that she 'had seen the minister, and had a prayer, and everything was all right'. And then she died. She had not said anything coherent for years, and she had met me, an unfamiliar woman minister, when she was already deeply into dementia. I have always been thankful that the Spirit had compelled me to visit her. Truly, it was not a waste of time.

A whole new area opens up when one begins to consider counselling in the context of the religious and spiritual care of those suffering from dementia, especially when the dementia itself may be quite advanced. Counselling may become more focussed on non-verbal communication, such as presence, and laughter, and touch, using not only words and story but also sign and symbol and sacrament as a means of grace. Surely the purpose of such counselling is likely to be the enabling of the older person to overcome any fear they may have, and to give them the reassurance that they are deeply loved by the Lord.

In Praise of Memory

Have you noticed that the images hidden within everyday words can sometimes reveal their deeper meaning? Thus 'recollection' becomes re-collection: a gathering of things together, and not for the first time. 'Remembering' conjures up the picture of a body, once dismembered but now with its limbs intact. And 'recall' suggests a summoning back of that which has once been present. Associated as they are with the function of memory, these words seem to invite us to take an active part in the process of bringing the past back to consciousness. They re-mind us that when we re-collect the past we are giving back a primal unity to separated particles, and that when we re-member the past we are restoring to its original fullness a body whose limbs have been severed. And so history is given a second chance, a new beginning – as our personal, ongoing story.

(Sheila Willson)

7

Advocacy and Communication

Sandra Williams

Editor's Introduction

At many times in our lives we need someone to help us practically or emotionally. Most of the time these aspects overlap. 'Simply' filling in a form may be too demanding of our energies, but unless the form is filled in, life cannot improve.

Sandra Williams and her team are advocates to people who need help. Before they can help, they need to know what the person's needs are, and these are often not so obvious. Advocates have to be independent, not in someone's pay and not representing others' interests, in order to help effectively. When they call on a person, they bring only themselves. That is why they have to be skilled in communication and in the use of counselling skills. That is why older people turn to advocates in the first instance. When they do this, they know that the help received is not biased but fair. The job of an advocate is not easy, but helping others never is; yet all of us are and can be advocates in given circumstances.

This chapter gives a different and even unusual slant to what communication and counselling is and is about. It may therefore need to be read with the wider context of the subject in mind. The fresh approach to a very complex process used by Sandra expresses her deep concern that all helping has to be relevant to the person and his or her individual needs.

Introduction

A broad definition of advocacy is, 'Taking action on behalf of and with the agreement of another individual'; it is arguably the most demanding of all citizenship roles. In *Collins English Dictionary* (1994) it is defined as 'active support' whilst 'counselling' is defined as 'systematic guidance in which a person's problems are discussed and advice is given'. Advocacy and counselling are similar, but they are also disparate.

There are varying interpretations put on the word 'advocacy' and it does convey different things to different people. In the context of this chapter it means empowerment of individuals. Empowerment is both a process and a goal by which individuals can have greater power to express their needs and decide how their needs should be met. Advocacy is about stating a case, influencing decisions, ending assumptions, getting better services and being treated equally. It aims to protect individuals from abuse and enable them to exercise their rights.

There are differences between advocating on behalf of an older person and advocating for someone with a disability or with learning difficulties. All too frequently old age produces marginalisation and, increasingly, older people whether through age or frailty, physical or sensory disabilities, mental infirmity, poverty or even social attitudes, are finding themselves in vulnerable positions and needing the service of an independent advocate to support their interests and, where necessary, intercede on their behalf.

The need for advocacy is increasingly being recognised and new schemes developed to help vulnerable members of society. Some schemes are generic and relate to people living within a certain area, others are specific to older people or people with mental health problems or learning difficulties.

I am employed by Age Concern Coventry as the Advocacy Project Co-ordinator. Over a period of time, we saw a marked increase in the number of older people approaching the agency who were in need of more than an information-giving service. Many of them did not have a partner or close relative who could support them or speak on their behalf and it was considered that an advocacy service would be highly beneficial to these people; this was borne out by the 152 referrals which we received during our first year of operation (1996–97). The service, which is free and independent, is aimed at people aged 55 or over living within Coventry City boundaries. Coventry has the third highest population of older people in the United Kingdom and demographic projections indicate that it will continue to rise in the future. We receive referrals from many sources, including social services, local health authorities, MPs and mental health services, in addition to self-referrals.

Who are advocates?

Advocates are ordinary people from a variety of backgrounds who are trained to work one-to-one. They are sympathetic to the problems of older people and have a commitment to their rights; whilst being supportive they must be able to represent the service user's view rather than their own. We provide on-going support and training in all aspects of our work.

Wherever possible, the volunteer advocates visit people in their own homes, as it is there that, in familiar surroundings, they are most relaxed. There we can pick up on photographs, treasured possessions, etc, in order to develop a conversation and start to build up a rapport. A great deal can be learnt from a home visit – not just visually. I used to visit a lady who, when I first met her, had been widowed for around three months. She had no children and her grief was further compounded by the fact that she had nursed her husband for the three years prior to his death. Her loss was therefore doubled – the loss of a much loved partner and companion and the loss of a purpose to her life. It was most poignant to see that his cap was still hanging on the corner of his armchair and his slippers were still warming in the hearth. This gave me far more of an insight than words could ever do. A visually impaired social worker told me that she always insists on making home visits; clearly she cannot pick up on the surroundings by what she sees but a good impression of the home environment, its occupants and general condition can be assimilated. There are, however, some circumstances when a home visit is not possible (for example when the person concerned does not wish any other person to know of their problems or in cases where they live in an area of the city where it would be unwise for one female to visit alone). In these circumstances we arrange to meet for a cup of coffee either in a local café or in a quiet room at the office.

We adopt a casual, relaxed and friendly manner. This can be achieved by not dressing formally or carrying briefcases, folders, forms, etc; notes can always be jotted down in a notebook kept in a handbag or pocket. An independent client satisfaction survey was carried out in 1997, and this revealed which parts of our service were felt to be of greatest value. Foremost on the list was the fact that our advocates were considered to be friendly and caring. The survey showed that users viewed the relationship aspect of the service as being as important to them as the professionalism demonstrated in the problem resolution. By adopting this attitude we are able to build up confidence and communication follows.

In order to establish contact we talk to the person about where he or she (or in the case of a widow, her husband) was employed and encourage them to tell us about what their work entailed; the majority of older people took a great pride in their work and love to have the opportunity to talk about it. Coventry was very heavily bombed during the war and large parts of the city were destroyed. People who knew Coventry pre-war love to tell us about what it was like before the Blitz; as none of us knew it then we, in turn, learn a lot about working practices and indigenous trades. Another good talking point is the fortunes, or otherwise, of our local football team.

It has to be recognised that older people do have a tremendous sense of pride and great resilience, and today's retired generation have experience of deprivation and lack of amenities which were acquired during war years and the consequent hardship resulting from this. Many circumstances and situations which to us appear almost intolerable may to them seem quite normal as they have not known any different. One very good example of this is a couple who are in their 70s and own their house. We first met them last year and, at that time, there was no bathroom in the house, the toilet was outside, and the kitchen area was a lean-to structure which leaked and was almost unbearable in the bad weather. There are no children and each week this couple would go to a family member's house for a bath and to take the washing; this state of affairs had existed for over 50 years! The couple in question could see no real difficulty in this and though they had a fair amount of savings they had never considered an alteration to the house to provide them with modern amenities. Earlier this year we helped them to get this work done and they are thrilled with the outcome. This is, of course, another good reason for meeting people in their own homes: we are able to see quite clearly when things are wrong and household repairs have not been carried out or food and heating are not in evidence. This cannot be conveyed in depth by talking to a person over the telephone or meeting them in the office. How an older person copes with these problems is very much on an individual basis which is dependent upon how he or she has coped with previous life experiences.

Types of advocacy

Our project incorporates two types of advocacy: **citizen advocacy** and **crisis advocacy**.

Citizen advocacy is an open-ended partnership whereby a volunteer advocate works closely with a vulnerable older person who, because of frailty, is isolated from services and frequently unable to express needs and wishes. One example of this is work with people experiencing dementia-type illnesses who are unable to comprehend what services and options are available to them.

Crisis advocacy is basically solving a one-off problem which is usually quite complex and made up of several issues. In these cases the client is quite able to manage the problems associated with normal everyday living but needs help when something out of the ordinary occurs. Examples of this would include: experiencing elder abuse, community care challenges, complaints against authorities or service providers.

We originally thought that the majority of our time would be spent on citizen advocacy work, the main principles of which are independence, loyalty, and a long-term one-to-one relationship between the client and an unpaid advocate. However, we are increasingly finding that a large proportion of our referrals require crisis advocacy.

The proposals of all political parties appear to concentrate more and more on self-sufficiency in providing for old age. Over recent years government legislation has greatly increased the need for advocacy and inequitable state economies in the provision of welfare services have disproportionately affected the elderly population. Phillipson (1993) argues that:

'There are a number of reasons for thinking that an advocacy approach would have benefits for work with older people. First, it may help restore people's confidence about asserting their rights. Secondly, it may highlight injustices in old age. Thirdly, restoring the voice of the consumer may help to influence an improvement in the quality of services received by older people'.

The need for advocacy

When considering the need for advocacy we should look at the attitudes of society towards older people. Clearly old age is a time when many changes do take place. Four basic characteristics of normal age-related changes are recognised: firstly, they are universal in that they affect all older adults – however, each individual is influenced differently; secondly, the onset of change is gradual, it usually happens very slowly; thirdly, these changes are progressive; and fourthly, normal age-related changes occur from within.

There are, however, many outside elements which affect the ageing process and it is therefore important to view ageing from a holistic point of view. Brearley (1977) felt that, 'An important task of ageing is to accept increasing dependence in a way that will still permit functioning as an independent individual'. When describing 'The Seven Ages of Man', Shakespeare considered the final stage to be 'second childishness, and mere oblivion, sans teeth, sans eyes, sans taste, sans everything'. This depressing and negative attitude is to some extent still with us at the end of the twentieth century, as evidenced in some of the terms commonly used to describe older people – 'geriatric', 'old biddy', 'old fogey', to name but a few. Old age is viewed by many as an anti-climax to life – a period of non-achievement, loss and deprivation. Many older people are well able to represent their own interests in everyday situations, but there are several inter-related issues which increasingly give rise to the need for advocacy. Some are described below.

Demographic changes

The number of people who are aged over 65 is increasing year by year and it is predicted that, by the year 2020, 37 per cent of the European electorate will be aged over 60 (figures supplied by Age Concern England). As a result of greatly improved living conditions and extensive advances in health care, we now have an increased life expectancy. In 1993 a man of 60 could be expected to live for another 17.8 years and a woman of the same age for another 21.9 years (ONS 1996). In 1994 8,000 people in the UK were aged 100 and over; in 2031 it is estimated that 34,000 people will be in this age group (ONS 1996). Whilst undoubtedly many people will welcome living to an ever greater age, there is a vast number to whom it will mean prolonged misery and deprivation. Resources will have to be stretched ever further and increasing old age does, in many cases, bring with it an ever increasing dependency upon others and the greater possibility of suffering with some form of dementia. The same forecasts show that there will be a rise of 16 per cent in the number of dementia sufferers in the UK by the year 2005.

Family structures are changing quite dramatically as, with changing work patterns, more people are moving away to find employment; to this must be added the number of family members who experience marital break-down. In addition, the percentage of women who now go out to work is higher than it has ever been (apart from war years). Older relatives are therefore having, out of necessity, to become more self-sufficient at a time in their lives when they are less able to do so. In these situations we are able to take on some of the tasks which erstwhile would have been carried out by a family member, for example setting up arrangements for the payment of bills, accompanying a person to hospital for an outpatient appointment, or arranging for household repairs to be carried out.

Legislation and policy

Legislation over the past decade and the ever-changing criteria involved with 'Care in the Community' has adversely affected older people. Current Government spending priorities on both health and education have meant a reduction in spending on social services. There are no specific laws relating to the treatment of older people or discrimination against them; this does therefore render them very vulnerable both to exploitation and abuse. As advocates we closely monitor legislation and its interpretation and implementation by the local authority, and wherever possible, we make representations on behalf of all older people.

Information

People of all ages need to be able to make choices based on information which is accessible, accurate and understandable. Organisational structures and systems have greatly increased the amount of bureaucracy which surrounds our lives. Even to very many professionals the amount of 'red-tape' is both confusing and often unnecessary, and so is likely to be daunting to an older person who has no-one to interpret it for them. One example of this is the completion of application forms for Attendance Allowance and Income Support. In every case where we, in the Advocacy Project, have assisted the applicant with the completion of these forms, we have been told, 'I am so glad that you were able to fill in the forms for me as I could not understand them and would not have done it for myself; I would have thrown them away'. It is hardly surprising therefore that benefits totalling over £1 billion go unclaimed.

Finance

Many people who have now reached retirement age were not able to put money aside for their later years. As a result of the introduction of the National Health Service in 1948, they erroneously believed that the state would take care of them 'from the cradle to the grave'. They considered that, as they had paid their National Insurance contributions and taxes, they could reasonably expect to be provided for when they were no longer able to provide for themselves either through age, infirmity, disability, or sickness. As people are living longer and the number of births and subsequent employed contributing individuals is decreasing, there is going to be a financial imbalance in the future. It has been made clear that we cannot expect to live in a 'nanny state' and must make provision for our own future. Whilst this may be feasible for today's younger generation who have been given much advance warning, it is impossible for someone in their later years to be able to accrue any savings. They are additionally penalised by the fact that the retirement pension does not keep pace with the rate of inflation. The Government's Family Expenditure Survey published in 1992 showed that 'retired households (however that is defined) depend on Social Security benefits for 41 per cent of household income in contrast to 11 per cent of all other households' (Oppenheimer 1993).

If the issue of how older people achieve an adequate income is not addressed urgently, we shall continue to see many older people facing hardship and worry because they cannot live on their income. In his study *Raising the Wage of Retirement* published as part of Age Concern's 1995 'Short Change' Campaign, Dr Eric Midwinter (1995) concluded that '£125 a week is the suggested personal cost for what passes as an active member of modern British society'. He goes on to point out that many older people cannot live 'ordinary' lives because they have insufficient income. 'They can stay alive, they can exist, but they are effectively excluded from much of what we would regard as normal life'.

The State Benefit system does ensure that people have a basic level of income, but surely everyone is entitled to 'live' as opposed to just 'survive'. It cannot be argued that older people should not rely on benefits but go out and seek a job if they wish to improve their standard of living and, as previously stated, many of them did not have the opportunity to save for their retirement.

As advocates we are able to ensure that people receive the benefits to which they are entitled. When visiting someone for the first time we complete a benefit check and, if there are any queries, we then liaise with the Benefits Agency and ask for their assistance.

Protection

It is a sad reflection on late twentieth century society that, on the whole, we do not consider the needs and wishes of others and have adopted a 'self-first' mentality. The present generation of older people was brought up, in the main, during war years and, as a result of that, experienced much hardship. They are far more trusting than younger people and believe in the trust and honesty of their fellow citizens; many of them (especially those living in inner cities) welcome strangers into their homes – often it is because they are so pleased simply to have someone to talk to. We have encountered several instances of older people handing over large sums of money in advance for repair work which they had been 'persuaded' by unscrupulous traders needed to be done; then either the work was never carried out or it was of a very inferior standard.

Elder abuse is a matter of great concern to many of us who work with older people (see Chapter 8). The abuse comes in many forms; sexual, physical, emotional, financial and neglect. The organisation Action on Elder Abuse is making great advances in bringing this matter to the attention of the wider public (many of whom cannot conceive that such things could possibly happen) and they have come a long way since Virginia Bottomley, as Secretary of State for Health, said in a 'Newsnight' programme in June 1991, 'I do not think that abuse against the elderly is a major problem'.

Advocacy versus counselling

The similarities between advocacy and counselling are many, the common denominator being that both have their roots in communication. Communication can be as basic as just knowing that someone is there; in some sense, communication forms the corner-stone of integration into a social world. It is an act by means of which human beings convey to one another their ideas, thoughts, needs or feelings. Communication (in whatever form) is a two-way process and advocacy on behalf of older adults relies very much on communication. Initially the individual seeking assistance needs to be able to convey where the problem lies. So often we are presented with the 'by-the-way' syndrome whereby we are told of all manner of minor difficulties and, on attempting to ascertain the facts, it eventually transpires that the main worry and concern is a completely different issue.

Communication

In both an advocacy and counselling capacity, if we are to help older people, we have to be particularly aware of the communication we use and receive. Many older people experience difficulties in communication with others as they get older and their hearing and/or vision deteriorates and they may not be as patient as once they were. Age strikes at a fundamental aspect of the information processing system: short-term memory loss. Morale can be lowered through ill-health, loss, loneliness or grief and to compound this there is a perceived lack of time to project forward. Older people are inclined to pass on a great deal of minutiae whilst withholding the more salient information. The art of communicating lies in the ability to elicit from them the information which is required whilst not appearing to dismiss as trivial what they want to say and they themselves consider to be significant. It has, at this point, to be borne in mind that many older people do not have anyone to talk to and, in some cases, they can go for days with their only contact with a human being represented by a character in a television programme or a check-up call from the warden of sheltered accommodation.

Communication is a set of skills both non-verbal (what you do) and verbal (what you say). Non-verbal communication is the first communication that we receive from and give to a person. Studies have found that the total impact of a message is about 7 per cent verbal (words only), about 38 per cent vocal (tone of voice, inflection) and 55 per cent non-verbal (gesture, body posture, eye contact, facial expression, etc) (Millar & Cameron 1994). Listening well involves being aware of our own non-verbal messages which could be creating barriers. Non-verbal prompts (eg a nod of the head which suggests agreement or understanding) demonstrate listening and also encourage the speaker to continue talking.

Eye contact is one of the most important ways in which we communicate full and undivided attention. It is possible to give both too much and too little eye contact; it should feel quite natural and it is important that a person is not made to feel that they have been put under a microscope. Another point to note is being aware of facial expressions; these should reflect what is being said, not what the advocate happens to be thinking at the time. It is also important to look comfortable without overdoing the appearance of being relaxed. Physical barriers should be avoided, it is not conducive to ease and relaxation if there is a table or desk between the two parties.

Developing confidence and building up trust are therefore the prerequisites of being able to communicate. However, equally important is the ability to listen, remembering that silence can be a useful prompt and can also convey a great deal of information. Listening is the area with which most practitioners are least familiar and comfortable. It is a complex skill involving attending, hearing and understanding the information which a person conveys both verbally and non-verbally. While it is quite easy for most of us to hear, it is much more difficult to listen and decipher the messages behind the words. A good listener is particularly sensitive to the concerns of the speaker and will encourage him or her to open up by creating a comfortable setting. This is done by paying attention in an unthreatening way and giving the speaker clues which convey that you are interested and encourage the other person to feel at ease. Good listeners avoid both unnecessary interruptions and taking conversations down blind alleys.

Ending the partnership

Another similarity between counselling and advocacy is the eventual need to end the relationship and the consequential difficulties caused as a result. Counsellors are able to overcome this in a more direct way, as usually, at the beginning of the sessions, the duration is fixed; in advocacy it is impossible to pre-determine how long our services will be required. In many cases it can be explained to the client that the work which we had set out to achieve has now been accomplished and, as the services of the advocate are required by someone else, then we shall no longer be able to continue visiting them. We always explain that we are there should they require our service in the future, but clearly the hope is that, over a period of time, we have helped them to gain confidence in their own abilities and be able to deal themselves with future problems.

This was superbly illustrated in the case of a woman who had broken her back; before his death her husband had bought an electric wheelchair so that she would be able to go out unassisted; she was, however, prevented from doing this by the fact that there was no ramp to enable the wheelchair to traverse from the house to the path. Despite requests for this to be attended to as a matter of urgency the council was unable to help as there was a long waiting list for work of this nature. However, her request to have a slab fixed outside her back door met with a more rapid response. When the workman arrived to set the slab, this woman managed to convince him that he hadn't come for that purpose but to build a ramp. She is now fully self-sufficient with regard to mobility, with the consequent vast improvement to the quality of her life.

Compatibility

A further similarity is the need to match the counsellor or the advocate with the person who is being helped. Clearly this is of great importance as, when there is not compatibility and respect, then nothing will be achieved and the time of all concerned will be wasted. When we introduce the advocate to the client we always stress that there is a possibility that the pairing may not work and, if this is the case, it is much better to deal with it straight away rather than let the matter drift with the inevitable result that either the advocate does not make sufficient contact or that the client does not fully confide in him or her.

It is very hard to convey to people that neither an advocate nor a counsellor possess a magic wand by which they can put everything right. When people do turn to either service most other avenues will have already been exhausted. We have had a few dissatisfied clients but, in most of these cases it has been because we did not have the powers to bring about what was required. This is most noticeable in cases concerning difficult neighbours where the law is such that a result favourable to the complainant cannot be achieved. We also have difficulty in the case of unscrupulous traders who have persuaded people to part with money for work which is of a very inferior standard. We do look into every possible means of pursuing these rogues but they deliberately set out to exploit vulnerable older people and then disappear without leaving any trace. The client is usually quite trusting when handing over money, always cash. We have even come across cases of an unscrupulous person driving an older person to their bank or building society to collect the cash from the account. In most of these cases it is only when, inevitably, things go wrong that they realise the mistake which they have made, and by then it is too late.

Conclusion

The joy of advocacy is being able to see an end result and to witness changes in a person's life style. This can come about in many ways, ranging from a relatively minor improvement to a quite profound change in lifestyle. Perhaps the most striking example of this is a man of 82 who, when we first met him, was experiencing abuse from his daughter in a variety of ways. Eventually he was able to accept the fact that there were people who would help and support him and he was not on his own. He was able to make the decision that he did not wish to have any further involvement with his daughter and, in future, he would be responsible for dealing with his own finances. Perhaps unsurprisingly, once that happened the daughter completely disappeared from the scene. He has daily assistance from a care agency who have cleaned up his home, he receives 'meals on wheels' each day and, in addition to providing him with clothing, we have accessed a Social Fund grant which has enabled him to purchase a fridge, a washing machine and washable floor covering. He now enjoys a good quality of life and, each time we see him, we find it hard to believe that it is the same man.

In this chapter I have attempted to show a link between advocacy and counselling with the aim of highlighting the many and varied similarities between them. We have also seen that in both cases relationship-building is arguably the most important part of the whole process. This is developed through communication and listening, which in turn leads to a build-up of trust and confidence. Other similarities are the difficulties which are encountered when ending the relationship and the very great need for accurate and sensitive matching of advocate or counsellor to the partner. The personal qualities required by both a counsellor and an advocate are compassion, genuineness, empathic understanding, confidentiality and non-judgemental acceptance. Advocates and counsellors aim to help people help themselves by building up their confidence and self-esteem, thus enabling them to develop their own strengths and resources. Advocates assist in a practical way, whereas counsellors assist in a listening role whilst supporting a person through changes.

Perhaps the best way in which I can sum up the true meaning of advocacy is in the anonymous comments of two of the people whom we have helped in reply to our recent client satisfaction survey. The first is from a man aged 82 who wrote, 'After three years of complaint by me to the landlord I approached Age Concern Advocacy Service and the immediate response was magnificent'. The second illustration comes from a couple in their 80s who describe how their advocate had helped them. 'She was a great help and sorted out the problems, we would have been lost without her. Without an advocate we would not have known what to do'.

References

Brearley C P (1977) *Residential Work With the Elderly*. London: Routledge and Kegan Paul.

Collins English Dictionary (1994) 3rd Edition. London: HarperCollins.

Government Actuary's Department Projections (1994) London: Office for National Statistics.

Government Family Expenditure Survey (1992) from 'Family Spending'. London: Office for National Statistics.

Midwinter E (1995) *Raising the Wage of Retirement*. London: Third Age Press.

Millar A, Cameron A (1994) *Active Listening: A counselling skills approach*. Milton Keynes: Open University Press.

ONS (1996) Social Trends Table No 7.3. London: Office for National Statistics.

Oppenheimer C (1993) *Poverty: The facts*. London: Child Poverty Action Group.

Phillipson C (1993) 'Approaches to advocacy'. In: Johnson J, Slater R (eds) *Ageing and Later Life*. London: Sage Publications.

Shakespeare W (1599) *As You Like It*. Act 2, Scene 7.

In Praise of Memory

If it is true that words have a secret life of their own and that they carry their own history, then we can expect them to reveal to us the assumptions, the fears and hopes imprinted on them by our ancestors, rather as old coins might bear traces of the countless fingers that have picked them up and handled them. Take the word *memory*. If we dig into the roots of this English word we find a Latin word *memor*, meaning mindful, a Greek word *martus*, meaning a witness, and an old Germanic word *murnan*, meaning to grieve. From earliest times, then, memory has been seen as a faculty enabling us to become aware of, and give witness to, that which causes sorrow. Other root words gather around these three, adding the idea of solicitude, anxiety, mourning and regretting. What nonsense, you may think – my memories are often perfectly happy ones, reminding me of good times, moments of pleasure and satisfaction and fun, events I enjoy recalling. That may be true, but perhaps we shouldn't too readily dismiss the wisdom of earlier generations, for whom memory was essentially bound up with sadness and the trappings of an unquiet mind.

For example, the ancient Greeks – whose grasp of psychological truth has never been surpassed – gave memory a name and a personality: for them she was Mnemosyne, one of the twelve children of Gaia the goddess of earth, and Uranus the sky god. Partnered by Zeus, the grandson of Uranus, Mnemosyne became the mother of the nine muses, whose gift to mankind was to inspire not only music but all the other forms of art and scholarship. It was said that the muses were born to bring about the forgetting of misfortune and a respite from sorrow; free from grief, their policy concern was to celebrate in song the victory of harmony over chaos. This idea is not as fanciful as it seems, nor is it irrelevant to our present civilisation in which so many creative individuals – from Schubert to Dickens, from Goya to Wilfred Owen – have shown that troubling memories can give birth to, be transformed into, inspired and inspiring works of the imagination. And, we could add, the same troubling memories can engender the urge towards self-healing, which ultimately might become the capacity to act as the agent of healing for others. There is, I promise you, no effective counsellor, therapist or analyst who has not first been through the fires of personal suffering, and has emerged a little wiser for the experience.

(Sheila Willson)

8

Elder Abuse

Tui Grimmer-Fleming

Editor's Introduction

Elder abuse, as Tui Grimmer-Fleming points out, is an uncomfortable subject which is subtle and pervasive and can be caused by anyone: people like you and me.

Because of the nature of abuse, talking about it is far from easy, especially for older people who may not be used to complaining or to making their feelings known. This chapter may need a 'health warning': reading about abuse can stir memories and bring us in touch with feelings which we may prefer to forget or not awaken. But as any of us, especially as older people, may hear stories of abuse, we need to be sensitive to the problem and how to deal with it.

While Tui's chapter gives details and insights about the subject of abuse, it opens the mind's eye to much that is potentially destructive in society and demeaning to the individual person. We are challenged at many levels by this chapter.

Introduction

>When I was a laddie,
>I lived with my granny,
>And many a hiding me granny gi'ed me.
>Now I am a man,
>And I live with my granny.
>And I do to my granny,
>What she did to me. (Anon) (Glendenning 1993)

Abuse of older people is not a comfortable subject; it shocks, it offends and is far easier to dismiss altogether than to accept (Tomlin 1992). It cuts across all social classes, ages and personalities. Consequently, it is much closer to home than many people might be prepared to admit.

Elder abuse is not new, it has always existed. Elder abuse can be described as the mistreatment of an older person which results in suffering and distress (Action on Elder Abuse (AEA) 1995a). The abuse of older people has been written about in literature for centuries, but the first articles in professional journals were published some 20 years ago (Burston 1975; Baker 1975). It is only in the last few years that there has been sustained pressure from interested groups and individuals and any public recognition of the problem. This recognition was voiced in a multi-disciplinary conference held in September 1988 in London, organised by the British Geriatrics Society, on the subject of elder abuse. Over 400 delegates, including consultant geriatricians, general practitioners, psychiatrists, nurses, specialist social workers and health visitors, heard a series of lectures that shared current knowledge about what was described as 'an unnecessary and preventable problem'.

A national prevalence study published in 1992 showed that up to five per cent of people over pensionable age could be victims of verbal abuse, while two per cent were victims of physical or financial abuse (Ogg & Bennet 1992: 24). Concern led to Department of Health reports, increasing research, social services writing policies and procedures and the founding in 1993 of Action on Elder Abuse, the first national organisation exclusively to address the issue of elder abuse. AEA was formed by a group of health and social care professionals, academics and representatives of the voluntary sector, concerned with the lack of help and assistance for those who are abused or at risk of abusing (AEA 1995b).

Elder abuse

Older people can be abused in different ways and in many different situations. Abuse may range from a spontaneous but extreme act to the systematic premeditated maltreatment of an older person. Abuse can be a single incident or a daily occurrence and the degree of harm experienced will depend on the person abused and the severity of the act of abuse. The nature, intensity and degree of the abuse or neglect will influence the effect on the older person. In some types of abuse a single incident may be harmful to some people, in others it may have no harmful effect unless the abusive behaviour is repeated over an extended period.

Elder abuse is the mistreatment of an older person and is more than an expression of anger or frustration; it is an extreme form of behaviour occurring in the context of established relationships. Any older person may be abused, but those who are physically, mentally or emotionally dependent on others may be the most vulnerable. People who have had a stroke or who have Parkinson's disease may be the least able to protect themselves (AEA 1995b). Dementia may affect the sufferer's intellect, memory or physical functions and cause unpredictable psychological or physical behaviour.

The intention of the person inflicting the abuse is an important issue; for example a carer who abuses an older person due to exhaustion and unrelieved stress is a different situation to that in which a carer has planned the abuse (Age Concern New Zealand (ACNZ) 1992). However, the focus should be on the effects on the abused rather than the intention of the abuser. It is important to keep in mind the effect on the older person. The effects of elder neglect by either wilful abuse or self-abuse may be as serious as that of any other form of abuse; the difference is the manner in which the harm is inflicted.

An older person may be abused in only one way, but in some cases a person may experience several kinds of abuse at the same time. This may be part of a continuum. Verbal abuse may escalate to physical abuse or it may be inter-related, for example demanding money with menaces (Support and Advice for Vulnerable Elders (SAVE) 1995). It is important not to make assumptions but to allow time to understand what is actually happening.

Some older people may be mistreated by strangers or casual acquaintances, or be the victims of crime or harassment and older people from ethnic minorities may also experience racial harassment. Although not commonly regarded as elder abuse, these incidents can cause considerable distress (SAVE 1995).

Elder abuse is a complex problem and each situation will be unique. Our personal and professional values and beliefs, as well as our social, cultural and family experiences influence our perception and views about what constitutes elder abuse. Deciding whether a situation involves elder abuse will be based on the knowledge, skills and judgement of the person assessing the situation. Persons making such judgements have a responsibility to ensure that they have the knowledge, skills and access to the resources and networks needed to make the best assessment of the situation and to respond positively and appropriately.

Types of abuse

There is a range of indicators which, if present, may suggest the possibility of some kind of abuse or neglect (AEA 1996). None of these mean necessarily that abuse has taken place but general signs are:

- Difficulty in getting access to the older person by independent (outside) agencies or concerned persons.
- Difficulty in having an interview with the older person alone.
- The older person may be found isolated or confined in one room of the house.
- The older person may refuse support or practice agency-hopping.
- Repeated visits to a GP or accident and emergency unit may be made by an older person for no obvious reason or where there is no change in medical condition.

The lack of a precise and comprehensive definition of abuse has, until now, hindered efforts to determine the extent of the problem and form a basic framework within which all disciplines can work together (Tomlin 1992). There are many different forms of ill treatment; the difficulty is in finding a definition which encompasses them under the umbrella of abuse. Some people, such as the American, James Callahan (1986), prefer to have no definition at all, finding that any single definition is too restrictive and might rule out some important abuse-related facets. Callahan says that the attempt to force the multiplicity of difficult human situations faced by older persons into an elder abuse framework is a waste of valuable time and energy that makes no sense. However, others regard this as evading the issue and would prefer a more positive approach.

Elder abuse is defined by Action on Elder Abuse as 'A single or repeated act or lack of appropriate action, occurring within any relationship where there is an expectation of trust, which causes harm or distress to an older person' (AEA 1995b). AEA's is the only definition that suggests that abuse involves a trust relationship. Many organisations talk of power; some include self-abuse and self-neglect, others have separate categories for deprivation of nutrition and the administration of drugs; and several do not recognise sexual or financial abuse or abuse within institutions or by workers outside institutions.

To provide a focus for its service, AEA has categorised elder abuse into the following main types (AEA 1995b):

Physical abuse can be hitting, slapping, burning, pushing, restraining or any action which causes physical harm. Indicators of possible abuse can be unexplained falls; fractures; injuries and finger marks; skin wounds; burns (especially if in unusual places such as inside of thighs or buttocks); old and new bruises at the same time (including bruising in well protected areas like the inner thighs or upper arms); malnutrition when not living alone; giving too much, too little or the wrong medication.

Pyschological abuse can be shouting, swearing, blaming, ignoring, rejecting or humiliating. The older person can exhibit such signs as unexpected or unexplained changes in behaviour, being depressed, frightened, withdrawn, agitated or anxious. Keeping an older person in isolation and/or trying to prevent access to the older person constitutes psychological abuse.

Financial abuse can involve the illegal or unauthorised use of a person's property, money, pension book or other valuables and assets. Signs include the unexplained shortage of money despite an adequate income, an inability to explain what is happening to the income and a reluctance on the part of family, friends or the person controlling funds to pay bills and to provide necessities.

Sexual abuse can occur in any relationship. An older person who is coerced to take part in any sexual activity without consent is being sexually abused. Signs of sexual abuse can be pain or itching in the anal, genital or abdominal area; difficulty in walking or sitting due to discomfort in the genital area; torn, stained or bloody underclothing; recurrent bouts of cystitis or unexplained problems with catheters.

Neglect abuse occurs when an older person in need of care is deprived of essentials for normal, everyday existence. Neglect abuse is when an older person is deprived of food, heat, clothing, comfort, hygiene, medication or access to necessary services. Signs such as unexplained weight loss, unkempt or unshaven appearance, poor hygiene, inadequate or dirty clothing, skin ulcers or bed sores, are cause for concern.

Where abuse occurs

Abuse can occur in an individual's own home. At home some of the causes of physical and psychological abuse would appear to include poor quality long-term relationships between those involved, and the capacity of the carer in the relationship to provide the level of care required or demanded by the individual.

In other settings, such as day centres, residential or nursing homes and hospitals, abuse may be a symptom of a poorly run establishment. It appears that it is most likely to occur when staff are inadequately trained, poorly supervised, have little support from management or work in isolation. Institutional abuse is widely held to be the fault of the institution: abolish or alter the institution and the abuse will cease. This fails to recognise that abuse is perpetrated by people. Failure to change people's attitudes will result in the continuation of the problem in the new setting.

Victims of financial abuse seem more likely to be socially isolated, with health problems and living on their own. Unlike other forms of abuse, the perpetrator is less likely to live with the older person.

The abusers

Both men and women abuse, and the abusers are often well known to the victim; they may be a spouse or partner, son or daughter, relative, friend or neighbour. In addition, abuse may be perpetrated by people whose work brings them into contact with older people, such as paid or volunteer carers, health, social or other workers.

We tend to think of the old in sentimental terms (Rowe 1996). A typical expression, Rowe argues, is 'she's good for her age'. Rowe states that sentimentality is a form of abuse. Children fear and hate adults. When they become adults they distance themselves from their hurt by venting their anger on the old, who were the cause of their pain. Rowe points out that in the same way the old envy the young and punish them.

The abused

Both older men and women may be abused and mutually abusive relationships and familial situations involving older people exist. Abuse is generally thought of as only physical mistreatment, but people can be ill-treated emotionally, economically, sexually and be wilfully neglected. If people are intimidated or frightened about what is happening to them, they have the right to get help and advice. Verbal bullying can be as destructive, upsetting and harmful to an older person as physical mistreatment. A minority of older people are mentally frail, but this should never be assumed and an assessment of mental capacity should be carried out by someone qualified to do so.

Self-abuse

Self-abuse (and self-neglect) is self-inflicted, and therefore is a different issue from elder abuse, but it is important to recognise that self-abuse does occur. Age Concern New Zealand (1992) points out that the problem of self-neglect highlights an important ethical issue. The right of the older person to self-determination must be respected. While elder self-abuse may cause considerable anxiety to those concerned about the older person, unless the older person is endangering himself or herself or others, the older person has the right to choose how he or she lives. It is important to respect this right.

Rights

The ethical issue of rights is important when dealing with elder abuse. We must ensure that we do not infringe the rights of the older person. These include the right to privacy, dignity, independence, choice, fulfilment and the right to live in personal safety and to take responsibility for that safety. The older person has the same entitlement of rights as any other person; just because a person is older, he or she does not have less rights or a special set of rights, as is the case for children.

Why abuse happens

Society is stratified in the way we mix (Rowe 1996) and most older people's only contact with the young is in terms of being a relative. Rowe claims that this age discrepancy creates distance to ageing and its meaning within the relationship.

The following predisposing risk factors have been identified as being associated with physical and psychological abuse: one or more may be present in any abusive situation (AEA 1995b):

- There is a history of a poor quality, long-term relationship between the abused and the abuser.
- The abuser is dependent upon the person he or she abuses for accommodation, and/or, financial and emotional support.

- The abuser has mental health problems or a personality disorder.
- The abuser has a drink or a drug problem.

There is an increased likelihood of abuse occurring when or where the older person has communication difficulties because of hearing, visual or speech disabilities, behavioural problems or major personality changes which result in repetitive behaviour, wandering or aggression. Conditions which can also lead to abuse are when a family undergoes unforeseen or unfavourable changes in circumstances or finances or is under stress due to poor housing conditions. An atmosphere can be created in which abuse can occur, when after frequent requests for professional help, this has not been provided or has not solved any problems.

Culture and abuse

Any older man or woman can experience abuse irrespective of culture, social class or gender. The old are sadly neglected in many cultures, and often there is a belief within the majority culture that a particular community looks after its own or that the older members of the family are more protected from privation than the rest of the population.

The facts do not bear out this assumption. John (1981) quotes from a survey of Asian families in the West Midlands, England, where older people were living with their younger relatives and where these relationships had become very strained. Some older people had unrealistic hopes of returning to their homeland, and became increasingly isolated and neglected in their adopted country. John says that these unfulfilled expectations are complicated by the loss of role and esteem where older people were no longer heads of households, nor financially independent.

Older persons in a transcultural setting are doubly disadvantaged, both by coming from an alternative culture and because they have less access to mainstream society. The formal education and employment settings provided for the young are simply not available to them, thus they have fewer opportunities to learn about their new culture (d' Ardenne and Mahtani 1989: 28).

Often there is an expectation of people to adjust to the perspective and values of the dominant culture (ACNZ 1992). This attitude is insensitive to the needs of people with other values and perspectives and can be abusive in certain situations. Acknowledging and respecting cultural differences by the majority culture can help to prevent elder abuse. The authors argue that each of us has a particular cultural perspective and we all need to ensure that we do not impose that perspective on people of other cultures or assume we always know best. Understanding our own cultures, values, norms, attitudes and decision-making processes, and the diversity and distinctive family or other values within our own culture should increase our awareness of the importance and sensitivity of cultural issues.

Older people from black and ethnic minorities may find it difficult to discuss the fact that they are being abused because of a strong commitment to family loyalty (SAVE 1995). In cases where abuse is suspected and English is not the abused person's first language, it is important to use an independent translator and not to involve family members as interpreters.

Carers and stress

The person looking after an older person is known as the carer or, in some cases, the supporter or care-giver. The carer is the person who is responsible, for meeting the basic living needs of another person (Tomlin 1992). This means ensuring the provision of warmth and food, and being responsible for the general well-being of the person dependent on them. There are both formal and informal carers; formal carers are paid and work in institutions and the community; informal carers are those who care for an older person, usually a relative, at home.

One of the most important points to realise about informal carers (Tomlin 1992) is that they are people like you or I, with no specific training in caring or nursing, yet they have to perform the duties of a nurse, 24 hours a day, week in and week out, often single-handed. They are also emotionally involved, which adds to the pressure. Most carers are naturally compassionate people; it is the constant pressure on them that may make frustration and anger spill over into violence.

Carers are defined by the Carers National Association (CNA) (1996) as 'people who look after relatives or friends who, because of disability, illness or the effects of old age, cannot manage at home without help.'

Caring for an older person is an extremely valuable yet undervalued role. For many carers it is a difficult task which offers few rewards but much stress. Very often a carer experiences role-reversal (AEA 1996) with the parent(s) becoming dependent on the adult child and the carer is forced to change his or her lifestyle as a result of caring. An older person may refuse or reject offers of help and this can leave carers feeling angry and resentful.

Carers may blame the older person for not being able to care for themselves because they may not understand the dependency. Coming to terms with dependency means adjusting to changing relationships (ACNZ 1992) and the balance of power between the dependent person and the carer. A former equal relationship between husband and wife may change as one becomes more dependent on the other.

Sometimes the dependent person is self-centred and does not consider the needs of the carer and in some situations nothing the carer does meets with the approval of the older person. When the relationship between the dependent person and the carer is strained or has broken down, the imbalance of power and the change of roles mean that abusive situations are more likely to occur.

Carers very often find that the family doctor and their social worker (if they have one) are too busy to give them the appropriate support that is needed (CNA 1996) to enable them to acknowledge and deal with their feelings about the demands of caring for the emotional and practical needs of the older person. Often the carer has no privacy or personal space. Carers may feel isolated and lack appropriate social support and the problem is compounded by the carer finding it difficult to have time out of the home. It is all too common that no help is offered until the carer is at breaking point, both physically and mentally.

Popular belief suggests that the majority of carers are women, yet the General Household Survey, United Kingdom, 1990 (CNA 1996) reported that of 6.8 million people who were carers, 43 per cent were men. The peak age for becoming a carer is 45 to 64 and 24 per cent of people in this age group said they had caring responsibilities. Survey work by the Health Services Management Unit at the University of Manchester (CNA 1996) suggests that there may be up to 40,000 children acting as primary carers nationwide. Commonly, these are children in families where the parent develops an illness or disability.

Some of the comments reported to Carers National Association are: 'After two heart attacks and a nervous breakdown, I wanted to kill my wife.' 'I'm depressed and hopeless and I'd like an absolutely unbroken night's sleep every two weeks or so.' 'If I knew some help was there – say two hours a week so I could get out of the house – I'd cope.' A young carer said, 'I can't talk to my friends because they don't understand. I don't talk to anyone, I just tell myself.'

Professional abuse

Abuse occurs in homes and hospitals and in both the independent and statutory sectors (Bright 1995). For reasons associated with culture, power and ignorance, all those affected by abuse find difficulty in expressing their concerns or in seeking appropriate help.

Older people entering residential care are susceptible to feelings of powerlessness. For many the decision to seek care is one made for them rather than this being a positive personal decision (Bright 1992). Becoming a client, as a prerequisite for becoming a resident, is acknowledged to be a disempowering process. Such lack of power to influence their environments has led to poor quality of services to the older person.

Homes and hospitals have written rules that may be minimal but it is the unwritten rules by which life is lived that may be abusive (Bright 1995). Deciding who uses the toilet facilities, how frequently, and how publicly may well be determined by a powerful individual who has little understanding of how to work through concepts such as dignity, choice and fulfilment. Brochures describing the home rarely contain such honest statements as 'You will be allowed to visit the toilet once during the post-breakfast period'.

The pyramidal hierarchy which places the manager or owner at the top may be replaced by a structure in which everyday rules of living are devised and implemented by the care assistants whose power to allow or deny access to a wide range of services is very formidable (Bright 1995). If the institution has allowed such behaviour to become established, the prevalence of such abusive behaviour is increased, stress builds up and staff fall into the easiest route to complete tasks. This is the way in which in some homes, residents have been humiliated, degraded and abused.

There is a growing recognition of the problem of abuse by health professionals, both in the United Kingdom and abroad (Prevention of Professional Abuse Network (POPAN) 1996). The abuse reported is often sexual, but may also take the form of emotional, physical or financial exploitation. Most of the allegations POPAN deals with concern abuse by psychotherapists, counsellors, psychiatrists and psychologists; and abusers are found to be working in both the statutory and independent sectors.

The impact of abuse within caring and therapeutic relationships is devastating (POPAN 1996). When they first come for help, most people are extremely distressed, disturbed and confused. In some cases they may even contemplate suicide. They also often develop a deep distrust of any caring and therapeutic relationship, thus cutting themselves off from any future help.

In the report *Homes Are For Living In* (Social Services Inspectorate 1989), the following values were established:

Privacy The right of the individuals to be left alone or undisturbed and free from intrusion or public attention into their affairs.

Dignity The recognition of the intrinsic value of people regardless of circumstances by respecting their uniqueness and their personal needs and to be treated with respect.

Independence Opportunities to act and think without reference to another person, including willingness to incur a degree of calculated risks.

Choice Opportunity to select independently from a range of options.

Rights The maintenance of all entitlements associated with citizenship.

Fulfilment The realisation of personal aspirations and abilities in all aspects of daily life.

Taking action

The community can no longer afford to keep elder abuse secret and hidden. To minimise the incidence of problems and the associated social costs, it is essential for people to understand the causes and the actions that can be taken to protect themselves and others from becoming either a victim or an abuser (ACNZ 1992).

If you are being abused you may feel frightened to talk about what is happening to you, but it is not your fault and you should not feel ashamed or guilty. It is very important to confide in someone you can trust (AEA 1995b). Charities such as Carers National Association, Counsel and Care, and Action on Elder Abuse which operates the Elder Abuse Response helpline, offer confidential and anonymous support and have information on services that you, or someone else on your behalf, can contact who may be able to help.

If you are concerned about someone else and you suspect that abuse of any sort is taking place, trust your instincts: they may be right. Never ignore your feelings, but try to get the facts to support them (AEA 1996).

Any form of direct intervention by a non-professional should only be taken with extreme care. Always speak to a suspected victim in private, as talking about your suspicions with others present may cause the victim to feel unable to speak about the abuse or they may deny it as they may be afraid or ashamed. Always respect the rights, needs and wishes of the victim and be sensitive to their religious and cultural background.

Don't discuss your concerns with a possible abuser at an early stage in your enquiry. This may cause difficulties or lead to further problems for the victim and may put them at greater risk. When responding to cases of abuse, don't put yourself at unnecessary risk and always try to ensure your own safety by making visits with a colleague.

If you are a resident of a care home and you are being abused or you are a friend or a relative of someone in a care home and you suspect they are being abused, it is important first to speak to an organisation such as Counsel and Care which has particular expertise in residential and nursing home care and can offer guidance on how to make a complaint.

If you are a worker in a care home you may be worried about repercussions of reporting what has happened, but it is important that you tell someone what is happening as the older person may not be able to raise the alarm himself or herself and the situation may continue or even get worse if you do nothing. If you know of a case of abuse, inform your line manager for guidance on how to proceed and make yourself aware of your employer's policy on elder abuse and follow its procedures. Should the situation not be resolved, do seek advice from your professional body or union. You can make your initial enquiry (anonymously if you are worried about 'whistle blowing') to Public Concern at Work, which is a legal advice centre, without breaching any terms of your employment or duty of confidentiality.

Summary

In recognising the sad reality that older people are abused, I wrote this chapter with the aim of helping to identify and prevent this abuse of some of the most vulnerable people in the community. In my research I was made aware that elder abuse was across cultures, classes, age, gender and relationships. I began to realise the need to raise concern in society of the actuality of what is to me a disturbing and little-discussed issue. I believe the way forward is to recognise and accept that the abuse of older people is everyone's problem.

Acknowledgements

A big thank you to Verena Tschudin, editor of this book, for all her help and encouragement.

References

Action on Elder Abuse (AEA) (1995a) *Everybody's Business: Taking action on elder abuse* (report). London: Action on Elder Abuse.

Action on Elder Abuse (AEA) (1995b) Information leaflets: *Action on Elder Abuse*; *Elder Abuse in Care Homes*; *What is Elder Abuse?* London: Action on Elder Abuse.

Action on Elder Abuse (AEA) (1996) *The Abuse of the Older Person at Home: Information for workers* (booklet). London: Action on Elder Abuse.

Age Concern New Zealand (ACNZ) (1992) *Promoting the Rights and Well Being of Older People and Those Who Care for Them* (report). Wellington, NZ: Age Concern New Zealand.

d'Ardenne P, Mahtani A (1989) *Transcultural Counselling in Action*. London: Sage.

Baker A A (1975) 'Granny Battering'. In: *Modern Geriatrics* i: 20–24. Cited in: Tomlin S (ed) (1992) *Abuse of Elderly People: An unnecessary and preventable problem* (report). London: British Geriatrics Society.

Bright L (ed) (1992) *From Home to A Home* (report). London: Counsel and Care.

Bright L (ed) (1995) *Care Betrayed* (report). London: Counsel and Care.

Burston G R (1975) Letter to the British Medical Journal. Cited in: Tomlin S (ed) (1992) *Abuse of Elderly People: An unnecessary and preventable problem* (report). London: British Geriatrics Society.

Callahan J J (1986) Guest Editor's Perspective, *Pride Institute of Long-term Health Care*, 5.3. Cited in: Tomlin S (ed) (1992) *Abuse of Elderly People: An unnecessary and preventable problem* (report). London: British Geriatrics Society.

Carers National Association (CNA) (1996) *Facts about Carers*. Ref: 23(IS) (briefing pack). London: Carers National Association.

Glendenning F (1993) 'What is Elder Abuse and Neglect'. In: Decalmer P, Glendenning F (eds) *The Mistreatment of Elderly People*. London: Sage.

John G (1981) 'Black self-help projects'. In: Cheetham J, James W, Loney H, Mayor B, Prescot W (eds). *Social and Community Work in a Multi-racial Society*. London: Harper & Row. Cited in: d'Ardenne P, Mahtani A (1989) *Transcultural Counselling in Action*. London: Sage.

Ogg J, Bennet G (1992) 'Elder abuse in Britain'. *British Medical Journal* 305: 24. Cited in: Decalmer P, Glendenning F (eds) (1993) *The Mistreatment of Elderly People*. London: Sage.

Prevention of Professional Abuse Network (POPAN) (1996) What is POPAN and what does POPAN do? (briefing pack). London: Prevention of Professional Abuse Network.

Rowe D (1996) The 6th Penny Edwards Memorial Lecture at the London Voluntary Resource Centre, 14 May 1996.

Social Services Inspectorate, Department of Health (1989) *Homes are for Living in*. London: HMSO. Crown copyright is reproduced with the permission of the Controller of Her Majesty's Stationery Office.

Support and Advice for Vulnerable Elders (SAVE) (1995) *Elder Abuse: Advice and guidance for anyone concerned about an older person being mistreated in Lewisham* (report). London: London Borough of Lewisham Social Services.

Tomlin S (ed) (1992) *Abuse of Elderly People: An unnecessary and preventable problem* (report). London: British Geriatrics Society.

In Praise of Memory

We find an interesting reflection on the nature of memory in the formal Jewish prayer book, where an ancient story – dating back to the Babylonian Talmud – has been preserved. It goes like this:

'Before a child is born, a light is held behind its head, with which it can see from one end of the world to the other, and they teach it the whole of the *Torah*.* But at the moment of birth, an angel touches it on the lips and it forgets all. So all of life is spent remembering what we once knew.'

(*The body of Jewish sacred writings)

Socrates would have liked this story, for it affirms his view as reported by Plato – that learning is nothing but remembering what we knew before we were born. I like the story too, because with characteristic Jewish subtlety it plunges us into paradox and makes us think twice about those curious moments when we don't know, yet feel we do know, what is about to happen, or when we recognise that a newly-acquired piece of information is unaccountably familiar. Could it be that, to tease us or to teach us a particular lesson, the angel sometimes removes his obliterating finger and just for a moment allows us to recapture our primal vision of reality, and so to remember precisely what we are up to?

(Sheila Willson)

9

What Counselling is and What it is Not:
Concepts, skills, theories and models

Verena Tschudin

Editor's Introduction

Although counselling has been practised for many years, it is a form of help which is all too often still not understood and even misused. This chapter intends to give an overview of the subject from both a practical and theoretical point of view.

Such a chapter can necessarily only pick up some of the most obvious points in a discipline which ranges ever wider in its application and whose theories are detailed in great tomes. Like all disciplines, it is evolving and changing constantly. Each practitioner is contributing to this process.

Counselling has more often been seen as being done *to* older people rather than done *by* them. The contribution which older people can make to counselling is considerable, and some of the topics addressed in this chapter are specific to the needs of older people, but some are universally applicable.

This chapter needs to be seen in the context of the other chapters in this book, and while reading the other chapters, it may sometimes be necessary to refer again to this chapter to clarify a certain point.

Introduction

What exactly is counselling? This question may have been asked by anyone who has ever tried to help another person. Or perhaps the question is rather, 'is what I am doing "counselling" or is it just being friends?'

A dictionary definition of counselling is 'giving counsel' or advice, or making recommendations. Those who work as counsellors regard this not only as inadequate but contrary to their practice. Hence, in many people's minds there is considerable confusion. Saying 'I had to counsel her' is a contradiction in terms. What is implied is 'I had to tell her off' and thus the specific characteristics of counselling – listening, reflecting, empathy and a non-judgemental attitude – have not been present. Saying 'you need to go for counselling' tends to imply that there is something wrong with the person addressed which a counsellor could sort out. This is derogatory of the person, and counsellors are not here to sort out other people; they provide a space and atmosphere in which it is possible for the client to take a closer look at herself or himself and so decide what changes may be necessary. Counselling is quite a specific activity which, confusingly, has little to do with the word 'counsel'.

Many situations can lead to counselling. Providing information (for example, on a product), advice (as nurses and GPs, etc, may give concerning health and lifestyle) and guidance (as may be given by a careers advisor) are all forms of communication in which there is a 'helping' relationship but which is not therapeutic in the sense of leading to more or better knowledge of one's inner nature and motives. These forms of communication are not binding, but given a specific context, they may lead to counselling.

The British Association for Counselling (BAC) has frequently rewritten its codes and statements about counselling. In the *Code of Ethics and Practice for Counsellors* (1996) the BAC gives this definition of 'The Nature of Counselling':

'The overall aim of counselling is to provide an opportunity for the client to work towards living in a more satisfying and resourceful way.

The term 'counselling' includes work with individuals, pairs or groups of people often, but not always, referred to as 'clients'. The objectives of particular counselling relationships will vary according to the client's needs. Counselling may be concerned with developmental issues, addressing and resolving specific problems, making decisions, coping with crisis, developing insight and knowledge, working through feelings of inner conflict or improving relationships with others. The counsellor's role is to facilitate the client's work in ways which respect the client's values, personal resources and capacity for self-determination. Only when both the user and the recipient explicitly agree to enter into a counselling relationship does it become "counselling" rather than the use of "counselling skills".

'It is not possible to make a generally accepted distinction between counselling and psychotherapy. There are well founded traditions which use the terms interchangeably and others which distinguish them. Regardless of the theoretical approaches preferred by individual counsellors, there are ethical issues which are common to all counselling situations.'

The *Code of Ethics and Practice for Counselling Skills* (1989) of the BAC states that:

'The term "counselling skills" does not have a single definition which is universally accepted. For the purpose of this code, "counselling skills" is distinguished from "listening skills" and from "counselling". Although the distinction is not always a clear one, because the term "counselling skills" contains elements of these other two activities, it has its own place in the continuum between them. What distinguishes the use of counselling skills from these other activities are the intentions of the user, which is to enhance the performance of their functional role, as line manager, nurse, tutor, social worker, personnel officer, voluntary worker, etc, the recipient will, in turn, perceive them in that role'.

Ask yourself the following questions:

a) Are you using counselling skills to enhance your communication with someone but without taking on the role of their counsellor?

b) Does the recipient perceive you as acting within your profession al/caring role (which is **not** that of being their counsellor)?

If the answer is **yes** to both of these questions, you are using counselling skills in your functional role.

If the answer is **no** to both, you are counselling.

If the answer is **yes** to one and **no** to the other, you have a conflict of expectations and should resolve it.

Only when both the user and recipient explicitly contract to enter into a counselling relationship does it cease to be 'using counselling skills' and becomes 'counselling'.'

The significant difference between 'counselling' and 'using counselling skills' is a contract. This can be anything from a signed document to the most simple of verbal agreements. This will be dealt with below.

Anyone is able to use counselling skills and no specific education or training is required. However, as with the word 'counselling' itself, reflection, empathy, listening and other skills and attitudes can be misunderstood and misused. It is therefore advisable that anyone who has contact with people who need some form of skilled help should have some background and training in the use of counselling skills. Those who call themselves 'counsellor' need not only to have a thorough training (generally between 400 and 500 hours; see Chapter 10) but are also bound by the Code to have regular supervision. Although supervision is not in the same way necessary for those who use counselling skills in their work, it is still advisable that they have someone with whom they are able to discuss work done with people, or situations which may cause problems. In every case of supervision, it is paramount that confidentiality is maintained.

Clearly, everyone can (and should) use counselling skills in many more situations than are perhaps current. Whenever you are with friends, family, colleagues and clients and you hear a story which needs to be told and heard, then counselling skills are essential. The listening and responding should ideally be such that both people in the interaction can be as natural and as much themselves as possible. When empathy has become a 'way of life', this becomes possible.

Core concepts of counselling

The person

One of the most important aspects of counselling is that the focus is on the person. What may be said and heard to begin with is a problem, but it is not the problem which is the centre; the person-with-the-problem is. The problem may be stated like:

'I just want to have a cry'
'I don't know what is going on but I don't feel right'
'I am so angry'
'I can't make up my mind'
'I would like to help him but he won't let me'
'Nobody is listening to me'

Very often such statements are not as clearly put, nor are they so obvious. Many a time clients are not sure what the problem is, or they feel unable to voice it for fear of being misunderstood, ridiculed or rejected. This is when a skilled helper is invaluable.

What is evident from the above statements is that in every case the person makes a personal statement, often implying that another or others are the cause of the problem. When unskilled helpers hear such statements, they are likely to concentrate on solving the problem, or concentrate on the 'others'. The one vital insight here is that we can never change others, we can only change ourselves.

The relationship

Egan (1994: 186) says that 'many, if not most, clients who seek help have trouble with interpersonal relationships'. It is therefore not surprising that the relationship between helper and client is of the greatest importance.

Problems with interpersonal relationships can cover many aspects. To start with, it is often the relationship with oneself which is unhealthy or lacking in some way. Most of us suffer from either a lack of self-confidence or an excess of it, causing problems for the people around us as we throw our weight around or are too timid – and all the variations in between. This causes problems with other people and we blame 'them', unable or unwilling to see that we may be the cause. When someone goes to a counsellor with problems in relationships, the first step is often to find the reason for the problem, and the realisation dawns that it is not 'they' who have the problem but 'I'. The admission of having a problem, and then finding that it is oneself who is the problem, can be a devastating revelation. The need for a non-judgemental attitude on the helper's part is therefore essential. More still, the beginning of a helping relationship must be marked by a stance of 'you're OK' towards the client. Clients can only be helped to give up certain 'bad' or unhelpful practices or attitudes if they are also helped to see that they already have 'good' or helpful attitudes and skills to draw on, though these may not be recognised or easily accessible.

'Rogers argued that the relationship that develops between counsellor and client is the most significant agent of change, not the counsellor's repertoire of techniques' (Bayne *et al* 1994: 31). This is obvious when someone says 'you have helped me so much, thank you' and the helper is baffled: 'What have I done? How have I helped? I said nothing; I just listened'. But that helper was there, just for this person, present in body and mind, giving the client an opportunity and space to hear herself or himself.

It is not possible to feel the same towards every client: we are more attracted to some than to others. But being willing to be attentive, whatever the 'vibes', can bring you to like people even when you did not feel drawn to them at first sight.

When the relationship between helper and client is open, co-operative and honest, then the clients can work on themselves in the way necessary. Such a relationship is then also the basis for other interpersonal relationships.

When two people meet – in any situation, not just for helping – the relationship is the third element. This is an invisible, untouchable and often indescribable element, but undoubtedly is that which keeps the two people together and makes them more human

The contract

A contract is the element which makes helping 'official' rather than part of a chance meeting or using your professional skills (as a social worker, GP, probation officer, nurse, etc) effectively.

Even in one-off or chance meetings, it may be useful to state some limits:

'Yes, I have a minute – ten minutes in fact.'

'I don't have time right now, but I can come back in an hour (tomorrow, etc).'

'Is it urgent or can you wait until tomorrow?'

When you are clear what is asked of you and what you can give, it is much easier to concentrate on the person and the task. When you have not set your limits, you may be more likely to have your mind on all the things you should be doing just now.

A contract for counselling is much more formal. Many counsellors offer a visit session free to the client to see if the two are able to work together. During that time they negotiate the number of times they will meet (often six meetings are arranged to begin with); how much this will cost; the method or theory which the counsellor uses; and the expectations the client brings and what the counsellor demands from the client.

Most contracts are verbal, or very simple written documents. It may be that a client recognises problems with keeping to commitments and brings this as a defining problem.

In such cases elaborate documents may be negotiated and drawn up and then worked on and evaluated regularly.

As counselling is essentially a relationship of trust and learning to trust, it is important that the contract expresses this in the most appropriate way possible.

Core conditions

The notion of 'core concepts' has largely been formulated by Carl Rogers, but others have developed these concepts further and therefore they are not necessarily always described in the same order nor are the same terms used.

CONGRUENCE

Genuineness or **congruence** is something which has to be learned, usually over many years. The more congruent (genuine, natural, open) a person is, the more effective that person is in helping. Rogers (1961) found that if he tried to be 'the counsellor', the relationship suffered. When he was able to be more himself, as one person with another, then both could be congruent and could trust each other. Genuineness or congruence here means that what you think and what you say are the same. Thinking 'I can't bear you' and saying 'I admire you' is not compatible in helping. You do not have to say 'you are an awful person' to the client when this is what you are feeling (you may have to ask yourself why you are feeling like this), but being honest and admitting that you are having difficulties in accepting what the other person is saying helps to remain grounded in the present, and is helpful for the relationship. How much is shared with the other person is crucial; it is also crucial that such situations should be discussed with a supervisor.

I was once seeing an older man with a different cultural background to mine. He made various references to love, giving me the impression that he had a sexual agenda. I felt very uncomfortable and did not quite know how to handle this. I discussed it with my supervisor who wondered how I had got myself into this situation 'with all your experience'. When I saw the man the next time I asked him every time he made some statement to clarify what he meant and it became clear that he was using religious language and expressions. I gradually relaxed and this helped both of us to explore what we expected of each other.

Egan (1994: 55) is ever practical in his approach to counselling, and he lists four aspects of genuineness:

- Do not overemphasise the helping role.
- Be spontaneous.
- Avoid defensiveness.
- Be open.

Perhaps these aspects indicate that the more human, 'ordinary' and unaffected you can be with your clients, the more your helping is real and effective.

UNCONDITIONAL POSITIVE REGARD

Warmth as an attitude has also been described as **non-possessive warmth** and **unconditional positive regard**. This means that in the first instance you respect the person with you and do not want to change her or him. It means loving a person unconditionally: you love someone even if she smells disagreeably or even if he uses words which you would not. The unconditional part of the warmth is that you try to see the whole person, not simply the obvious parts. It does not mean having to be effusive, but rather in being consistently accepting, valuing the humanity of the person first of all.

People who come for counselling or who ask others to help them are vulnerable and perhaps unsure. Such people do not need reassurance or generalisations like 'everybody feels like that', but they need someone who accepts them for who and what they are as an individual and unique person.

Sometimes counsellors feel or give the impression that they have to be perfect role models and never say the wrong thing. When people are vulnerable and unsure, perhaps the last thing they need is someone perfect: that would make them feel even worse. Hurt and suffering people need others who also feel hurt and make mistakes: such people are real. Not only admitting this, but being able to share with others the humanity of these situations conveys non-possessive warmth and a regard for others which is unconditional. The skill in counselling is that helpers and counsellors can either put aside their own hurts for the time of the session or use them in such a way that it is helpful. Telling your clients about your hurts and so reversing the situation – you being the client and the client counselling you – is not only bad practice but is most likely destructive. This is one of the real reasons for supervision.

EMPATHY

Much has been said and written about **empathy**, and it was again Rogers who used the term first and who later (1980) insisted that empathy is not only a skill but 'a way of being'.

The following story may illustrate what is meant:

> 'A person has fallen into a ditch and is unable to get out of it. A **sympathetic** person comes along, sees the victim, goes to him and lies in the ditch with him, and both talk of this terrible misadventure and of other similar ones they had both experienced in the past. An **unsympathetic** person comes along the road, sees the person lying there and shouts to him 'Don't just lie there, pull yourself together, do something!' But the victim has broken bones, and he cannot move, and the helper neither sees nor hears what the victim is saying because she is standing too far away. An **empathic** person who comes that way climbs down to the victim and gives what first aid is necessary. Then she listens to what the victim has to say, how the accident happened, what led up to it, and what he now feels and experiences. This helper is completely present, but figuratively she has one foot on the bank, the firm ground. This eventually enables her to help the victim get out of the ditch on to his own legs, and to the way he wants to go, the way that is right for him' (Tschudin 1995: 77).

Helping relationships have to be established, and empathy can often mean at first doing something practical: filling in a form, telephoning a person or agency, or just staying with a person. People who are shocked from accidents or bereavement are not able to work on their emotions to begin with, but they need someone who is physically there in a supportive way.

Empathy has also been described as going the second mile, walking in someone's moccasins, and knowing someone from the inside. These are at best approximations. It is probably not right that we can walk in someone else's shoes, but it is right that we have the capacity to feel and imagine what it may be like for that person to walk in her or his own shoes. What matters is not only that you can feel this, but that you can *communicate* this to the other person. This gives clients the assurance and the knowledge that you have heard them and that they are accepted.

Clearly, this is more than a skill, because in that communication you are sharing something of yourself, and in the responses each makes to the other, both are enhanced as human beings.

Helper skills

If the aim of helping and counselling is that the other person, the client, can lead a more satisfying and resourceful life, this person has to be helped to do that. Counselling is therefore essentially goal-oriented and the aim is that sooner or later the client does not need the counsellor any longer; the client has become his or her own counsellor. This means that the helper's skills will enable the client to develop certain skills, particularly those of self-awareness, self-assessment and self-challenge. The initial skills used by helpers and counsellors therefore have this goal in mind. Some of the essential and basic helper skills will be considered here.

ATTENDING

However or wherever you start in helping someone, you need to give that person your attention. This can sometimes be easier said than done. You might have been in the middle of some job when your client arrived, or you were called away from going somewhere when someone asked you if you have a minute. Even when your client has booked an appointment, you may have been with another client before and your mind may still be somewhere else. Giving someone your full attention is a precious gift. Answering the telephone or being otherwise interrupted is not only impolite but gives the client the impression that you are not really there for her or him. From experience I also know that when my counsellor yawns I no longer have his attention, whatever excuse he makes. At the beginning of any encounter there is always a time of adjusting to the other person, hence the usual question 'how are you?' to 'reach' each other. This may not be the appropriate opening on meeting a regular client, though, and you may need to go much deeper straight away.

Attentiveness is a basic stance vis-à-vis anyone; it is not restricted to counselling. You have to be attentive to other drivers on the road, to colleagues at work and certainly to family and friends. There are different levels of attention and some could be described as therapeutic, ethical, or spiritual ways of being. When you are attentive to a person you are also attentive to the environment (the room, sitting in similar chairs or at similar height) and the space between you (how close or far you are). Most of all, though, attention is a 'way of being': you are there for the other, knowing that in that stance, you are also rewarded as a person.

LISTENING

Listening is clearly the most important skill in any helping and counselling. But it is not just listening to the words spoken: it is listening to the whole person of the client and with the whole person of yourself. You listen to hear the client, but what is perhaps most important is that because you listen, the client can hear herself or himself.

What is the person trying to communicate? What is she saying? How is she saying it? Why is she saying it now?

In order to be human we have to communicate. We have to respond to others and be responded to. We grow through the story of our lives and we have to tell parts of the story to others at specific points in order to make sense of this story. We need someone to hear our story.

Listening to others is hard work. Not only have you to pay attention closely to the words, but you also have to hold yourself in check and not let your own feelings and thoughts intrude. This can make for tension and therefore you get tired. Listening to another person's (usually) sad story means that you are, in the words of the allegory, with the client but having one foot on firm ground. It means being all there but also being able to withdraw when necessary. An example would be:

Client: 'I don't really know where to begin, there are so many things I want to say.'

Helper: 'Just say what comes first to mind.'

Client: 'Well, I have two sons and a daughter and they all have children and two of them constantly bring them to me to look after them.

I love children and I love my children, but I also want my freedom. I don't want to hurt them and I don't want to be selfish either. Tell me what I must do.'

Sometimes it is not easy to listen because either a story is disjointed or it is told in a way which may be rambling or with seemingly no aim or content. Some people are keen to say as much as possible and others have to be coaxed to say anything. Some people are so wounded that they will not trust anybody with their stories and yet you sense that this is what is needed. Some people want you to tell them what to do. Much as most of us love to do that, it is not what helps. The firm ground here may be knowing that this is not what is helpful.

In most stories there is some significant word or phrase which you can pick out and reflect (see below) back, and this may be the clue to further work. Your listening in this case is for something specific. Perhaps the words in the example may be 'freedom' and 'selfish'.

REFLECTING

Together with listening, reflecting is perhaps the most important counselling skill. It is the skilled part of empathy and good reflecting is therefore also part of being empathic.

Depending on the situation and the emphasis on the words in the example above, a skilled helper might have reflected:

'You want your freedom?'

or

'You don't want to be selfish.'

This type of paraphrasing uses the words which the client spoke. This gives a sense of being at the same level as the client, respecting his or her story, expression and pace. It must be done sensitively, though, as too much paraphrasing can appear to be a parrot-like repetition, giving the impression that the helper is not capable of entering into more constructive dialogue.

It is possible to reflect what you see:

'You say that you are alright, but I can see 'tension' written all over you.'

Drawing attention to a client's body posture or language usually brings about an immediate change. As a helper you can glean much information from this. It also means that the client is made aware of the fact that she or he is seen and heard as a person.

A deeper and more advanced level of reflection moves the conversation forward. In this instance you reflect something unspoken but implied, or something hinted at but not fully expressed. Using again the example above, a helper might have said:

'These are only the obvious problems and what I guess is really happening is that you are taken for granted. You like to be needed but like them, you also like to lead your own life.'

Such reflection can sometimes elicit the remark that you 'read' someone 'like a book'. It is not that you have supernatural powers (you may, of course), but being as a human being with another human being, this is what you 'hear' your client saying. You say it in such a way that it can be seen as exactly what applies or it can be denied: 'No, this is not quite right. What I feel is …'. and in this response is the advance towards more insight.

If you are helping another person at an emotional rather than practical level, you need to stay with the emotions. This is not easy. In many instances a conversation can go something like this:

'How do you feel about this?'

'Well, I think I have a problem.'

'How do you *feel* about that problem?'

'I think I can't handle it.'

'You don't seem to have heard my question.'

'You asked me about my problem.'

'I asked you how you are feeling.'

'I told you how I feel, I think I can't cope.'

Many people mix up feeling and thinking. We can control our thinking, but very often we are at the mercy of our feelings, even without being aware of them. Anger, fear, helplessness and many other feelings characterise us and our relationships and they need to be addressed so that change can happen. Therefore to reflect the 'feeling' words in particular is often the most helpful and the most empathic way of being with someone.

GIVING SPACE

Many different skills or aspects of skilled work with people can be summed up under this heading. A helping relationship is intended to be a safe relationship in which different aspects of living and being can be explored. This means that there needs to be room for emotional and physical expression. If you can be comfortable with long silences with clients, with clients crying or shouting or hitting pillows or taking on body postures which express their state of being, such as curling up in a foetal position, you help the other person to grow.

Mentally staying open to the needs of the clients may sometimes bring you into unexpected situations where you may find yourself laughing or crying with the client, or discussing a poem or picture created by the client. It may also mean that you risk being hurt, becoming involved, getting tired and being exploited and used, sometimes for much longer than you had envisaged. But by 'hanging in' – always considering that it is right – you are not only helping another human being, but you are also likely to see changes in the other and you know that without your vulnerability and willingness to stay open, this might not have happened.

Beginning, maintaining and ending relationships

Helping relationships have clear phases: they begin, they have to be maintained, and they end. Each of these phases needs different skills, but what skills are most useful depends on the length of the relationship.

Attending, listening and reflecting are skills which will be necessary in any helping, if this be for ten minutes or many sessions.

Attending, a non-judgemental attitude, and encouraging the person are specifically necessary at the beginning of a relationship. Conveying, in whatever way is most appropriate, that you are willing to hear a story, gives another person a sense of being valued, that you have time and have committed yourself to that person and are respecting her or him. Sometimes a gentle 'I'm all ears' or 'I would like to hear your story' may be helpful. Very often it is more prosaic: 'What has been happening?' Such questions give the client the necessary invitation to talk – and encouragement, if needed.

Accurate and advanced empathy is the means of maintaining a relationship. It is through empathy that a person can grow and increasingly become aware and hear herself or himself. In a helping relationship both people learn and grow. The impact of the client on the helper is sometimes as big as the other way round. Helping and counselling is not detached and value-free; on the contrary, it is work done in a relationship and that affects both people. While you may need to learn to keep your own feelings and thoughts at bay for the duration of the meeting, there will be many instances when both are affected and you find that a client has unknowingly helped you to make a connection or given you an insight. This in turn can be used for further helping.

When the helping occurred in a one-off situation and you are not likely to meet the person again for the same reason, the ending should normally be focused on something practical or good:

'Do you see where you are going now?'

'Are you clearer now what you need to do?'

These questions need not be put in this way, but it is important that a session is rounded off and that both of you can say 'goodbye' to each other in a way that is satisfying.

A long-term relationship will inevitably run into difficulties of one kind or another from time to time. At such times it is important that both people should be prepared to look at *their* relationship, or 'you-me talk', as Egan (1977: 234) calls it.

'What is happening between us?' is a question which may have to be asked at difficult moments. What is happening between the two people is often also a reflection of how the two people separately communicate with others and is therefore a mirror of their relationships. Clients who use counselling because of problems with relating to others may therefore learn specific skills from such questions and ways of working.

When the relationship has been long and in-depth, preparation needs to be made for the ending. Such a relationship will have had some contract, either that you are meeting for a specific number of times, or that it is long-term and on-going. The time for parting has to be negotiated, as both people in the relationship have commitments to each other. When clients simply fail to turn up for an appointment, helpers and counsellors inevitably feel bereft. They may not know the reason why a person has not come and may wonder if something happened to the person; or they may feel guilty that perhaps they were considered not good enough; or they may worry that they had upset the client in some way. The end of a helping relationship can be like a bereavement, and for older people who have often been bereaved already, this can bring elements to the surface which may need to be looked at, hence the need to prepare for the ending.

Skills for ending are, particularly: focusing, summarising and reflecting. Focusing on a goal or aim makes the helping process specific and oriented towards growth; summarising can be helpful for clients to see where they have come from; and reflecting can enhance the empathy and help clients to see that they are growing in the skills which they needed or wanted to learn and in living more satisfyingly and resourcefully.

It may be obvious that to praise a person gives her or him more impetus, but it is also one of those things which we are not used to doing naturally in our culture. Leaving a person, therefore, with a 'well done' at least at the end of a meeting can sometimes do more good than much theorising.

It is never possible to list or discuss all the helper skills necessary. You may find that in certain situations you need different skills from those mentioned here. This means that you may need to be well acquainted with the client needs in your sphere of work and develop the specific skills necessary for you. This is beyond the scope of this book.

Blockages to helping

There may be obvious reasons why helping is not easy, such as deafness on the part of either person, different accents or speech problems. When one person has a visual impairment, additional skills are needed to get and stay in touch with the other.

It may be that a counsellor lives on an upper floor and there is no lift and clients who have problems with breathing or walking may find it difficult or impossible to visit such a counsellor. Such details may have to be mentioned or negotiated before appointments are made.

Apart from the more obvious blockages to helping, there may be many psychological reasons why it may not be successful. Some of the reasons have already been touched on, such as the different expectations or understandings of what counselling is. There may be deep-seated mistrust about 'spilling the beans' or taking skeletons out of cupboards. Helping and counselling is not the same as confession (though it may lead to that), and clients should not feel under any obligation to reveal all. Sometimes this has to be made clear at the beginning of a relationship. Perhaps just because the permission was given *not* to disclose all, there is more trust to do so. We have to be invited into people's hearts and soul; we cannot get there by force.

There are many possible reasons why counselling is not helpful in certain situations. False expectations, unwillingness to change and personality incompatibility are perhaps the most common. This is where it is important that helpers are skilled in recognising what is happening, can challenge effectively, and use supervision sessions to discuss the situation. Counsellors who have many such situations may need to consider their attitudes, values and skills.

Client skills

Counselling is not a spoon-feeding business, and it is necessary that clients get out of the 'ditch' on their own legs and choose the direction in which they want to go. Empathic helpers go towards them but keep one foot on the firm bank because they also have their own way to go. As the process of helping goes on, so the clients need to become more and more skilled to live in that satisfying and resourceful way which is the aim.

According to Egan (1994), counselling is a 'problem-management approach', meaning that counselling is goal-oriented. At the end of a session or a time of counselling, there should be a goal towards which the client strives and which, with the help of the counsellor, he or she can realise. The goals vary from person to person and may vary over time, but the important thing is that there is a focus for the meeting.

The skills which clients need to develop, therefore, are particularly concerned with goal setting: using the imagination, visualising possibilities, planning for change, and setting realistic goals. The skill of the helper is to encourage the development of these tactics by demonstrating them:

'You might think of trying to speak to him when you next see him, or you could write him a letter, or you could call him tonight. These are just the obvious possibilities, and you may think of other ways of tackling this problem. What might be most useful for you?'

As helpers and clients we can and must use our experiences to help, but this should be done in a way which is not disturbing or burdening the client. An example may be:

'I often find myself in a similar situation to what you are describing here, and I do … which I find helpful. Is this something which might also be helpful for you?'

The goals envisaged and set have to be realistic: not too big and not too small, but there must also be an element of self-challenge in it, otherwise nothing will change.

The reason why nothing changes in our lives is often that we think others should change, not we. Therefore to do something which challenges the blind spots, which manages a particular feeling, or which tries to overcome some personal resistance is always a brave act. When such a goal has been reached, perhaps unspectacularly for the other people concerned, an important step has been taken. This is always a reason for some celebration – whatever this might mean – to mark these events. If we do not mark such events, they do not mark us.

As with helper skills, there may be many more skills which clients need to develop and which are beyond the scope of this chapter. For more information you may need to read more about the subject, or for more experience you may need to consider a course of training.

Theories and models
Theories

There are different approaches to helping and counselling individuals and a short overview of the main theories involved and the models used follows. Nelson-Jones (1982) describes these theories under the broad headings of humanistic, psychoanalytic, behavioural, and occupational choice and developmental.

Perhaps the best-known of the humanistic theories is **person-centred therapy**. This theory is intrinsically linked with Carl Rogers. The starting point here is that human behaviour can be considered from the objective angle, that is, as others see someone, or from the subjective angle as the person him- or herself experiences the world. Rogers believed fundamentally that people live essentially in their own personal and subjective world, and that even such objective functions as science and mathematics are the result of subjective purpose and choice. 'It is this emphasis on the subjective, perceptual view of clients which has led to the term "client-centred". The perceptions of the client are viewed as his version of reality' (Nelson-Jones 1982: 18). An important point of departure for this theory is that clients have the capacity for change and for fulfilment within themselves. Mearns and Thorne (1988: 18) describe the 'Person-Centred Counsellor's Creed'.

The person-centred counsellor believes that:

- every individual has the internal resources for growth;
- when a counsellor offers the core conditions of congruence,

unconditional positive regard and empathy, therapeutic movement will take place;
- human nature is essentially constructive;
- human nature is essentially social;
- self-regard is a basic human need;
- persons are motivated to seek the truth;
- perceptions determine experience and behaviour;
- the individual should be the primary reference point in any helping activity;
- individuals should be related to as whole persons who are in the process of becoming;
- persons should be treated as doing their best to grow and to preserve themselves given their current internal and external circumstances;
- it is important to reject the pursuit of authority or control over others and to seek to share power.'

In this theory it is therefore important that counsellors can enter into the client's frame of reference, expressed and experienced in the relationship. According to Stewart (1992: 199), client-centred therapy aims to answer two basic questions: 'Who am I?' and 'How can I become myself?'

Two well-known theories, **reality therapy** and **rational emotive therapy** (RET), are similar in starting points and concepts. Reality therapy 'emphasises the importance of acknowledging reality as the basis for responsible behaviour' (Nelson-Jones 1982: 38). Stewart (1992: 228) sums up the main tenets of the theory by saying that the client has two choices: 'To deny reality, with its irresponsible behaviour, loneliness, pain, and lack of involvement' or 'To face reality, with its responsible behaviour, love, worth, and involvement'.

RET's basic principles are that 'while present behaviour is related to the past, it is beliefs about the events and not the events themselves that cause problems in the present'; people actively reinforce faulty beliefs from the past; and 'only repeated rethinking of ... irrational beliefs and repeated actions designed to undo those beliefs ... are enough to create lasting change' (Stewart 1992: 223). RET teaches clients to transform their irrational beliefs and ideas into positive wishes, wants and preferences.

Transactional analysis (TA) is widely known by its set of 'OKness' which describes the basic three positions (scripts) which the young child experiences and which the adult can change (the fourth stance):

I'm not OK – you're OK

I'm OK – you're not OK

I'm not OK – you're not OK

I'm OK – you're OK

This theory was developed by Eric Berne who recognised different 'ego states' in behaviour. When in any groupings, individuals will exhibit either a parental, adult or child state. Such roles can be maintained throughout life, by 'games' such as 'I never do' or 'Yes, but', depending on the OKness of the person. The last position (I'm OK – you're OK) is deliberately learned and acquired and relates to the adult stance.

The aim of TA is to achieve autonomy which means regaining the three basic capacities of awareness, spontaneity and intimacy. When these are present, the person is said to be an integrated adult who is attractive, responsive, objective and responsible (Nelson-Jones 1982: 79).

The **psychoanalytic** theories are best known for grouping human instincts into erotic or life instincts and death or destructive instincts. This theory has been mainly developed and expounded by Sigmund Freud.

The **behavioural** theories are marked by proponents in each category: Ivan Pavlov (classical conditioning), John Watson (conditioned behaviourism), Frederick Skinner (operant behaviourism), Joseph Wole (reciprocal inhibition), Hans Eysenck (incubation theory of neurosis) and Albert Bandura (social learning theory). To work with these theories, considerable degrees of psychological knowledge are necessary.

The **occupational choice and development** theories are much more directly geared to career choices and education and are therefore only mentioned here.

Of the therapies notably used in and with groups, **Gestalt** therapy needs to be mentioned specially. The German word means either 'pattern' or 'form', pointing to the idea that any analysis of parts cannot lead to an understanding of the whole. Gestalt is known for its activities and for concentrating on the present experience. Fantasy plays a large part, as does also how things are said, that is, the language used. One of the features of Gestalt which many people recognise is the use of the chair. Clients are asked to sit in different chairs when addressing different parts of themselves, other people, or dream objects. It is an effective therapy in groups because of the activities, giving large numbers of people the possibility to experience different scenarios to which they can possibly relate.

Models

So that theories can be applied practically, various models have been established. Two of the most popular ones are briefly detailed here.

Gerard Egan's model of helping (1994: 23–40) has evolved and changed over the 20 years since his book first appeared. Egan is problem-management oriented and therefore his aim is to help clients to formulate goals and put them into action. His model has three stages, with each stage further divided into three steps.

Stage 1: The current scenario. Clients are clients because they are stuck in a particular situation from which they cannot escape by themselves and which they experience as painful or problematic. Reviewing this scenario leads to a) telling the story, b) recognising the blind spots present, and c) finding the leverage to action.

Stage 2: The preferred scenario. The principle here is to help clients to identify what they want and formulate this in terms of goals and objectives. This means that a) new possibilities have to be envisaged, b) the agenda has to be set, and c) a commitment is made to the goal. This leads to:

Stage 3: Getting there. The model here helps counsellors to see that clients need to be helped to a) develop strategies for accomplishing the goal, b) finding the best fit from among the strategies, and c) devising the plan for action.

When these steps have been accomplished, the goals should not only have been achieved, but the outcomes should be valuable and valued.

Egan is very clear that this is not necessarily a linear model, that is, clients do not necessarily move smoothly through these stages. Sometimes much time is spent considering some aspect, and in terms of the model, some steps may have to be repeated several times before forward movement can take place.

Richard Nelson-Jones' model (1993: 33) intends that helpers and clients should collaborate to attain the goals at each stage of his 'Lifeskills Helping Model'. Helpers and clients use both 'thinking skills' and 'action skills' at every stage. To help counsellors to remember the steps of the model, Nelson-Jones uses the acronym DASIE. Each stage is characterised by a specific task.

> **Stage 1:** Develop the relationship, identify and clarify problems. The task is to build the rapport between helper and client and to help clients to tell their stories.
> **Stage 2:** Assess the problems and redefine or rename them in terms of skills. The task is to elicit the information needed to define the problem in terms of skills.
> **Stage 3:** State working goals and plan interventions. The task is to state the goal and to negotiate self-helping interventions to attain them.
> **Stage 4:** Intervene to develop self-helping skills. The specific task here is to work at developing and strengthening self-helping skills in problem areas.
> **Stage 5:** End and consolidate self-helping skills. The helping contact is terminated and self-helping skills are consolidated.

The lifeskills which Nelson-Jones (1993: 30) mentions are 'personally responsible sequences of self-helping choices in specific psychological skills areas conducive to mental wellness. People require a repertoire of lifeskills according to their developmental tasks and specific problems of living'.

This idea of developing lifeskills makes this model attractive as it aims to leave clients not only in a better space, but with better skills to stay well and in good spaces.

In many years of practice I have developed my own model which I have widely used and written about (Tschudin 1994; 1995). This model consists of four questions:

1) What is happening?
This question invites the client to tell the story. The question is in the present tense which points to the fact that what is happening at this moment is important. The present feelings and emotions matter as they reflect memories and anticipations.

2) What is the meaning of it?
Behind a story there is a sense of a meaning. When we can see the sense, purpose or meaning of an event or action we are free of the tyranny of it and can direct our lives into fulfiling the meaning we want to give them.

3) What is your goal?
Knowing something is not enough to put it into practice. It is too easy in counselling either to go round in circles or to stop at the crucial moment without a commitment. This question commits the client to move forward.

4) How are you going to do it?
The most difficult thing for most people is to bridge the gap between inner and outer, and understanding and action. Therefore this question encourages clients to be specific and challenges them to be responsible to themselves.

These questions are applicable in most short- and long-term situations. They are also useful for helpers and clients to apply to themselves and their evaluation of their helping and also their daily situations.

Conclusion

An overview of concepts, theories and skills like that given in this chapter is inevitably deficient and very black-and-white. But having some ideas of some of the points involved can help you to go and look up some item which may seem interesting or important.

Perhaps the most important thing to remember is that no two people would help another person in the same way; no two people would use the theories, models or skills of helping in exactly the same way. Helping and counselling is about the therapeutic use of self, and this changes and adapts. The best that we can hope for is that with age we have come to more insights, have learned to listen less defensively and have gained some wisdom which we can share perhaps more freely with others than when we were younger. Helping others is never dull because we see not only that they are changing, but we also see ourselves change – hopefully also towards more satisfying living and more resourcefulness.

References

BAC (1989) *Code of Ethics and Practice for Counselling Skills*. Rugby: British Association for Counselling.

BAC (1996) *Code of Ethics and Practice for Counsellors*. Rugby: British Association for Counselling.

Bayne R, Horton I, Merry T, Noyes E (1994) *The Counsellor's Handbook*. London: Chapman & Hall.

Egan G (1977) *You and Me: The skills of communicating and relating to others*. Belmont, CA: Wadsworth.

Egan G (1994) *The Skilled Helper: A problem-management approach to helping* (5th Edition). Belmont, CA: Brooks/Cole.

Mearns D, Thorne B (1988) *Person-Centred Counselling in Action*. London: Sage.

Nelson-Jones R (1982) *The Theory and Practice of Counselling Psychology*. London: Cassell.

Nelson-Jones R (1993) *Practical Counselling and Helping Skills* (3rd Edition). London: Cassell.

Rogers C R (1961) *On Becoming a Person*. London: Constable.

Rogers C R (1980) *A Way of Being*. Boston: Houghton Mifflin.

Stewart W (1992) *An A–Z of Counselling Theory and Practice*. London: Chapman & Hall.

Tschudin V (1994) *Counselling. A primer for nurses.* Workbook and Workshop Guide. London: Baillière Tindall.

Tschudin V (1995) *Counselling Skills for Nurses* (4th Edition). London: Baillière Tindall.

Further Reading

Axline V (1971) *Dibs: In search of self.* Harmondsworth: Penguin.

Berne E (1964) *Games People Play: The psychology of human relation-ships.* Harmondsworth: Penguin.

Holmes P, Paul S, Pelham G (1996) 'A relational model of counselling'. *Counselling* 7 (3); 229–231.

Hough M (1994) *A Practical Approach to Counselling.* London: Pitman.

Knight B (1986) *Psychotherapy with Older Adults.* London: Sage.

Rogers C R (1951) *Client-Centred Therapy.* Boston: Houghton Mifflin.

Rogers C R (1980) 'Growing old – or older and growing'. *Journal of Humanistic Psychology* 20 (4); 15–16.

Scrutton S (1989) *Counselling Older People: A creative response to ageing.* London: Edward Arnold/Age Concern.

Truax B, Carkhuff R R (1967) *Toward Effective Counselling and Psycho-therapy.* Chicago: Adline.

In Praise of Memory

There is another way of defining memory, and that is by its absence. Some time ago I called to see an elderly friend – let's call her Sybil – who has for many years acted as a beacon of civilised living, wise and witty, cultured, humane and shrewd. But on that occasion the real Sybil, or perhaps I should say the familiar Sybil, had slipped away and in her place I found a charming, carefree, younger woman, appreciative of the gift I brought her, friendly, eager to question me about my present life and my past, almost as though we were meeting for the first time. The old Sybil would have been a little bored by facts she already knew; the new Sybil seemed to relish my story and to find it interesting. It is not yet clear whether Sybil will emerge from this phase of forgetfulness and recover her old identity. In the meantime I, along with her family and other friends, must hold it for her, as I might look after a winter coat for a friend on a summer outing. The pain I felt on leaving Sybil's house, the sense of loss, are mine and not hers. Perhaps her vanished gravitas – the interest she had always shown in art, in politics and in the deeper issues of our time – has now become my own grave sadness? And shall I, next time we meet, be able to match her lightness with lightness of my own? In the absence of shared memories, shall we be able to build a bridge of another kind, more playful, less purposeful, but one that can still carry the traffic of an enduring friendship?

If there is an expert in this field, it is the neurologist Dr Oliver Sachs, whose books – in particular *The Man Who Mistook his Wife for a Hat* (1985) – show a consistent sensitivity to the plight of his patients, some of whom suffer from a loss of memory so severe that they are obliged to put together the assorted fragments of their lives and to reinvent their world every few minutes. Some of them may be described as victims of Korsakov's syndrome (Korsakov being the Russian neuropsychiatrist who in the late nineteenth century studied this pattern of memory loss), but to Sachs each patient is an individual whose world he enters with respect, tenderness even, and a warm good humour. But he does not minimise the drastic effect that severe loss of memory must have on the human personality. 'We have', he says, 'each of us, a life-story, an inner narrative – whose continuity, whose sense, *is* our lives. It might be said that each of us constructs and lives a "narrative", and that this narrative is us, our identities.' And he goes on, 'To be ourselves we must *have* ourselves – possess, if need be repossess, our life-stories. We must "recollect" ourselves, recollect the inner drama, the narrative, of ourselves. A man needs such a narrative, a continuous inner narrative, to maintain his identity, his self.' (Sachs 1985: 198)

It would be quite improper to suggest that anyone in Sybil's situation, possibly moving into a further stage of the ageing process, can be helped back through the skill of even the most experienced counsellor. She and others like her are on a journey, and those who accompany them are required to draw on their human resources of cheerfulness, loyalty, affection and imagination, which are qualities shown by Sachs when confronted by the pathological extremities of the patients under his care, and which supplement his professional insight and judgement.

Memory loss, an inherent part of the process of dementia, is a spectre haunting the thoughts of many of us as we approach old age. It will be there in the corner of the consulting room whenever a counsellor of senior age meets with a senior citizen, and as with all spectres, it is best to admit its presence and to take a hard look at it: spectres that are ignored or denied quickly become monsters. At the very least, the prospect of losing one's memory should trigger gratitude for the memories that remain – a readiness to relish this personal treasury and to take responsibility for befriending its contents and putting them into good order.

(Sheila Willson)

Reference

Sachs O (1985) *The Man Who Mistook his Wife for a Hat*. London: Duckworth.

10

The Training of Counsellors

Francesca Inskipp

Editor's Introduction

When undertaking any new work or signing up for a course, we can imagine what it might be like, but we can never have that 'fly on the wall' experience. Francesca Inskipp comes as near as possible to it, though, in this chapter.

As older people we are inevitably more hesitant about learning and studying than younger friends and colleagues. Life has taught us a lot, and experience can be more valuable than any certificate. When counselling others, we literally walk around in their lives, and to do this effectively, with benefit and without hurting, we have to learn a certain number of things which even the best experience alone cannot teach us. To do a counselling course is therefore a requirement. But which course, and where, are important questions when the choice is real.

This chapter helps us to look at the many possibilities and decide what may be the right starting point. Francesca's own long experience in teaching courses gives an invaluable insight and makes such courses inviting and stimulating.

Introduction

When I started to write this chapter I imagined myself back at the age of 60, wanting to continue to lead a useful life and thinking that counselling could be helpful to my community and that I would find it interesting. I had heard that counsellors have to have training, so what were the questions I would want to ask to find out about it: Why would I have to train? What would I have to do? How would I find a course? How much would it cost in money, time and effort? How would my age affect being accepted on a course, or affect what I might be required to do? This chapter explores some of those questions – and a few more.

Why training?

Counselling is about helping another person by communicating on a personal level and building a relationship – human activities that most of us have been doing throughout our lives, so why do we need to learn how to do it? Counselling aims to help the person being helped – the client – to **discover and use their own resources and strengths** so that they can live more effectively, learn to deal with their difficulties and find purpose in their lives. This means that we, as counsellors, have to put aside our own purposes, learn to listen intently to what the client is saying and feeling, and be able to respond to and communicate what we are hearing and what we imagine they are feeling, without intruding our own ideas or suggestions. We also have to learn how to create a warm helping relationship which is like friendship but is not friendship because it has boundaries and will end. It is therefore important not to create dependency in the client – and not to get over-involved.

Learning to counsel is about developing ourselves as competent and caring human beings and the training is both about 'doing' and 'being', it is both professional and personal development. We need to learn what to do – the skills of good interpersonal communication – and also learn to become more aware of ourselves. To counsel others we need to be very aware of our own beliefs, values and attitudes, of how to listen to others without judging them, how we experience and deal with our own sadness, anger, fears and joys. So training is an opportunity to learn more about ourselves as human beings, to work on our personal development, and to practise the skills which are needed to be able to help others on their life's journey.

Counselling, then, makes great demands on us as human beings. Our longer life, hopefully, has brought us wider experience and wisdom to bring to our counselling, but also, possibly, more fixed ideas and resistance to relearning what we may feel sure we already know! In one sense training for counselling never ends: after an initial course a practising counsellor requires ongoing training and supervision.

Where to train?

One of the simplest ways to train is through voluntary organisations which run their own training for the counsellors they employ (see Chapter 11). This is usually an initial course followed by supervision and ongoing training. These organisations may be concerned with, for example, bereavement, alcohol or drug dependency, young people (some will not accept older volunteers), cancer or AIDS help, marriage problems, or a counselling service provided by a church. There are a wide range of helping organisations in most localities. Your local Council of Voluntary Service or Citizen's Advice Bureau will probably be able to give you details.

Some organisations do not run their own training and will only employ people who have already completed a counselling course. In the last ten years, counselling courses have multiplied and can be found in most towns, often run by the local college or further education institute, or by private organisations. Brochures detailing courses can be obtained from colleges or institutes and sometimes from your local post office.

There are two main kinds of training course, one for **counselling skills** and one for training as a **counsellor**. The courses for counselling skills are shorter, maybe between 30 and 100 hours, and usually aim to train you to use counselling skills in a variety of helping roles, either paid or voluntary. The courses for training as a counsellor for those who will work specifically in that role are usually at diploma level and extend over two or three years part-time, 400–500 hours attendance, often one day a week for three terms each year. Most of the diploma courses expect you to have done a counselling skills course before embarking on a diploma. These courses require a large commitment of time and money and it is wise to explore thoroughly before deciding on a particular course. The British Association for Counselling (BAC – address on p 245), the professional organisation for counsellors which monitors standards, has a list of longer courses. Many of these are advertised in the BAC journal *Counselling* (your local library may have a copy).

There are also some distance learning courses, for example those provided by the National Extension College (address on p 248) or College of Counselling (address on p 247) which can provide some basic learning about counselling. These need to be backed up with attendance on a practical course where you can practise counselling and get feedback from a qualified tutor, and also have an opportunity to work in a group and explore attitudes and beliefs with others who are learning to counsel.

What would I do on a training course?

You may be thinking as you read about counselling training that you have been doing most of those things during your life, you have learnt a lot about yourself through your experiences, and have been communicating with others over a lot of years. You may wonder how it would be having to learn, relearn and share experiences, possibly with younger people – and probably learning from a younger tutor. At the end of this chapter the probable contents of courses you might join are listed. What follows may be useful to give you some idea of what a training course is like, and some comments made by older men and women who have taken counselling courses are included.

Selection

Unless you take a very short course you will have to fill in an application form and may have an interview with one of the tutors on the course. The tutor will want to know about your motivation for taking the course. She or he will want to explore whether you are likely to be a committed learner, willing to face the possible discomfort of having to relearn ways of listening and responding. Will you be willing to talk about yourself and your values and explore your attitudes to a range of issues, such as death, sexual orientation, parental responsibilities, abuse – physical, sexual, emotional – and listen to others without judging? How flexible are you? Some people get more set in their ways and views as they get older, some are far more flexible and wiser than younger people. Be prepared to explore this.

You may be asked about educational qualifications, although these may not be relevant unless you are taking a diploma course which involves a lot of reading and writing. Many people feel anxious about writing if they have not done any formal writing for many years, but if you are prepared to commit the time and energy, most courses provide help for anybody struggling with this. All accredited courses have a policy of equal opportunities, which means they do not discriminate on the basis of educational background, age, race, disability, etc, and that they endeavour to adapt the course to accommodate motivated students.

The selection criteria for courses differs, depending on the level and length of the course, but generally they concern issues of motivation, commitment and openness to learning about self and others, an ability to reflect on your life experiences and learn from them, and a caring for humanity and social justice. They will also be checking that you are not dependent on counselling others to meet your own emotional needs. There is a fine balance between wanting to help others and only feeling worthwhile if you are a helper.

That is what they will be seeking from you, but you, in turn, should look carefully at the course to see if it will give you the training you want (suggestions of things you should look for and ask about are given on pages 195–196).

What is it like to be on a training course?

Once you have been selected, what happens on the course? Three examples follow.

1 Rosemary

Rosemary is a widow of 61 whose family have grown up and left home. She has a part-time job in a chemist shop. She often finds people talk to her about their problems and she would like to know more about helping them, and would also like to do some voluntary counselling. She was accepted on a Counselling Skills Certificate course in her local further education (FE) college. It is 80 hours, 2 terms of 11 weeks, 3 hours per week (with a choice of evening or afternoon) with one whole day at the beginning and at the end of the course.

Rosemary wrote the following description of her first day on the course:

'There were 18 students in my course group – mostly women in their 30s to 40s – and two tutors. I felt excited and anxious – was I too old to be a student, how would the others see me, would the other students be much more knowledgeable than me?

'The tutors introduced themselves, said a little about the course and about the structure of the day. We were asked to stand up, find a partner and talk to each other about ourselves for two minutes in turn. We had to change partners several times, and were asked to tell new partners different things about ourselves. In between, we were asked how it felt finding a partner, talking to a stranger, deciding who would start.

'We then introduced ourselves to the whole group: name, why we had joined and something we were good at – anything from jogging to telling stories. The tutors then asked us to talk in fours about what would help our learning, how could we help ourselves, how could others help, how could the tutors help, and what would hinder our learning – self, others, tutors?

'The tutors then helped us make a group contract on how we would work together to maximise the helping and minimise the hindering. This included issues like confidentiality within the group, being open to listen to each other, keeping to agreed times, asking for help, giving feedback to the tutors on what helped or hindered our learning.

'One tutor then gave a brief talk about counselling and asked us in threes to write up our definition and then share it with the whole group. We did several exercises like this, the tutors talking, using a board or flipchart to clarify points and asking us in different twos or threes to discuss and clarify for ourselves. The morning went very quickly – I found I had talked to most of the others in different small groups by the end of the morning and was losing most of my anxiety. I felt I had taken part and found it easy to talk, already noticing how good it was to be really listened to. The tutors emphasised this many times during the morning: the importance of giving complete attention as we listened to each other.

'In the afternoon we started with what the tutors called a 'check in'. We sat in a large circle and anybody could bring up anything left from the morning – queries, feelings, observations. It was an interesting session. We learnt that we would start each of our weekly sessions with 20 minutes for this check-in; it became an important feature of the course.

'We then went on to do some exercises on listening and responding, the tutors demonstrating skills to us and getting us to practice in threes, one person talking about themself, one responding and one observing We also learnt how to give feedback in the observer role.

'We had a short break for tea and then the tutors talked about the "learning journal" we are asked to keep. We had been asked to bring a large notebook or file to write in. This would contain a brief account of every session, what we had learnt, what we found useful or not useful, what raised questions for us, what emotions we experienced. It was to be a record of our development throughout the course. We spent ten minutes recording thoughts and feelings so far, and then five minutes each way with a partner talking about our recording. We were told the tutors would ask to see the journals twice each term, not to mark them but to check we kept them up to date, and to help them get feedback on our progress. Keeping this weekly journal would be part of our assessment for the certificate at the end.

'We finished the day with a relaxation exercise, imagining ourselves in a warm, safe place and breathing slowly. Lastly we went round the circle saying one word, how we felt at that moment. Mine was "full". I felt I had received a lot from the tutors and from the others on the course – a good start!'

When Rosemary talked with me at the end of her course she said it had been very different from how she imagined, and although she had been very anxious at times, she had enjoyed the informal way the teaching and learning was done. She had learnt a lot from the other students and had also realised how much she could contribute to her own and others' learning, especially from her life experiences of two marriages, three children, the death of her second husband, and caring for her own elderly parents until they died. As a result of the course she had applied and been accepted to do some counselling with a local team working on alcohol dependency, and was having some further training specifically on working with people with alcohol problems.

2 William

William is a retired builder and at 63 had already done a counselling skills course which he had enjoyed. He found excitement in learning new things and working in a group. He was counselling in a centre set up by his local church and wanted to feel more confident, particularly in working with some of the depressed people who came to him. He applied and was accepted on a diploma course at his local university. This was five hours weekly over two years, a whole Saturday each term and with a residential weekend at the beginning of the second year and a full day at the end of the course. He was also working two half-days at the counselling centre and attending there two hours a fortnight for supervision of his counselling.

I asked him to tell me what had been most important to him on the course:

'All the course was important, but there were some highlights. What I enjoyed most were the small groups we worked in throughout the year. We were eight students in our Skills group with a tutor. In this group for the first year we practised counselling each other with the rest observing us and giving feedback. As the client we used issues from our own lives, and this was important in teaching us how it felt to be a client. We also learnt a lot about each other which created a very close group, and it opened my eyes to lives very different from mine. The tutor was good at pushing us to listen and observe at different levels and also shared her own experiences of working with clients, which was very helpful.

'In the second year, it became a supervision group and we brought issues from our work with clients, sometimes part of a tape-recording, sometimes we role-played being our client with another member being the counsellor. I felt this group helped me the most to improve my counselling at the Centre, especially when I felt stuck with very depressed clients.

'Throughout the two years I also found the Self Development group very rewarding, although very painful at times. This group had nine members and a tutor, and aimed to help us become more aware of our-selves, our values, beliefs and prejudices and how we stereotyped other people. Also to become aware of how we interacted with each other, how we developed more empathy and acceptance for each other and how genuine and open we were, how we were perceived by others in the group. I made some good friends, especially in this group. It was very good to be accepted as an older man – the rest of the group were between 28 and 49, mostly young enough to be my children, but I learnt a lot from their views of the world and ways of living in it.

'The other area that was very useful to me were my sessions with a pro-fessional counsellor. The course required us to have 30 sessions within the two years. I was resistant at first but then found I was doing a lot of looking back on my life, and how past experiences affected me now, especially when I worked with clients who raised similar issues. The counselling I received helped me to be more open in all my relation-ships and this has benefited my work and my personal life.'

William completed his Diploma and is continuing to work at the coun-selling centre. He is extending his work by providing counselling in their homes for older people who are unable to travel, including resi-dents of a local care home.

3 Elizabeth

Elizabeth is 68 and had been a worker in a Citizen's Advice Bureau. She had given that up but still wanted to do some voluntary work. She had done some counselling skills training as part of her work at the Bureau and applied to work with a bereavement counselling service which counselled people mainly in their own homes. She did a short course of two weekends and ten evenings specifically working with bereavement and loss, and then started working with one client. She continued her training by having individual supervision with an experienced counsellor every four weeks and attending a supervision group every four weeks. As she gained confidence and approval from her supervisor she took on more clients. The bereavement organisation also organised a training evening every two months, and a whole Saturday every six months. To work in the organisation she had to agree to attend the supervision and the training sessions.

She said:

'I found the training rather different from previous sessions with the CAB as it was mainly experiential or lectures in a small group of eight with different tutors. I found some of the experiential sessions very hard, although I learnt a lot from them. One was an exercise to imagine I had been given six months to live. What would I do? Then to imagine the last two months: what were my feelings and how would I spend the time? And finally I was dying, what was I feeling? Who did I want with me? How did I want to die and what did I imagine would happen? Fortunately we were a supportive group and this session took place after we had got to know each other a bit. Other sessions were on normal and abnormal grief, how to help people talk about their feelings and how to keep boundaries when counselling people at home: keeping to time and not encouraging too much dependency. We also had a session on working with children.

'The individual supervision made me anxious at first, having to talk about the client and how I worked with her, but I gained a lot from it. The group supervision is very interesting as we hear about each other's cases and how each works on them, and I feel I am learning all the time. I enjoy the people I meet in the supervision and training sessions and have made new friends.'

Elizabeth is now 70 and is continuing to counsel for the bereavement service. She finds a lot of satisfaction in her work and hopes to go on for as long as she can continue to drive her car. She found that some clients still needed some support after finishing counselling, so she helped to set up, and works with, a fortnightly group for people who wish to continue.

This should have given you some idea of the content and flavour of some of the different counselling courses available. It is important to make sure that you choose the course you want to take. The questions you should ask will depend on how you want to use counselling, how much time and money you have available, and whether you want a qualification.

Qualifications

At present there are no legal qualifications necessary to practise as a counsellor in the UK. The most widely accepted qualification in this country is Individual Accreditation as a Counsellor by the British Association for Counselling (more information on this is available from BAC at the address on p 245). Some counselling courses are validated by the university or college responsible for the course and there are a number of other examining bodies validating courses, for example, Royal Society of Arts (RSA – address on p 249) Associated Examining Board (AEB – address on p 245), CENTRA (address on p 246), etc and the standards laid down for these can be quite variable. Some training institutions award internal certificates which may be only certificates of attendance. It may be important to find out if the course is assessed and has a qualifying certificate or diploma if that is what you want. A system of National Vocational Qualifications in counselling is being set up and these will have European recognition. Some courses are beginning to offer this qualification route. Readers can get more information from the AEB.

What should you ask about a course?

You should consider carefully what it is you want at this point in your life. It is often a good idea to do some work with a voluntary organisation to see if counselling is for you – you can always go on to further training. Working in a voluntary organisation is a help to being accepted on a diploma course if that is your aim.

If you do aim to become an Accredited Counsellor with BAC, you should try for a place on a BAC accredited course if one is run locally. You can obtain a list of Accredited Courses from BAC (address on p 245).

If no course is within reach, BAC suggests that anyone aspiring to be an Accredited Counsellor should aim to have:

- been trained by trainers at least some of whom are practising counsellors and who adhere to the BAC codes of ethics and practice;
- had in-depth access to at least one model of counselling, and have been able to compare it with other models;
- had an opportunity for systematic development of appropriate self-awareness;
- had a minimum of 24 sessions of counselling with an experienced counsellor;
- engaged in substantial and regular supervised counselling practice (both during training and subsequently);
- had regular opportunities for observation and practice of counselling skills with feedback from both staff and fellow students together with progressive monitoring and assessment of skills development;
- had access to learning about and applying relevant concepts from the social sciences in counselling-related work;
- gained an understanding of professional issues.

Experiential learning and its implications for the participant

The British Association for Counselling (BAC) gives the following information in its guide to selecting courses:

'Participants in counselling courses are likely to be involved at times in experiential learning. This learning is designed to heighten awareness of an experience or give experience of a familiar happening. Subsequently workshop members will be asked to reflect on that experience and to make sense of it, either in their own terms, or in the light of an offered framework. Experiential learning can be personally challenging for participants in a number of ways:

'**1** Counsellors attempt to recognise and respect the ways others see and feel about their situation and the sense they make of it. In training, the process of suspending judgement and continuing to listen can raise anxiety, as can being asked to tolerate and encourage the expression of sometimes taboo thoughts and feelings.

'**2** Most courses expect students to share with other group members some of the difficulties and problems that they face in their lives. This work gives a personal insight into the opportunities and discomforts of sharing (and working to resolve) thoughts, situations and feelings that are problematic. It also provides an opportunity to give and receive direct feedback to each other as counsellors.

'**3** The process of learning more about our own values and the ways that we communicate with, relate to, and cope with others in our life may result in initial self-consciousness, self-questioning and some discomfort. Beyond that, most students experience new personal understanding and confidence in life and work which is energising. This can affect life outside the course and lead to personal and social reappraisal.

'Because of all these factors, it is important to try and discover, before paying money or making a long-term commitment, whether such a course suits you, or whether it will be too stressful. The quality of such a course for everyone depends on sufficient commitment to attendance and learning on the part of each participant.' (Chaytor 1998: X)

You will notice that the three case examples previously described mention anxiety about experiential learning and all say it was useful in their development as a counsellor. One way of finding out more about a course is to talk to students who are doing, or have done the course. Some courses run an open evening with an opportunity to talk to ex-students, or if this is not available, you could ask if you could meet and talk with an ex-student – possibly someone older who has experienced the course.

Content of training

A **counselling skills** course of up to 100 hours may involve a selection process, which will involve completing an application form and attending an interview.

The content of the course will include:

- exercises to learn and practice a variety of counselling skills with opportunities to practise in small groups, getting feedback from tutors and from fellow students;
- counselling theory: what helps people change; theory on human development, with opportunities to explore our own development; the effect on us of the environment we live in (family, neighbourhood, culture, etc);
- explanation and discussion on counselling codes of ethics; responsibilities for standards; setting up clear contracts with clients; boundaries; confidentiality; protection of clients; and the importance of monitoring your work by recording and supervision;
- opportunities in a safe situation to explore values, beliefs, attitudes, especially attitudes about differences. How we react to, and communicate with, others who are different in age, class, race, religion, sexual orientation, etc;
- opportunities to reflect on your learning and its implications for you and your work.

If it is an assessed course you may be required to:

- keep and present a 'learning journal' which records your learning from the course, both what you learn about counselling and what you learn about yourself and as a member of the group;
- do a short counselling session with a colleague demonstrating the skills you have learnt and your ability to evaluate yourself;
- do some reading and possibly some short written work on counselling or human theory.

A course run by a specialist voluntary organisation would include some or all of the above, and would also include training for working with the specific client group, for example on bereavement, drug dependency, etc. Training would also cover information on the aims,

objectives, ethics and structure of the organisation, systems of recording and general administration such as intake of clients, referral, etc. It
is also likely that some form of assessment would be included.

A counselling diploma course would contain all the above. There
would also be a selection process involving references, an application
form, and attendance at one or more interviews, possibly taking part in
a group exercise. A diploma course would also cover:

- more counselling theory, probably based on one particular orientation, eg person-centred, psycho-dynamic, Gestalt, or a combination
  of these theories or others, sometimes called integrated theory;
- more theory about human beings, human systems, equal opportunities and working with difference;
- more reading and written work, papers, essays on theory work for
  assessment, case studies on clients, and probably audio-tapes of
  work with clients with evaluation of your skills and way of working;
- more skills training, more practice with observation and opportunities to give and receive feedback from colleagues and tutors;
- more work on professional issues – assessing and intake of clients,
  making contracts, building and maintaining a counselling relationship, recording (written and audio) endings with clients, etc;
- more personal development work, probably in a specific group and
  integrated into all areas of the course work;
- more work on ethics – codes of ethics and guidelines for practice;
- more 'experiential work' – that is, work with 'real' clients out in the
  community, probably within a counselling agency;
- structured supervision of client work, possibly within the course,
  with the counselling agency, or possibly individual supervision outside the course;
- some work on specific client issues, such as depression, bereavement
  and loss, stress, relationship problems, drug dependency, anger,
  abuse.

Cost of training

A voluntary organisation may offer you free training, conditional on your agreeing to work for the organisation for a certain length of time. Some voluntary organisations expect you to pay part of the costs of training. Counselling skills courses will probably cost between £50 and £200 depending on the length of the course and where it is run. Further education courses usually cost less than those put on by private organisations. Diploma courses are usually between £800 to £1,600 per year; you may have to pay extra for supervision which could be another £300 per year. Some courses also recommend or require you to have counselling during the course: the cost of this will depend on the number of sessions required. You should make careful enquiries of total costs before deciding on a course.

Conclusion

I hope this chapter has given you enough information – and perhaps inspiration – to think about taking up some training for counselling. With an increased life expectancy, and often a long period of life after finishing full-time work, there are opportunities for older people to enter counselling. I am now in my late 70s and still working part of the week on counselling and supervision, both of which give me an opportunity to give something back to my community and enliven my life. I am frequently approached by older people seeking an older counsellor and have difficulty in finding good referrals. There is a need out there, especially for voluntary or low-cost counselling. Training is a challenge, an opportunity to open up to a new world, and to find yourself. I hope you will consider it.

References

Chaytor D (ed) (1998) 'Experiential learning and its implication for the participant'. In: *The Training in Counselling and Psychotherapy Directory*. Rugby: British Association for Counselling.

In Praise of Memory

In her fine and perceptive book on the nature of memory, *A Collection of Moments*, the Russian-born scientist Esther Salaman (1970) tells us that towards the end of his life Dostoyevsky recorded his belief that a man could not go on living without his memories, especially the 'sacred and precious' memories of childhood. 'Some people,' he wrote, 'appear not to think of their memories of childhood, but all the same preserve such memories unconsciously. They may be grave, bitter, but the suffering we have lived through may turn in the end into sacred things for the soul.'

In his 80s, the great Swiss psychologist C G Jung – who liked to call himself 'a doctor of the soul' – reluctantly agreed to write his autobiography, which was later published under the title *Memories, Dreams, Reflections*. He was assisted in this task by his friend and colleague, the analytical psychologist Aniela Jaffé, and it was she who, in her introduction to this book, recorded Jung's observation: 'This autobiography is now taking a direction quite different from what I had imagined at the beginning. It has become a necessity for me to write down my early memories. If I neglect to do so for a single day, unpleasant physical symptoms immediately follow. As soon as I set to work they vanish and my head feels perfectly clear.' (Jung 1961)

So here are two deep thinkers, through whom we glimpse the idea that memories, especially memories of childhood, represent both a demand and an enrichment, with the power to heal or disturb us according to how we treat them. In *A Collection of Moments*, Esther Salaman introduces another point of view when she recounts the striking story of a childhood event which set the scene for a dominant pattern of reaction in later life. It concerns the writer Leo Tolstoy, who at the age of 50, she tells us, recorded an infant memory: 'I am bound; I want to pull out my hands, and I can't. I scream and cry, and I myself don't like my screaming, but I can't stop. Someone is bending over me, but I cannot remember who. And all this is happening in semi-darkness. But I remember there were two people. My screams affect them; it makes them anxious, but they do not untie me, and I scream louder. They think it is necessary (that is that I should remain bound), whereas I know that it isn't, and I want to prove it to them, and burst into more screams, disagreeable to me, but uncontrollable. I feel the injustice and cruelty, not of people, because they are sorry for me, but of fate, and I feel pity for myself.' Tolstoy believed that he was possibly swaddled at this early age to prevent him from scratching a sore; in any case he regarded this first impression as the strongest in his life. He goes on to say: 'What is memorable is not my cry and suffering, but the complexity and contradiction of impressions. I want freedom, it would disturb nobody, but I lack strength, while they are strong.' Esther Salaman makes the point that awareness of this memory was not enough in itself to change the adult man. 'He continued,' she says, 'to demand his freedom. His wife and others continued to deny it him, though they loved him; he felt – he said so in letters – that he was weak and they were strong, and he continued to "scream" and to hate his screams. The recovery of memories does not result in our altering our pattern, but in recognising it.' (page 104)

If the recovery of a memory is not enough to change our pattern of behaviour, is there anything more to be done about it? I believe there is, and that the power of imagination can be brought to bear on a traumatic memory in such a way as to transform, first the memory and then the pattern it has created.

(Sheila Willson)

References

Salaman E (1970) *A Collection of Moments*. London: Longman.

Jung C G (1961) *Memories, Dreams, Reflections*. Recorded and edited by Aniela Jaffé. London: Collins, Routledge and Kegan Paul.

11

Dimensions of a Counselling Service

Hugh D Mackay

Editor's Introduction

How does a counselling service work? What sort of things do counsellors do? Hugh Mackay's chapter sums up and brings together many of the topics discussed in the earlier chapters.

This is a chapter giving us insight into one counselling service which has grown and expanded and which aims to be as holistic as possible in answering the various needs of its users. The beginning and end of counselling and all true human relationships is listening, and hearing what is being said. It is therefore both stimulating and comforting to read that the Age Concern local group in Bath is able to get locks changed on doors as well as transforming lives with counselling help: all because a person was heard and the right response made to what was heard.

Hugh writes with the passion of the involved person and so gives us a fascinating glimpse into the work of one counselling service.

Introduction

Many Age Concern (AC) centres made a name for themselves in the 1960s by providing community support for older people needing practical help through information and advice centres, befrienders and carers, etc. However, many older people and their carers also often have emotional problems – such as those stemming from bereavement, anxiety, depression or emotional fatigue – about which they need to talk privately with someone.

In a number of places, therefore, it was felt necessary to meet this need by forming counselling services of trained volunteers. This chapter is a description of how one such service was developed in Bath, the basic essentials found to be necessary and some of the difficulties encountered.

Early days

In the City of Bath, where a quarter of the population is over 60, there was a growing number of older people living alone who had no one with whom to discuss things – often because their partners had died or their families moved away – as they tried to come to terms with their failing abilities or other losses. Befrienders went to lonely people for a chat over a cup of tea or to do odd jobs, but when emotional or relationship problems were discussed, they felt out of their depth. So in 1987, the Counselling Service was brought into being to fill that gap, using start-up grants from the local District Health Authority and Age Concern England.

The Counselling Service began with four volunteer counsellors, who had some rudimentary counselling training, and a part-time paid co-ordinator. Three years later, new offices were made available for it, together with three other care services, in a Care Centre at St Martin's Hospital, Bath, refurbished and equipped through a generous legacy (the care services moved to new premises in 1998). By 1992, the number of counsellors had increased to six and supervision was kindly undertaken by two sympathetic local professional counsellors and a community psychiatric nurse (CPN).

Following the NHS and Community Care Act of 1990 which came into effect on 1 April 1993, it was realised that if the increasing number of people being referred to Age Concern by hospital staff, health visitors and social services were to be adequately helped, then an expanded programme was needed, incorporating regular training in counselling of older people and addressing their specific needs and problems, coupled with a larger supervision support network. This task, it was felt, should be undertaken by a manager who was not only able to organise and administrate, but was also a trained counsellor, capable of making objective assessments of clients, teaching counselling skills, providing supervision and stimulating a team spirit.

The mechanics of growth

Training

A key factor in the expansion of the scheme has been the holding of an annual six-month Induction Course in Counselling Older People, which includes a period as a probationary counsellor. There is now a core of some 30 trained counsellors and half a dozen follow-up befrienders seeing about 100 clients weekly – the maximum number with which the service can cope.

Counselling in general consists of two basic levels:

Level one is the provision of a listening ear and support to people who have a need to off-load their problems or talk through difficult situations with someone who can give an outside objective viewpoint, perhaps because they have no family or friends in whom they can confide. Many older retired people with a natural gift of sympathy and experience of life can prove to be ideal listeners and counsellors on this level.

Level two is the application of counselling skills and theory to people with deeper emotional problems, such as feelings of guilt, anger, depression or grief, for which a fuller understanding of human nature and expertise in gently probing to expose inner feelings is required. For this, more specialised training is needed.

In any counselling service for older people, counsellors who are skilled on both levels are required and the Induction Course seeks to train volunteers in both areas of understanding and professionalism.

The course follows a pattern of giving practical listening and counselling skills in part one, and, in part two, a basic understanding of the medical problems that often occur in older people. The counsellor needs to know how such problems affect someone's emotions and the appropriate response (see the course programme, Appendix A, on pp 221–222). The Age Concern Handbook *Counselling Older People* (Scrutton 1989) serves as an ideal textbook for the course, covering both counselling and medical aspects. The course also introduces the volunteer to the attitudes and policies of Age Concern and uses a person-centred holistic approach to appreciate and address the needs of the whole person – emotional, physical, mental, spiritual, social and financial. At Age Concern Bath we have a number of other departments and services to refer to for practical help, for example: an information centre; community, advocacy and carers' support schemes; as well as various luncheon clubs and day centres.

This broad approach to counselling has encouraged three groups of people to attend the course. The first group includes those who have a general interest in helping people in the community. Some of these have taken early retirement and/or are financially independent, and have ranged from bankers and solicitors to nurses, teachers and social workers, housewives and carers of older relatives. They may or may not have had counselling training, but can draw on a vast experience of life, and we recommend that they should have attended an Introductory Course in Counselling before the Induction Course. These volunteers often prove to be excellent listeners on Level One and go on to become some of our best long-term counsellors.

The second group includes people who want counselling experience. They already hold Counselling Skills and Theory certificates and wish to go on to get a diploma in their third year. However, to do so, they are required to undertake a minimum number of counselling hours, generally around 100. Some ask if they can be taken on as volunteers with Age Concern. To this we will agree, but request that they first complete the Induction Course in order to acquaint themselves with the particular needs, problems and approaches necessary for work with older people. We also ask them to commit themselves to a further year of voluntary work for us after they achieve their diploma.

The third is a smaller group of people who apply from the statutory and other voluntary bodies wishing to better their own understanding of and dealings with older people without becoming volunteers. These have come from other network agencies, the RNID (Royal National Institute for Deaf People), Help the Aged, Society for the Blind, local councils, community nursing or other caring professionals.

A nominal fee to cover the costs is charged to each participant. In order to develop personal contact and team spirit, numbers are restricted to ten volunteers and two non-Age Concern applicants in each course. This costs £250 for the first two parts of the course and is halved for those who apply to become volunteer counsellors for Age Concern.

Team spirit

In order to stimulate a team spirit and to prevent volunteers feeling that they are single individuals out on a limb, a monthly newsletter is sent to all the counsellors and past course members detailing items of local counselling news, information and policy changes, etc.

There is also a regular support group meeting, which all counsellors are expected to attend one afternoon a month. At these meetings, information about Age Concern services and changes in legislation or other local news is given, problems or progress in cases are discussed and a short teaching spot is included. This last named may include anything which may broaden knowledge to help volunteers to improve their counselling skills.

Supervision and accountability

In the early days, the Counselling Service was managed by a co-ordinator who matched clients to counsellors and utilised local professionals to provide support, advice and supervision. However, with the expansion of the scheme, the number of sympathetic qualified counsellors who could give of their time and expertise in this way became limited.

The only practical answer was to provide the necessary supervision in-house by senior counsellors within the organisation who had achieved a counselling diploma or had more than five years' experience in counselling and supervision.

Each two counsellors are now paired up by the manager to meet for an hour each month with their personal supervisor, who is at a higher level of training and experience than the supervisees. Each counsellor shares any concerns they may have about their case(s) with the supervisor for half an hour and then listens to the case(s) of the other counsellor. Thus the knowledge and experience of each is doubled.

Supervision is highly important, having three main benefits:

- It ensures that the counselling is in keeping with our organisation policies and that practical issues are being helpfully dealt with or referred on appropriately.
- It improves one's effectiveness as a counsellor by maintaining ethical and professional standards, helping to focus on key issues, enhancing confidence and constructive thinking about the client.
- It is also a good measure to prevent stagnation and burnout.

In 1994, the Counselling Service became a member organisation of the British Association for Counselling (BAC) and conforms to its *Code of Ethics and Practice for Counsellors* (1996), giving special emphasis to supervision and confidentiality. This accountability increased the respect and status the service held in the eyes of local medical and social services.

After the referral of a client, the manager makes an initial assessment in the person's home, which can give more insights into aspects of their personality, self-caring attitudes and needs than an impersonal interview in an office. In addition, it has been found that the client's home provides a more relaxed atmosphere for carrying out an assessment and the subsequent counselling sessions.

After initial assessments, the manager allocates counsellors of suitable background, training and experience to clients. Counsellors are asked if they are able and willing to take on the people concerned, taking into account their overall workload. As a general rule, we suggest that the maximum number taken on is four at any one time, bearing in mind that past clients from whom they have disengaged may request further help.

Referral sources

Since the nationwide local health authority directives to GPs in 1989, it is to the advantage of GPs to have contact with all their registered patients over the age of 75 at least once a year in order to qualify for a performance payment. Consequently, busy GPs went through their lists of patients and sent health visitors to see those with whom they had no recent contact.

It may be that some of these people are semi-immobile and unwilling to go outside their homes. There are those who have not visited their GPs for many years though they may have medical conditions, such as chest pains, arthritis, eye or ear problems which have slowly deteriorated until they reach dangerous levels and then prevent the sufferer from going out. On checking, the health visitor may find needs which are complicated and a mixture of medical and emotional problems. Ten per cent of our referrals come, therefore, from GPs or their health visitors, who may feel that counselling is a more effective and cheaper therapy than quantities of tranquillisers or anti-depressants. Although some surgeries now employ their own counsellors, we still get a fair proportion of referrals this way, especially for home visits.

A larger number of referrals come from hospitals. In conversation with nurses or the registrar, the older person's home circumstances are investigated, possibly revealing that they are very anxious about the future, living by themselves without homecare, or perhaps suffering from unresolved grief. Thirty-two per cent of our referrals come from ward sisters and key nurses who recommend the Counselling Service to these patients.

Social workers in hospitals are also concerned to ensure that a care plan is in place when the patient returns home. Other clients are visited by social workers at home through requests to their local offices. We co-operate closely with both of these departments in a two-way process.

A further 13 per cent of our referrals come from them and similarly we make referrals to them for practical help when it is beyond our means.

A further 25 per cent are self-referrals – individuals who either know of the service or are recommended to it by neighbours, friends or family. Some are at their wits' end and search through the business section of the phone book or *Yellow Pages* for someone to ask for help. Others pick up our information leaflets in hospital wards, GP surgeries or the local library. We are now also on the local MIND, Community Voluntary Services, Citizen's Advice Bureau and Disability Information Service databases, which supply information about local organisations and services in the area.

One of the objections to the establishment of such a counselling service, especially for older people, is that there are already other voluntary agencies dealing with similar problems – for example, Cruse for bereavement, MIND for mental illness, RELATE for marital difficulties, ACAD (Alcohol Advisory Centre) and AA (Alcoholics Anonymous) for alcohol abuse and the Samaritans and Victim Support for despair and the follow-up of trauma. In such clear-cut situations, we refer a client to the appropriate agency. But conversely, a final 20 per cent of referrals come *from* these other voluntary groups when Age Concern's broader range of services is more appropriate.

Some of the referrals come concerning those who act as carers for an older person, often a housebound relative needing care 24 hours a day, seven days a week. These carers are often stretched to the limit but do not readily ask for help, though facing difficult problems and in need of respite care and encouragement to manage their task sensibly.

Practical considerations

Guidelines

Because the Counselling Service was a small operation it was possible at the beginning to keep informal checks on what everyone was doing, but as the service enlarged, more organisation and structure became necessary. Consequently, a set of guidelines was drawn up to formulate the way in which we wished the service to function. These were not hard-and-fast rules, but a statement of procedures, support network and reporting back that we had proved to work well. The guidelines are reviewed annually and changes made when necessary.

The present guidelines include statements on each of the following areas:

- the requirements of training, appointment and resignation;
- our commitment to Age Concern;
- client referrals, assessments, contracts and reviews;
- the number of clients recommended for each counsellor;
- visiting procedure and charges;
- respect for personal beliefs;
- supervision and support group meetings;
- disengagement from clients;
- suicide intervention;
- confidentiality;
- complaints and complements procedure;
- identity card;
- insurance;
- expenses;
- a declaration for the counsellors to sign affirming their acceptance of the guidelines.

Most of these are commonsense and generally-accepted procedures, but it is important and helpful to have a signed written agreement, especially regarding requirements of confidentiality.

General organisation

In the year from January 1996, the Counselling Service received and dealt with over 1,250 general enquiries, often of a practical nature, by phone, averaging 100 per month. Such enquiries range from requests for information about mobile hairdressers to finding a gardener or someone to change a light bulb. Most are dealt with immediately over the telephone or passed on to our Community Support Scheme, or other appropriate action is taken. But when an enquirer or referral warrants an assessment visit because of an emotional problem, contact is made with the prospective client within 24 hours and an appointment made to visit them for a counselling assessment as soon as possible, usually the same week. In the year 1996/97, 128 such visits were made and the people concerned taken on as clients or referred elsewhere. After the visit, the referee is advised by telephone or letter of the result and the action being taken. (See 'Flowchart of Client Referrals', Appendix B, on p 223).

For daily review, a dry-wipe wall chart, showing the names of all the counsellors with their clients, is kept privately in the manager's office. This greatly helps the selection and allocation of available counsellors. Visits to clients by counsellors are generally for approximately one hour weekly. A verbal contract is made with the client to visit initially for a six- to eight-week period and certain actions and goals are agreed with the client on the understanding that the counsellor will withdraw when these have been achieved. We try to make our counselling short to medium term (three to six months), with reviews every six weeks. However, some situations, especially involving bereavement, may well take up to a year or more.

Feelings of non-compatibility between clients and counsellors are important and taken into account. Should the counsellor discover that the client or client's family is known to him or her, it is likewise reported to the manager who will allocate another counsellor if appropriate.

Counsellors are also asked to forward brief monthly reports summarising the sessions and detailing all visits, phone calls and letters. The records are kept in a locked filing cabinet and destroyed after seven years. Some volunteers may at first feel that this has bureaucratic overtones, but we have found it essential to maintain accurate records which are the mark of an accountable and professional service. Statistics gained from these enable the total operation of the service to be evaluated and the tasks of producing annual reports and local funding applications are made easier.

We expect to reimburse out-of-pocket basic travel expenses, phone calls and postage to counsellors. Some who kindly do not wish to receive reimbursement nevertheless complete the claim form with a request to treat the amount as a gift to Age Concern Bath funds so that a full and reliable costing of the service can be made.

Problem areas
Finance

With the introduction of local Care in the Community plans on 1 April 1993, which put the emphasis on sustaining and supporting older people in their homes, client demand rose and the cost of administration and travel went up proportionately. This posed an increasing problem. At that time, the overall cost of running the service was £10,000 per annum (now £14,000), which included salaries, rent, stationery, publicity and volunteer expenses. About a quarter of the income needed came directly from course fees and gifts from grateful clients. But the remainder had to be made available from the general funds of the Mayor of Bath's Age Concern (MOBAC) which was being sorely overstretched.

The Executive Committee of MOBAC therefore decided to introduce a nominal charge of £3 for every counsellor visit to those clients who could afford it. Those receiving Income Support were automatically exempt and the manager had discretion not to charge others receiving Housing Benefit. This was in line with charges that were introduced at that time by social services for homecare workers. However, it was not in keeping with the older persons' culture to think of paying someone 'just to sit and talk' as they viewed it. Furthermore, it proved difficult to request payment from people with suicidal tendencies and those in shock after a traumatic event such as a bereavement or a burglary.

A number of clients reacted by deciding that they could manage without further counselling. As news of the charge was passed on to the referring agencies, the number of people willing to be referred also dropped off dramatically. From a peak of 72 active clients in October 1993, the numbers fell to 21 over the next five months. As this was proving counter-productive, leaving clients without help but still with their needs, we found ourselves forced to drop the charges and encourage clients to make a donation as and when they were able.

In the following year, 1994, approaches were made to all the GP surgeries suggesting that fund-holding GPs might like to avail themselves of our extremely cost-effective service by means of a contract for counselling their less mobile older patients at home. This evoked some interest but no takers. However, they, along with our other main referees, continued to refer clients to the service – at no cost to themselves.

In appreciation of our work, social services made a grant to us of £2,320 the following year, but unfortunately, because of council cutbacks, this has now been withdrawn.

Under the new county boundary re-organisation, we are now asked to extend our service to meet the unmet needs in North East Somerset. This means even more referrals and the recruitment and training of more volunteers from the area itself, as the service is presently stretched to the limit coping with Bath alone.

If individual Care in the Community plans are to work in practice, then the appropriate funding has to be made available to those who have proved their value over the years. The measure of support we will be able to give to others will be in direct proportion to the support that is given to us. As a registered charity, most of our income comes from gifts, legacies or donations from local businesses and trust funds. We also receive a few grants which involve time-consuming lengthy applications, but which are rarely successful. Without funding, however, it is not possible to do the job – and unfortunately our National Lottery application never came up! Nevertheless, we are determined to carry on and do the best we can.

Confidentiality

Another problem area is the subject of confidentiality. In this, we follow the British Association for Counselling (BAC) *Code of Ethics and Practice for Counsellors* (1996). We stipulate in our guidelines that clients should be informed at the outset that whatever they tell us is in the strictest confidence and will not be passed on *outside the organisation* unless it is in their best interests, and then only with their permission. Two exceptions to this rule are:

- In order to prevent serious harm to the client or another person, especially in life-threatening situations.
- When legally required to break confidentiality, for example, if there are criminal implications in cases of serious fraud, abuse, murder or terrorism.

However, it is also made clear to clients that as part of the support and supervision structure *within the organisation*, counsellors are expected to discuss individual cases with their supervisors, the manager and with other counsellors at support group meetings. These discussions will, however, be anonymous and the other members are similarly bound by confidentiality.

Though it is debatable whether volunteers can be asked to sign a formal work contract, in order to protect ourselves legally as far as possible, we ask all counsellors to sign a declaration in which they undertake to adhere to the principles and policies contained in the guidelines while they are voluntary counsellors for Age Concern Bath and that they will also agree to the restrictions regarding confidentiality in perpetuity.

Practical examples

Many examples could be given of how the Counselling Service has been helpful to older people. Of the many hundreds we have been able to help over the past ten years, the following examples will give some idea of the kind of situations we have been involved with and how effective counselling has proved. To preserve anonymity, no names are given and some of the details have been changed, but the stories are based on actual clients and given here by permission.

Loneliness

Mrs A, aged 84, had been taken into hospital after falling unconscious in the street. It was suspected that she had a drink problem. She did not talk much, but when she did, she mainly complained that she was very lonely. She said that all her family and friends had died and that she was the only one left. It was difficult to contact her because she had no telephone, but a visit to her home found her sitting by herself and having little or no contact with the neighbours. She had no heating apart from a coal fire which was alight in May when the outside temperature was 75°F. The flat was poorly lit and in need of redecoration. Though quite active, she complained that the younger locals who had moved into the neighbourhood flats were not very friendly. Altogether, she presented a sad and forlorn picture.

We contacted a local Healthy Homes Energy Scheme with a view to having her flat upgraded and arranged a weekly visit by a counsellor to whom she was able to off-load her feelings. After three months, she became much more relaxed and chatty. No evidence of a drink problem was found. She was very independent and liked to fend for herself. When it was suggested that she might like to go to a nearby luncheon club, she made excuses, and, as she was happier staying at home and seemed to welcome visitors, a befriender was found to call in for a chat periodically, to provide support and seek to encourage eventual greater socialisation.

Real anxiety

Mrs B, in her late 70s, walks with a stick and is registered blind (though she can make out blurred images). She lived in a flat over some shops in town, but became 'a bundle of nerves' after the shops downstairs were burgled twice in a fortnight. Although she heard and saw the intruders through a window, she did nothing for fear of reprisals. When visited by Age Concern, she was almost hysterical about the vulnerability of her flat. However, she calmed down when assurances were given that we would contact the council to provide greater security than a common night latch on her front door. She was very independent and had lived in the flat for 17 years. The sense of security this familiarity gave her was now threatened.

The council agreed to put in a higher grade security lock on the front door immediately and promised to fit a door-entry system eventually. Counselling in this case went on for two years as the process opened up many old wounds with which she was slowly able to come to terms through cognitive therapy. However, the fear of further burglaries kept re-appearing and after carefully going into all the alternative options, she was helped to apply for and move into sheltered accommodation nearby. She has now happily settled there where she has made a few new friends and her old friends can still visit. She feels secure and thankful that, as her health is getting worse, she is in a place where she feels safe and looked after, whilst retaining the independence of her own flat.

Perceived anxiety

A local city councillor took up the case of Mrs C, aged 78, referring her to us because she was very distraught and worrying him with letters and phone calls. She imagined that someone was entering her flat through the loft and stealing things at night. This became an obsessive fixation and when we tried to reason it out with her, she would just curl up against the wall and cry. Her growing obsession and the involvement of the police (whom she habitually called out at night) frightened her daughter who was getting blamed for disbelief and leaving her in the lurch. The daughter could not cope with what was happening so also asked for counselling. Ultimately, the mother's GP and social services were called in and 'sectioned' her under the Mental Health Act (1983) and she went into hospital.

The daughter experienced a backlash of guilt (wondering what she could have done to prevent it), fear (for her mother's future and possibly her own) and confusion (the unknown possibilities). She needed help to understand that she was in no way responsible for her mother's actions which were due to a medical condition now being successfully treated. The support at that time from one of our counsellors gave her the re-assurance she needed to pull through and see the situation objectively.

On the mother's discharge from hospital into sheltered accommodation, we were asked if we could help her to settle in there. A community psychiatric nurse and a social worker continued to monitor her medication and moods and we helped her to come to terms with the situation and develop a happier frame of mind through positive thinking and the release of some of her past hurts. She still has occasional doubts and depression, but overall is moving forward now to enjoy the rest of her life. Happily, the relationship with her daughter is much improved. They accept that they each have their own lives to live, but their friendship is restored and the daughter visits regularly.

Depression

Mrs D, in her early 80s, was referred to us by a social worker because her husband, to whom she had been married for nearly 60 years, had been taken into a nursing home with dementia. It had left an enormous gap in her life as she had spent all her time in recent years caring for her husband. She now felt empty and exhausted. She did have a son, but was not on very good terms with him. She had no other family or friends to tell how she felt, which she described as 'desperately alone and bereaved'. She fell into severe depression and did not want to go out or do anything. She merely sat at home alone and cried day after day.

A counsellor went to visit her every week for six months, enabling her to talk through her feelings and adjust to the situation. The counsellor made sure that she was eating properly and organised meals-on-wheels for her. She also encouraged her to resume happier relations with her son, which, though traumatic to begin with, ended with a satisfactory solution. This lifted her mood of despondency considerably and the counsellor was able to disengage after the client started going to a day centre twice a week.

Bereavement

Mrs E, aged 76, lost her husband about four years ago. They were a devoted couple who did almost everything together, so when he died she was devastated and saw no point in living any more. Soon after his death, she was offered alternative accommodation in a warden-controlled complex and moved there a month later. However, having moved away from friends and neighbours, she found herself in a new community where she did not know anyone and found it difficult to talk to people. So she retired into her shell and became even more lonely.

The following Christmas was a particularly difficult time for her and the warden contacted Age Concern to see if we could provide counselling for her – this was the first Christmas without her husband and she talked several times about 'putting an end to it all.'

Her bungalow flat was at the end of a cul-de-sac, so she rarely saw anyone but her immediate neighbours. When attempts were made to encourage her to make contact with them, she complained, 'Everyone around me is over 80 and so old'. She looked out at the walls of other houses at the front and a bare fence at the back. She felt that moving somewhere else was the only answer.

The counsellor found that whilst her main problem seemed to be loneliness, she had not been able to talk properly about her grief with anyone and she was very anxious about the future. She was sinking deeper and deeper into depression.

Encouraging her to talk about the many happy experiences she had shared with her husband in the past enabled her to accept his death and she began making the most of the present by linking up with a local club. This provided her with the social contact and new friends she needed. The view at the back was improved by having the garden planted with bulbs and bushes so she could look forward to seeing flowers in the spring.

Now she has been there for three years and is more contented and comfortable – with a beautifully decorated home that she takes pride in keeping clean and neat and which she knows would have pleased her husband. She recently said to someone, 'Age Concern was an absolute godsend to me at the time. I had just about given up all hope and I certainly wouldn't be here now if it wasn't for them.'

Conclusions

Our experience in Bath has convinced us of the vast need everywhere for counselling services specialising in the needs of older people. In an ever-increasing ageing population, more and more older people will have very demanding emotional as well as practical needs. Sometimes these people will be on their own or have families who feel inadequate to deal with the situation and will therefore require professional help.

This support for older people can be given in large measure through counselling services. Ideally, this can best be done by organisations like Age Concern who have the other resource services necessary to cope with the practical issues.

An adequate on-going training and support network are the keys to an effective and flourishing counselling service. However, it is better to provide a good quality service for a fewer number than to spread resources too thinly and prove less effective.

If 'Care in the Community' is to work in practice, then the appropriate funding has to be made to those who are trained and equipped to undertake it. This in turn necessitates adequate Government funding being ring-fenced for the provisions of its own legislation.

Appendix A

The Induction Course in Counselling Older People Programme for Age Concern Bath and North East Somerset

The course, consisting of two parts, with a week's break expected in-between for half-term, is as follows:

PART ONE		COUNSELLING PRINCIPLES AND PRACTICE
Week	Session	Subject
1	1	Introduction to Age Concern (B&NES) What is Counselling?
	2	Guidelines for Volunteers What Makes a Good Counsellor?
2	3	The Psychology of Ageing Life Stages
	4	Problems Affecting Older People Age and Identity
3	5	Self-awareness Relative to Counselling
	6	Stages in Counselling
4	7	Active Listening & Questioning Skills
	8	Reflecting Back & Summarising
5	9	Egan's Model of Counselling & Challenging Skills
	10	Video of the Egan Model
6	11	Counselling Dangers – Emotional Fatigue (Burnout)
	12	Counselling Dangers – Emotional Dependency
7	13	Helping People with their Emotions
	14	Body Language Summary Review

Appendix B

Flowchart of Client Referrals to Age Concern Bath and North East Somerset Counselling Service

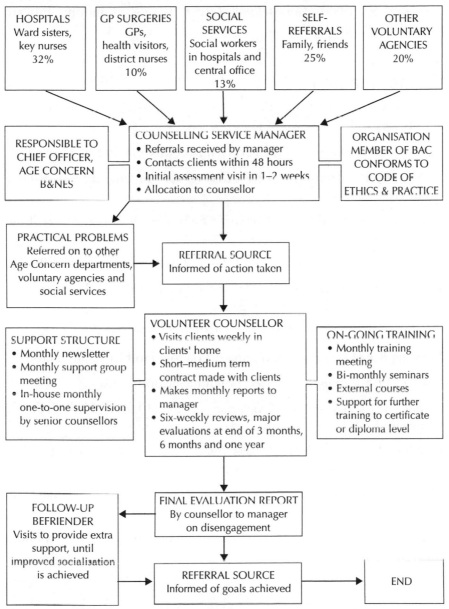

HOSPITALS
Ward sisters,
key nurses
32%

GP SURGERIES
GPs,
health visitors,
district nurses
10%

SOCIAL
SERVICES
Social workers
in hospitals and
central office
13%

SELF-
REFERRALS
Family, friends
25%

OTHER
VOLUNTARY
AGENCIES
20%

RESPONSIBLE TO
CHIEF OFFICER,
AGE CONCERN
B&NES

COUNSELLING SERVICE MANAGER
• Referrals received by manager
• Contacts clients within 48 hours
• Initial assessment visit in 1–2 weeks
• Allocation to counsellor

ORGANISATION
MEMBER OF BAC
CONFORMS TO
CODE OF
ETHICS & PRACTICE

PRACTICAL PROBLEMS
Referred on to other
Age Concern departments,
voluntary agencies and
social services

REFERRAL SOURCE
Informed of action taken

SUPPORT STRUCTURE
• Monthly newsletter
• Monthly support group
  meeting
• In-house monthly
  one-to-one supervision
  by senior counsellors

VOLUNTEER COUNSELLOR
• Visits clients weekly in
  clients' home
• Short–medium term
  contract made with clients
• Makes monthly reports to
  manager
• Six-weekly reviews, major
  evaluations at end of 3 months,
  6 months and one year

ON-GOING TRAINING
• Monthly training
  meeting
• Bi-monthly seminars
• External courses
• Support for further
  training to certificate
  or diploma level

FOLLOW-UP
BEFRIENDER
Visits to provide extra
support, until
improved socialisation
is achieved

FINAL EVALUATION REPORT
By counsellor to manager
on disengagement

REFERRAL SOURCE
Informed of goals achieved

END

References

British Association for Counselling (1996) *Code of Ethics and Practice for Counsellors*. Rugby: British Association for Counselling.

Scrutton S (1989) *Counselling Older People*. London: Edward Arnold/Age Concern Books.

Further reading

Eastman M (1994) *Old Age Abuse - A new perspective*. London: Age Concern Books with Chapman & Hall.

Egan G (1994) *The Skilled Helper*. CA: Brooks/Cole, Pacific Grove.

Eunson K, Henderson M (1997) *Coping with Shyness and Loneliness*. Edinburgh: Chambers.

France R, Robson M (1997) *Cognitive Behaviour in Primary Care*. London: Jessica Kingsley.

Gibson F (1994) *Reminiscence and Recall*. London: Age Concern Books.

Gillett R (1987) *Overcoming Depression*. London: British Holistic Medical Association and Dorling Kindersley.

Hughes S (1987) *A Friend in Need*. Eastbourne: Kingsway.

Hurding R F (1985) *Roots and Shoots*. London: Hodder & Stoughton.

Lake T (1985) *Living with Grief*. London: Sheldon Press.

Madders J (1979) *Stress and Relaxation*. London: Optima, Little Brown & Company.

Marriott V, Timblick T (1988) *Loneliness: How to overcome it*. London: Age Concern Books (now out of print).

Meredith B (1993) *The Community Care Handbook*. London: Age Concern Books.

Mitchell L (1988) *The Magic of Movement*. London: Age Concern Books (now out of print).

Murgatroyd S (1985) *Counselling and Helping.* London: British Psychological Society and Methuen.

Nelson-Jones R (1995) *The Theory and Practice of Counselling.* London: Cassell.

O'Leary F (1996) *Counselling Older Adults.* London: Chapman & Hall.

Scrutton S (1989) *Counselling Older People: A creative response to ageing.* London: Edward Arnold.

Tennyson L (1996) *Developing and Running Counselling Services: A 'how to' guide.* London: Age Concern England.

Worden J W (1991) *Grief Counselling and Grief Therapy* (2nd Edition). London: Routledge.

In Praise of Memory

In the practice of counselling, memories form a vital part of the material we work with. Along with dreams, moods, fantasies, affections, antipathies and habits of behaviour, they can bring to light patterns buried in the unconscious mind, some of which are positive and life-enhancing while others have a destructive quality and, if not addressed, can damage relationships, hamper creativity and create psychological blockages that will prevent an easy flow of energy through the past and the present towards the future.

The experience of sharing your memories in a therapeutic setting, when you will be telling your story to a relative stranger and at the same time hearing it afresh yourself, can in itself bring relief and a change of attitude. But that is just the start of the process. In order to demonstrate one way of working effectively with memories in therapy (there are of course other ways) I am asking you to accept for a moment a set of hypotheses. The first one is that we are the product of our past, at any given moment living the sum total of what has gone on in earlier stages of life, decisions we have made, risks we have taken or avoided, problems we have or have not faced, injuries we have sustained or caused. To change our present circumstances can therefore demand a change in our attitude towards, and our involvement in, our own history. That statement may well seem self-evident. But the second hypothesis could prove more challenging: that the past is still in some sense alive – more like an enactment taking place behind closed doors than it is like the pages of yesterday's diary. And the third hypothesis – more startling, perhaps – is that if we go about it in the right way we can open the closed doors and enter the theatre, and by so doing interrupt the drama that is being enacted and change forever the shape of that particular story.

Let me bring this down to earth by returning to the story of Tolstoy and his recovered memory of having been, as a baby, prevented from stretching his limbs. In recounting the incident, Esther Salaman (1970) had noted the effect this episode evidently had on the patterns within his marriage in later years, when the tension between domesticity and the desire for liberty became extreme. Now, if you were Tolstoy and you decided to talk to me professionally I would naturally regard this memory as a very important part of your background. I would also hear the story, not just as a sad tale of ineffectual childcare, but as a plea, a petition that had now become a repetition, a part of your nature begging for attention and doing so, not simply through the recovered memory, but also through its echoes in later patterns of experience. I might therefore ask you to imagine what you would want to do if you were to hear the cries of a child next door, whose parents were exercising undue restraint on its movements. And having made that connection with your compassion and your readiness to act as a mediator, you would then be invited by me to imagine entering, in your own memory, the room where the baby is fighting to free itself, and to imagine living as fully as possible your role as the rescuing newcomer, giving central importance to the plight of the baby whose champion you have become. Perhaps you would argue with the two adult figures, perhaps ignore them? But you would certainly want to pick up the baby, comfort him, remove the trapping garments and restore his freedom to move his body as he pleases. You would watch his face, sharing his joy and his sense of relief. Finally, you might possibly replace the garments, but with kindness and accompanied by an explanation. After that I would ask you to repeat exactly the same episode, but this time from the point of view of the baby, whose rage, surprise and delight would then become your own. By moving the story on in this way two mighty forces, freedom and restraint, will begin to become partners, no longer needing to work out their quarrel in the repeated tangles of everyday life. The exercise – a form of what Jung (1961) called 'active imagination' – would probably have to be repeated over a period of time, but each time the new pattern would become stronger, the transformation more perceptible.

I sometimes think of such memories – and Tolstoy was not alone in being at their mercy – as black balloons, intact and self-perpetuating, exercising a baleful influence only until the skin has been punctured and the toxic energy allowed to disperse. Then and only then can the story cease to repeat itself. Imagination is the ally that helps us to penetrate the balloon, to visit the memory and thus allow the troubled story to take a new direction. A fourth hypothesis then presents itself: that the baby you once were is still alive and fully conscious, as is the older child, the teenager, the young adult, and so forth, and that these earlier consciousnesses, though lacking an appropriate body, are in every other way utterly real. They are, I believe, asking for a symbolic second chance, the opportunity to shed the traumas of the past in which they have been cocooned and to contribute their gifts – for example playfulness, trust, assertiveness or enthusiasm – to the life we are currently living. I am suggesting that we can use our memories as opportunities to reach earlier selves, trapped as prisoners in a wasteland of unresolved moments of pain and injustice. The liberation we offer comes in the form of respect and recognition, warmed by that most elusive yet simple of energies – love. It may be that love alone can heal our relationship with our past selves, just as it can heal our relationship with the world around us.

Our memories and our dreams point us to the need for transformation, while imagination gives us the power to make it happen. As we have seen, a memory can become the basis for a dialogue with the diverse inhabitants of our inner world, the 'people' who compose our nature, rather as individual planets form part of our solar system. So your memory of an unfair punishment, say, or mine of a broken promise, can become springboards, moving us through the pain into a state of reconciliation, beyond which lies the psychic wholeness that is our destiny.

And by the way, I am thankful that Tolstoy, that great and gifted writer, never as far as I know came near a consulting room like mine. The path of a genius is not to be defined, and therapy is after all only one of many ways leading towards inner harmony. And for all we know, the price of Tolstoy's freedom from conflict might have been – no *War and Peace*.

(Sheila Willson)

References

Jung C G (1961) *Memories, Dreams, Reflections.* Recorded and edited by Aniela Jaffé. London: Collins and Routledge and Kegan Paul.

Salaman E (1970) *A Collection of Moments.* London: Longman.

Telephone Helplines and Support Work

Tui Grimmer-Fleming

Editor's Introduction

The telephone can be a very impersonal machine, but this very fact can also be helpful. Tui Grimmer-Fleming has worked for several years as a volunteer on a telephone helpline, and this has led her to train further in counselling and psychology.

Many older people rely on the telephone for their contact with 'the world'. Even when we know a person well, it is possible to use telephone support skills in a conversational setting with friends, neighbours and relatives. We may think we know our friends and relations well, but when we really begin to listen, we may be able to perceive the feelings behind the words.

In this chapter, Tui shares with readers her insights and skills in a way that confirms what we know already and encourages what we may need to learn.

Introduction

The telephone is an integral part of our lives and for many older people it is their only contact with the 'outside world'. In this chapter on telephone helplines and telephone support work I shall outline the different types of helplines and consider what help they offer. I will discuss volunteers and training. Most of us, whether as friend or relative of a troubled person, have at some time acted as a trusted advisor during a telephone conversation, so in the last part of the chapter I shall explore the skills necessary for effective telephone support work. These skills do not require any particular areas of expertise and are based on common sense.

For many older people the decision to telephone a helpline is the first step they have taken (for some the first in their lives) in seeking help. It may be stating the obvious, but the help that is available depends on the help that is sought by the caller and on the resources and abilities of the organisation called. Most agencies restrict their work to one issue and become experts in that field, but funding will often dictate the extent to which they can offer practical help. The *Telephone Helplines Directory* contains details of around a thousand national, regional and local telephone helplines throughout the UK. All the organisations listed offer telephone services which include advice, information and listening support on a wide range of subjects. (For more details on the *Telephone Helplines Directory*, contact the Telephone Helplines' Association at the address on p 249.)

There are also a huge number of commercial organisations which have renamed their 'hotlines' as 'helplines' (how to programme your video recorder, etc), so caller expectations can be confused as to the outcome of any call. Some of the confusion arises because implied in the name 'helpline' is the expectancy that the agency will do something on the caller's behalf. This is rarely the case, as most agencies have a philosophy of enabling and empowering callers to help themselves. It may therefore be useful to consider the different types of helplines.

Some helplines, such as those set up by hospitals, are information lines only. As an example, most hospitals have a pharmacy helpline operated by a trained pharmacist who can give qualified information on dosage or side-effects of prescribed medicines. Other medical helplines which deal with a specific illness are usually staffed by volunteers who have suffered, or cared for someone who has suffered, from that particular illness and so have intimate knowledge of the caller's problem.

Helplines which deal with State benefits, legal matters or civil rights usually have paid staff who have the expertise necessary to explain the law. The anonymity of the telephone is particularly helpful for these agencies who are able to give impartial advice to callers about disputes or bad practice at work.

Probably the best-known helpline is the Samaritans, whose work could be described as 'therapeutic listening'. Most helplines are operated by a mixture of trained volunteers and paid staff who are able to give detailed information and offer listening support.

Volunteers and training

Some helplines advertise for volunteer operators and others use the services of counselling students who are gaining work experience; most, however, rely on the goodwill of people who have a personal interest in the work of a particular charity. Often a volunteer's involvement with a helpline will begin with a telephone call to an agency asking if they need any help. There are no particular qualifications or experience necessary to become a helpline operator, but it is important to take all callers seriously and to let them know you are prepared to listen and care.

All charities or agencies operating helplines offer training for the skills that the agency feels are necessary for a 'helpliner' to respond effectively to calls. Essentially these skills include being able to:

- respond to callers in a calm and mature manner;
- listen effectively;
- maintain confidentiality;
- possess good verbal communication skills;
- cope with distressing information.

Agencies which use volunteers are careful about giving advice. Most will train their volunteers to offer information or to suggest options, because the volunteer is not an expert. A volunteer who spends most of his or her time preaching or telling callers what to do for their 'own good' would not make an appropriate helpliner. The acceptance necessary in supportive telephone work means putting aside these feelings and allowing people to help themselves.

Telephone support skills

By its nature, the telephone allows the lack of intimacy that many people would find daunting or frightening in a face-to-face interview. The telephone gives the caller control and creates a distance. The anonymity of the telephone can in some cases allow the caller to breach family loyalties and confidences which would not be possible if the caller could be seen.

Many people call a helpline when they feel desperate, helpless, isolated or powerless (Rosenfield 1996). The main difference between talking to someone on the telephone and being a helpliner is in the approach. A helpliner does not have a conversation with a caller; her or his role is to give support by sensitively reflecting the caller's concerns.

The main reason why some people prefer to talk about their problems on the telephone is that they can release emotion in private, and this privacy should be respected. Egan (1995) points out that in the social nature of humankind the deepest need is the need for respect. Respect is such a fundamental notion that it eludes definition. Egan calls it 'prizing' people, just because they are human.

Although there is no specific approach or model given to the practice of telephone support work, the concepts of person-centred counselling are practised in that the skills are based on the core values of the Rogerian approach (Rogers 1967); that is, empathic understanding, congruence and unconditional positive regard (see Chapter 9, pp 163–166, for more about core values). A formula for demonstrating telephone empathy is suggested by Rosenfield (1996):

'It sounds to me as if ...'

'What I'm hearing from you is ...'

'You seem to be saying ...'

These phrases convey to the caller that the helpliner has an accurate perception of what the caller is feeling and why.

If the telephone is held in your left hand, you are more likely to use your right brain function for feelings and to explore (Stewart 1992); if the telephone is held in your right hand, you are more likely to use your left brain to analyse and be precise. Empathy is more right than left brain orientated.

Congruence and unconditional positive regard can be difficult to convey over the telephone and the helpliner needs to be aware of attitudes which can affect the warmth of acceptance and genuineness. Some of these attitudes are:

- mind-reading: assuming or finishing sentences;
- rehearsing: preparing what to say or thinking of what to say;
- filtering: avoiding comments, hearing only what you want to hear;
- dreaming: only half-listening, trigger words set off memories;
- identifying: referring everything back to your own experience;
- advising: you hear a few sentences and you have the answer;
- sparring: arguing and debating, quick to disagree;
- derailing: suddenly changing the subject;
- placating: being indifferent – 'Right', 'Absolutely', 'How awful'.
(Rowe 1996)

Active listening

All telephone support work requires active listening. It is the fundamental skill of listening with a purpose. Listening is a complex and multiple skill. It involves attending to, hearing and understanding the messages which the caller is sending, both verbally and non-verbally. The purpose of listening is to facilitate understanding between you and the caller and to reach a common agreement about what concerns them and how they experience their concerns. However, when you are listening, you are not a sponge, soaking up information and messages indiscriminately (Munro *et al* 1983). The amount of information passing between you will be too great for you to pick up and respond to every cue and clue, therefore you will be doing several things: you will be sorting the information and deciding what to respond to; you will be forming hypotheses about what the caller is saying as well as what he or she is omitting, and you will be seeking clarification of aspects which are unclear. In other words, you will be listening 'actively'.

Active listening is no different whether on the telephone or face-to-face. However, there are difficulties on the telephone due to the lack of visual clues, making it essential not only to listen to what the caller says but also to hear what is not openly said – the non-verbal language and non-verbal messages. This is sometimes referred to as the 'background music' and it is necessary to tune into what the caller is not saying, as sometimes the tone of voice and the words do not seem to be saying the same things. For example:

Caller: 'He's driving me crazy, he questions everything I do.'

Helpliner: 'I can hear the despair in your voice, it sounds to me as if he is always under your feet.'

Although the helpliner may be actively listening, blocks to effective listening can occur when:

- their culture, education or life experience is different from yours;
- they speak with a strong accent or use words you do not understand;
- you have heard the same story before or the outcome is not good;
- you decide you dislike the person or their views;
- your emotions get in the way or your values are under attack;
- the thoughts or feelings expressed shock you or cause anxiety;
- you realise you are out of your depth or have to admit an error;
- you are experiencing discomfort (physical, emotional, social).

(CancerLink 1996)

Use 'Mmm', 'I see' and 'Aha' to convey you are listening during pauses when the caller speaks, otherwise the caller can feel as if you are 'not there'. This is sometimes referred to as the equivalent of maintaining eye contact. To understand the importance of these interjections, try this simple exercise. Place two chairs back-to-back, have another person sit on one chair and yourself on the other. The other person remains silent for two minutes while you talk. You know the other person is there, but what is he or she doing? Is she interested, bored or what? Is she even listening?

The helpliner should be aware that non-verbal language is always being transmitted and too much note-taking or doodling can sometimes be 'heard' by the caller.

Essential skills

Reflecting, paraphrasing and summarising are techniques which are used to convey active listening. These are essential skills which anyone involved in supportive work must develop, but whereas in face-to-face counselling these skills may be used only occasionally during a session, reflecting and paraphrasing are in constant use in telephone support work as they help to replace body language (eye contact, facial expression and nodding).

In telephone work, reflecting conveys to callers that you have heard correctly and accurately. Paraphrasing can be useful to simplify what a caller is saying. For example:

Caller: 'It's so easy to talk about my feelings to you. My family thinks I'm just being a silly old woman.'

Helpliner: 'So you prefer not to talk about your feelings to your family because they dismiss them but you feel you can talk to me.'

It can be helpful to preface reflecting with a phrase such as 'It seems as if …', 'It sounds like …', 'So, what you are saying is …' which give callers a non-threatening opportunity to correct you if you are wrong or if they disagree with what you are saying.

Call structure/framework

Most calls are handled using a version of Egan's (1995) three-stage helping model of clarification, forming new perspectives and devising new strategies (see pp 178–179). The call should loosely follow such a three-stage framework:

1 Establish rapport. Active listening.
2 Exploration and clarification. Gather information, open questions.
3 Action and end. Caller options. Summarising.

The immediacy of the telephone means that accepting and believing what the caller says is vital if the helpliner is to offer effective help. It is also necessary quickly to establish a rapport with the caller to enable them to talk freely, bearing in mind it may have taken a great deal of courage to make the call. The best way to do this is to imagine you are meeting the person face-to-face, so look welcoming and greet the caller with warmth.

In responding to a caller, follow the caller, do not try to lead the call. If the caller seems to be incoherent or muddled and you feel confused, say so, being careful not to blame the caller, for example: 'You've told me such a lot, I'm feeling confused.' Be careful not to give advice or your opinion as this can sound judgemental and it is important for callers to work towards resolving problems themselves.

The middle part of the call, sometimes known as the 'body' of the call, is where most of the supportive work is done. Here the helpliner will try to establish what the issue is and what the caller is feeling and thinking. By actively listening and gently questioning the caller, the helpliner can (by reflecting) clarify the caller's needs and what the caller wants from the call or for himself or herself.

The end of the call consists of summarising what has been said so far. It is used to focus the caller's mind on the issues involved, what action or options are open to the caller and to indicate the end of the call. At the end of a call, be careful not to include such remarks as 'I hope I've been helpful' or 'I hope you feel better now', as these are not helpful to the caller and serve only to boost your own ego.

The use of questions

During the course of most calls, as in a counselling session, it will be necessary to ask questions. Sometimes questions will be needed to clarify the caller's presenting problem or to highlight the caller's most pressing problem if several have been mentioned.

Questions usually fall into two categories: open and closed. Closed questions ('is', 'are' and 'do' or 'does') are those which can be answered with 'yes' or 'no' and are not usually helpful as they will require further questions if more information is needed, and they can make the caller feel as though they are being interrogated.

Open questions ('which', 'who', 'when', 'how' or 'where') can encourage the caller to say more and to explain and explore a situation. 'Why' questions, although open questions, can feel like an accusation or an order. Open questions invite a fuller response, for example: a caller who is talking about arguments with his wife might be asked, 'What happens when you argue?' or 'How do your arguments start?'.

Take care with leading questions or with questions which can put answers in the caller's mouth. Leading questions can make a caller feel that a certain answer is expected or that they are expected to conform to certain beliefs and values. For example: a caller says, 'He's driving me crazy, sometimes I feel that if he doesn't stop shouting at me I'll hit him with something heavy.' The helpliner's non-verbal attitude can seem to say, you shouldn't think or feel like this, if she replies, 'You can't do that, have you seen your doctor?' A better response would be 'Are you saying you feel like harming your husband?'

Some questions can be described as helpful and encourage the caller to say more, for example: 'Is there anything else you would like to say?' Some, such as, 'How do you feel about …?' or 'What are your feelings when …?' can allow the caller to express feelings and emotions. Be aware of making assumptions. Check out what you think might be going on for the caller and begin any clarifying question with, 'I'm wondering if …' or 'I'm not sure, but it sounds to me as if …'

Challenging and confronting – techniques used in some counselling approaches – are almost never used in telephone support work. Challenging is when the helpliner feels the facts presented are not right, and confronting is when the helpliner feels the facts are hidden. These techniques sound hostile on the telephone and rarely prove productive.

Third party calls

The bulk of the calls received by some agencies (those dealing with drug or alcohol misuse, violence or abuse, illnesses and carers, etc) will be third party calls – that is, someone calling on another's behalf or someone concerned about another person. In responding to these calls it is necessary to ensure that the third party is aware of the first party's feelings and takes these into consideration. The first party's rights must be taken into account and the person called about should be consulted and their agreement sought before any action is taken. If an agency specialises in children's welfare, mental disorders or dementia, there may be specific laws which empower a third party to act on another's behalf. In most cases, however, the carer or concerned person just needs someone to talk to.

Referrals

When you suggest that a caller contacts another agency, tell them why you are making the suggestion so that they feel heard by you and not rejected. Acknowledge that it is extra work to make another call and never say 'I'm sure they will be able to help', as this may give false expectations.

Difficult calls

It is important to be sensitive to the caller's language and not to respond patronisingly or to use jargon which the caller might not understand. Angry callers are perhaps the most difficult callers to work with, but even the most irate callers will calm down if they want to. Bear in mind that it is probably not you that the caller is angry with. Acknowledge the anger: 'I can hear you are very angry', and explore it. No one should be expected to put up with abusive language but it is important to remember that some callers may only be able to express themselves through language which may be offensive to you. Restating (repeating) what the caller has said, often taking out the emotional attachment, can be helpful. This tells the caller that it is acceptable to talk in their own words without meeting embarrassment or judgement on your part.

Hearing someone crying or sobbing on the telephone can be painful, but if you are patient and let the caller know you are there, crying can be very therapeutic.

It can be hard to get used to silences in telephone work, because it is not always clear why they occur, but they allow thinking time for both the helpliner and the caller. Accepting and allowing silences can indicate to callers that they are controlling the call, but you need to be sensitive to timing. If possible, allow the caller to break the silence; reassure the caller that you are there and ready to continue when they feel able to talk again. Callers will sense your non-verbal attitude should you not be genuine or be disinterested.

Calls concerning suicide or euthanasia can be disturbing. Remember the caller is in control and you cannot intervene to take any action. Callers may talk of suicide or euthanasia to indicate their desperation. Explore the situation and decide with the caller if another specialist agency, such as bereavement counselling or those working with suicidal or euthanasic callers may be of more help. Often 'being there' and allowing the caller to talk and to express any feelings can relieve the situation.

Repeat callers

Most agencies discourage repeat callers, not because they do not care about the plight of the caller, but because the agency is unable to ensure that the caller will be able to speak to the same helpliner, meaning the caller may have to repeat the problem to a 'new set of ears'. While this may have benefits for callers in that they can get a different perspective on their problem, it can also cause conflict and resentment in emotional terms.

Most repeat callers use an agency for someone to talk to and it is this aspect of helpline work which causes real dilemmas for some agencies. All telephone calls have to be paid for and agencies which offer freephone calls or reduced rate calls have constantly to balance available funds against what is effective call time. Some agencies will practise an 'end of contract' session (see also Chapter 9, p 162) with a repeat caller by pointing out that they have done all they can for the caller by reviewing other options and resources available.

Self-awareness

Some calls can leave the helpliner emotionally drained and some calls can be disturbing, so it is important that you receive appropriate emotional support. Be aware of yourself and your reactions to what the caller says and what the caller's feelings are. Transference happens easily down a telephone line and it is important to be very clear about what you 'own' yourself and what you pick up from the caller. Remember, you are not the important one here (Rosenfield 1996).

Summary

Telephone work is in many respects no different from face-to-face counselling. The helpliner 'sees' callers and provides a safe environment in which to allow the caller to express thoughts and feelings, and enables the caller to change and make choices. The main difference is in approach. Telephone counselling has some parallels to crisis counselling in that it is very short-term work – therefore the beginning, middle and end of counselling, which can take many sessions or even years to evolve, are brought sharply into focus in one session if the call is to be effective. In telephone support work the physical environment is just as important as in counselling – it must be quiet, safe and comfortable, and you must ensure that you are not disturbed during a call.

Conclusion

Writing this chapter and getting my knowledge 'down on paper' has helped me in the application of being an empathic and anonymous 'listening ear'. I hope that my experience as a mature volunteer will give other older people some awareness of the basic skills of support work and will enable them to use the telephone as an effective tool in helping others.

Acknowledgements

With much love to Trouble my cat and to my best mate, my husband Ted, for their patience and understanding while I was writing this chapter.

References

CancerLink (1996) *Counselling Skills Training Course*. London: Cancer-Link.

Egan G (1995) *The Skilled Helper* (5th Edition). Monterey: Brooks/Cole.

Munro E A, Manthei R J, Small J J (1983) *Counselling: A skills approach*. New Zealand: Methuen.

Rogers C (1967) *On Becoming a Person*. London: Constable.

Rosenfield M (1996) *Telephone Training Information*. London: Broadcasting Support Services.

Rowe C (1996) Tutorial. Royal Society of Arts Certificate 'Counselling Skills in the Development of Learning'. Hammersmith and West London College.

Stewart W (1992) *An A–Z of Counselling Theory and Practice*. London: Chapman & Hall.

In Praise of Memory

Here is one last word on the subject of vanishing memory, and the consequent erosion of personality caused by the onset of dementia. I need not speak of the tragedy inherent in such circumstances, the pain, the rage, the sense of loss and abandonment, the struggle – possibly harder for those in attendance than it is for the sufferer – not to give way to despair or to a self-protective withdrawal of feeling. But I do wish to share with you my own experience as a daughter, and to tell a story that I would find it hard to believe had I not been there myself.

My 89-year-old mother, Marie, had led a vigorous and independent life until the last year or two before her death, when her deteriorating mental state meant that decisions had to be made on her behalf; the cottage she was so fond of had to be left behind, and she was obliged to move into a nursing home, comfortable enough but greatly disliked by her. To some extent she was able to adapt to her new circumstances, and I think she continued to take pleasure in visits from family and friends, though she was increasingly unable to concentrate and to converse with her visitors in any meaningful way. And so a new lifestyle was established, while her house remained empty but not yet stripped and sold. One day, when I was visiting her some two or three months before her death, and when a friend of her own age happened also to be present, suddenly and without warning she emerged from her shadow world and 'came to'. Turning to me, she said: 'Have you got your pencil and paper? Right, then let's begin.' And she proceeded to move in imagination through the rooms of her small house, noting in each room her most valued personal possessions, and stating how she wished to dispose of them. Her mind was as clear as a bell, her memory for names and for preferences as sharp as it had ever been, her judgement as sound. 'I think so-and-so would like that picture,' she said, 'and what about this piece of furniture for your sister? My goddaughter must have the chair I promised her, and I want you to have the framed sampler.' At one point I reminded her that she had not yet included her grandson, and I suggested that he might like the antique chest at the top of the stairs. 'Good idea,' she said, and gave her assent. When all the rooms had been visited, all the choices made, she began to flag, saying just before her twilight state returned: 'That's all. It will be on a Wednesday.' And sure enough, when the time came, she died very early on a Wednesday morning.

There is no way of accounting for this unexpected and brief return to normal consciousness, and certainly no theory can be built on a single experience. But I remain convinced that when an individual is living in a state of mental exile, the old self has not been permanently eclipsed but is simply inaccessible, perhaps – who knows? – because it has been drawn into a mysterious phase of transformation in which the unconscious mind plays a central role. Be that as it may, when conversing with that individual I would always want my words to convey respect for the dignity of the absent self – the silent listener to our conversation.

In this area, proof cannot be expected. We choose our hypothesis and live by it, and mine includes the notion that individuality is never finally lost, and that in the fullness of time memory will return, transfigured and transfiguring. It is then, I believe, that the pieces of our puzzle will come together and the meaning of the whole will be revealed.

(Sheila Willson)

USEFUL ADDRESSES

AA (Alcoholics Anonymous)
See your local telephone directory.
For those with problems related to alcohol.

AEB (The Associated Examining Board)
Staghill House
Guildford
Surrey GU2 5XJ
Tel: 01483 506506
Providers of short courses in counselling skills.

Action on Elder Abuse
Astral House
1268 London Road
London SW16 4ER
Tel: 0181 764 7648;
Elder Abuse Response Line 0800 731 4141 (10am-4.30pm weekdays)
Aims to prevent abuse of older people by raising awareness, education, promoting research and the collection and dissemination of information. Action on Elder Abuse operates the confidential helpline service providing information for anyone and emotional support for those involved.

Age Concern New Zealand Incorporated
3rd Floor
150 Featherston Street
PO Box 10-688
Wellington
New Zealand
Tel: 006404 471 2709
Fax: 006404 473 2504

British Association for Counselling (BAC)
1 Regent Place
Rugby
Warwicks CV21 2PJ
Tel: 01788 550899
To find out about counselling services in your area.

British Geriatrics Society
1 St Andrews Place
London NW1 4LB
Tel: 0171-935 4004
Campaigning to make sure that all district health authorities provide well-equipped, fully-staffed, centralised departments of geriatric medicine and adequate day hospital and assessment facilities.

Broadcasting Support Services
Union House
London W12 8UA
Tel: 0181-735 5000
Telephone training and consultancy service.

CancerLink
11–21 Northdown Street
London N1 9BN
Tel: 0171-833 2818
Freephone information: 0800 132 905
Asian freephone: 0800 590 415
Information and advice about all aspects of cancer.

Carers National Association
20–25 Glasshouse Yard
London EC1A 4JS
Tel: 0171-490 8818
Adviceline: 0171-490 8898 (1-4pm weekdays)
Information and advice if you are caring for someone. Can put you in touch with other carers and carers' groups in your area.

CENTRA
Duxbury Park
Duxbury Hall Road
Chorley
Lancs PR7 4AT
Tel: 01257 241 428
Validates counselling and counselling skills courses.

College of Counselling
6 Dixon Street
Glasgow G1 4AX
Tel: 0141 204 2230
Fax: 0141 221 2841

Provides a wide range of counselling skills courses via home study, using text, audio and video tapes.

Counsel and Care
Twyman House
16 Bonny Street
London NW1 9PG
Tel: 0171-485 1566
Advice for elderly people and their families; can sometimes give grants to help people remain at home or return to their home.

Cruse – Bereavement Care
126 Sheen Road
Richmond
Surrey TW9 1UR
Tel: 0181-940 4818/9047
Comfort in bereavement. Can put you in touch with people in your area.

Help the Aged
16–18 St James's Walk
London EC1R 0BE
Tel: 0171-253 0253
Seniorline: 0800 650 065
Winter Warmth Hotline: 0800 289 404
Advice and information for older people and their families.

Jewish Bereavement Counselling Service
PO Box 6748
London N3 3BX
Tel: 0181 349 0839
To offer emotional help and support to members of the Jewish community who have been bereaved, to be a resource and information centre to both the Jewish and the non-Jewish community within London and around the UK.

Lesbian and Gay Bereavement Project
Vaughan M Williams Centre
Colindale Hospital
London NW9 5HG
Tel: 0181-200 0511 (3-6pm weekdays)
Helpline 0181 455 8894 (7pm–12midnight)
Counselling, support and advice for gay men, lesbians, and their friends and families.

MIND
Granta House
15–19 Broadway
London E15 48Q
Tel: 0181-519 2122
Information, support and publications about all aspects of mental illness, depression, etc.

National Association of Bereavement Services
20 Norton Folgate
London E1 6DB
Tel: 0171-247 0617
Has a directory database of local and national services UK-wide and runs a referral helpline manned by trained bereavement counsellors who give information, advice and onward referral to a caller's nearest, most appropriate service.

National Extension College Trust Ltd
18 Brooklands Avenue
Cambridge CB2 2HN
Tel: 01223 316644
Provides distance learning courses and publications for a wide range of subjects including counselling and counselling skills.

POPAN (Prevention of Professional Abuse Network)
1 Wyvil Court
Wyvil Road
London SW8 2TG
Tel: 0171-622 6334
Work with victims of professional abuse.

Public Concern at Work
Suite 306
16 Baldwin Gardens
London EC1N 7RJ
Tel: 0171-404 6609
Fax: 0171-404 6576
Legal advice centre and an independent charity. Public Concern at Work are popularly known as the Whistleblowers' Charity.

RELATE
See your local telephone directory.
For advice and guidance on problems concerned with marriage and relationships.

RSA (Royal Society for the Encouragement of Arts, Manufacturers and Commerce)
8 John Adam Street
London WC2N 6EZ
Tel: 0171-930 5115
Provides certificates for two counselling courses.

Samaritans
See your local telephone directory.
Someone to talk to if you are in despair.

Telephone Helplines' Association
4 Deans Court
St Paul's Churchyard
London EC4V 5AA
Tel: 0171-248 3388
Publishes the Telephone Helplines Directory.

ABOUT AGE CONCERN

Counselling and older people: An introductory guide is one of a wide range of publications produced by Age Concern England, the National Council on Ageing. Age Concern cares about all older people and believes later life should be fulfilling and enjoyable. For too many this is impossible. As the leading charitable movement in the UK concerned with ageing and older people, Age Concern finds effective ways to change that situation.

Where possible, we enable older people to solve problems themselves, providing as much or as little support as they need. Our network of 1,400 local groups, supported by 250,000 volunteers, provides community-based services such as lunch clubs, day centres and home visiting.

Nationally, we take a lead role in campaigning, parliamentary work, policy analysis, research, specialist information and advice provision, and publishing. Innovative programmes promote healthier lifestyles and provide older people with opportunities to give the experience of a lifetime back to their communities.

Age Concern is dependent on donations, covenants and legacies.

Age Concern England
1268 London Road
London SW16 4ER
Tel: 0181-765 7200
Fax: 0181-765 7211

Age Concern Scotland
113 Rose Street
Edinburgh EH2 3DT
Tel: 0131-220 3345
Fax: 0131-220 2779

Age Concern Cymru
4th Floor
1 Cathedral Road
Cardiff CF1 9SD
Tel: 01222 371566
Fax: 01222 399562

Age Concern Northern Ireland
3 Lower Crescent
Belfast BT7 1NR
Tel: 01232 245729
Fax: 01232 235497

PUBLICATIONS FROM AGE CONCERN BOOKS

Health & Care

CARERS HANDBOOK SERIES

The Carers Handbook series has been written for the families and friends of older people. It guides readers through key care situations and aims to help readers make informed, practical decisions.

Caring for Someone at a Distance
Julie Spencer-Cingöz

There is now a wealth of much-needed information for carers living with their dependants, but little on that increasingly common situation of trying to care for someone at a distance. This book examines the particular difficulties which can be encountered and provides detailed practical advice and support on how best to help a loved one from a distance.
£6.99 0-86242-228-0

Caring for Someone who has had a Stroke
Philip Coyne with Penny Mares

Supportive and positive, this book is designed to help carers understand stroke and its immediate aftermath and contains extensive information on hospital discharge, providing care, rehabilitation and adjustment to life at home.
£6.99 0-86242-264-7

Caring for Someone with an Alcohol Problem
Mike Ward

More people drink alcohol than smoke, gamble or use illegal drugs. When drinking becomes a problem, the consequences for the carer can often be so physically and emotionally exhausting that it is difficult to

see any way out of the situation. This book will be of invaluable help to anyone who lives with or cares for a problem drinker, with particular emphasis on the problems of caring for an older problem drinker.
£6.99 0-86242-227-2

Caring for Someone who has Dementia
Jane Brotchie

Caring for someone with dementia can be physically and emotionally exhausting, and it is often difficult to think about what can be done to make the situation easier. This book shows how to cope better and seek further help as well as containing detailed information on the illness itself and what to expect in the future.
£6.99 0-86242-259-0

Finding and Paying for Residential and Nursing Home Care
Marina Lewycka

Acknowledging that an older person needs residential care often represents a major crisis for family and friends. Feelings of guilt and betrayal invariably compound the difficulties faced in identifying a suitable care home and sorting out the financial arrangements. This book provides a practical step-by-step guide to the decisions which have to be made and the help which is available.
£6.99 0-86242-261-2

The Carer's Handbook: What to do and who to turn to
Marina Lewycka

At some point in their lives millions of people find themselves suddenly responsible for organising the care of an older person with a health crisis. All too often such carers have no idea what services are available or who can be approached for support. This book is designed to act as a first point of reference in just such an emergency, signposting readers on to many more detailed, local sources of advice.
£6.99 0-86242-262-0

MONEY MATTERS

Your Rights: A guide to money benefits for older people
Sally West

Written in clear and concise language, *Your Rights* guides readers through the maze of benefits available and explains all of the main areas of interest to older people. The book contains up-to-date information on all key changes and provides specific sections on:

- Retirement pensions
- Housing and council tax benefits
- Income Support and the Social Fund
- Paying for residential care
- Help with legal and health costs

For further information please ring 0181-765 7200.

Using Your Home as Capital: A guide to raising cash from the value of your home
Cecil Hinton

Many older people own increasingly valuable homes but would like more income or capital to make the most of their retirement. This best-selling book for home-owners in their 70s and 80s, gives a detailed explanation of how to safely capitalise on the value of your home and obtain a regular additional income.

Written in clear and straightforward language, Using Your Home as Capital provides all the information older people need when considering this complex area.

For further information please ring 0181-765 7200.

The Pensions Handbook 1999–2000: The pensions system explained
Sue Ward

Many older people in their later working lives become concerned about the adequacy of their existing pension arrangements. This annually updated title addresses these worries and suggests strategies to enhance the value of a prospective pension.

For further information please ring 0181-765 7200.

Your Taxes and Savings 1999–2000
Sally West and the Money Management Council

The definitive annual guide to financial planning for older people, this popular book:

- is fully revised and updated
- explains the tax system in clear, concise language
- describes the range of saving and investment options available
- includes model portfolios to illustrate a range of financial scenarios

Your Taxes and Savings explains how the tax system affects people over retirement age, including how to avoid paying more tax than necessary.

For further information please ring 0181-765 7200.

If you would like to order any of these titles, please write to the address below, enclosing a cheque or money order for the appropriate amount made payable to Age Concern England. Credit card orders may be made on 0181-765 7200.

Mail Order Unit
Age Concern England,
1268 London Road, London SW16 4ER

Information Line

Age Concern produces over 40 comprehensive factsheets designed to answer many of the questions older people – or those advising them – may have, on topics such as:

- finding and paying for residential and nursing home care
- money benefits
- finding help at home
- legal affairs
- making a Will
- help with heating
- raising income from your home
- transfer of assets

Age Concern offers a factsheet subscription service that presents all the factsheets in a folder, together with regular updates throughout the year. The first year's subscription currently costs £50; an annual renewal thereafter is £25. Single copies, up to a maximum of five, are available free on receipt of an sae.

To order your FREE factsheet list, phone 0800 00 99 66 (a free call) or write to:

Age Concern
FREEPOST (SWB 30375)
Ashburton
Devon TQ13 7ZZ

INDEX